Dynamics of
World Development

POLITICAL ECONOMY OF THE WORLD-SYSTEM ANNUALS

Series Editor: IMMANUEL WALLERSTEIN

Published in cooperation with the Section on the Political Economy of the World-System of the American Sociological Association.

About the Series

The intent of this series of annuals is to reflect and inform the intense theoretical and empirical debates about the "political economy of the world-system." These debates assume that the phenomena of the real world cannot be separated into three (or more) categories—political, economic, and social—which can be studied by different methods and in closed spheres. The economy is "institutionally" rooted; the polity is the expression of socioeconomic forces; and "societal" structures are a consequence of politico-economic pressures. The phrase "world-system" also tells us that we believe there is a working social system larger than any state whose operations are themselves a focus of social analysis. How states and parties, firms and classes, status groups and social institutions operate within the framework and constraints of the world-system is precisely what is debated.

These theme-focused annuals will be the outlet for original theoretical and empirical findings of social scientists coming from all the traditional "disciplines." The series will draw upon papers presented at meetings and conferences, as well as papers from those who share in these concerns.

Volumes in this series:

Dynamics of
World Development

Edited by **Richard Rubinson**

Volume 4, **Political Economy of the World-System Annuals**
Series Editor: Immanuel Wallerstein

SAGE PUBLICATIONS   Beverly Hills   London

For information address:

SAGE Publications, Inc.
275 South Beverly Drive
Beverly Hills, California 90212

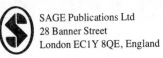

SAGE Publications Ltd
28 Banner Street
London EC1Y 8QE, England

Printed in the United States of America

Library of Congress Cataloging in Publication Data
Main entry under title:

Dynamics of world development.

(Political economy of the world-system annuals; v. 4)
Bibliography: p.
1. Economic history—Addresses, essays, lectures.
2. Economic development—Addresses, essays, lectures.
I. Rubinson, Richard. II. Series.
HC26.D95   338.9   81-1437
ISBN 0-8039-1591-8   AACR2
ISBN 0-8039-1592-6 (pbk.)

FIRST PRINTING

Dynamics of
World Development

CONTENTS

PREFACE

The papers collected in this volume were presented at the Fourth Annual Political Economy of the World-System spring conference at Johns Hopkins University, Baltimore, Maryland, June 1980. This conference was sponsored by the Political Economy of the World-System Section of the American Sociological Association and by the Departments of Social Relations and Anthropology of Johns Hopkins University.

Most of the preparations for the conference fell upon the staff of the Department of Social Relations, particularly Binnie Bailey, Pam Skalski, and Anna Sielaff. The task of ensuring that the two-day conference operated smoothly was carried out by several graduate students in Social Relations, Patricia Arregui, Deborah Holtzman, Jeff Kentor, and Pam Walters.

Richard Rubinson

INTRODUCTION

Richard Rubinson
Johns Hopkins University

Understanding the dynamics of development requires theoretical conceptualization. That point is common knowledge. The problem is what kind of theory. The papers in this volume represent one solution: The kind of theory that is most useful is a theory of the totality of the process of development. The particular theoretical approach they all share is that of the world-system perspective. This perspective is now well-known; there is no need to summarize its basic ideas. What is important is to continue the process of studying the development of the world-system in all its forms and to continue to theorize and reconceptualize. That is the task of the papers in this volume. They share a common set of assumptions, a common theoretical perspective. But their task is not to defend or test their common starting points, but to understand the particular problems on which they focus. In analyzing its particular problems, each paper proceeds from its initial theoretical assumptions and continues the process of theoretical development.

The dynamics of development refer to those processes which operate to maintain and transform the world-economy. That is, the unit which is developing is the world-economy and the processes which maintain and transform it form the basic dynamics. The assumption, then, is that the history of the modern world is the history of capitalist accumulation; and that capitalist development is the development of a single system, the modern world-system. We can group the dynamics of development into three sets of processes: those affecting and maintaining the structural features of the system; those representing the cycles of the system; and those that represent the secular trends of the system (see, for example, Chase-Dunn and Rubinson, 1977; Hopkins and Waller-stein, 1977).

BASIC STRUCTURES

To analyze any social system one must first understand its basic structures. In analyzing the modern world-system, we can distin-guish three analytically separate but empirically interrelated struc-tures: the structure of capitalist accumulation, the core-periphery division of labor, and the state system. The understanding that the history of the modern world is the history of capitalist accumula-tion distinguishes world-system theory from modernization theories, but it does not distinguish this theory from most Marxist theories. What does differentiate this theory from other Marxist theories is the theoretical centrality of the other two basic struc-tures, the core-periphery division of labor and the state system.

While it is possible to imagine these as three separate structures, in the actual empirical development of the modern world all three components have operated together. In fact, it seems impossible to imagine understanding our modern world without giving equal theoretical weight to all three as the basic components of the world-system. Capitalist development, as Polanyi argued, leads to constant political attempts to destroy capitalism itself. Only if capitalist accumulation occurs within a multiple political frame-work, as in the state system, can it survive. It is the creation and expansion of the stratified state system, then, that allows for the process of capitalist accumulation. However, it is equally difficult to imagine the modern state system in the absence of capitalism. The tendency of capitalism to expand has caused the state system to expand, so that now the entire globe is both capitalist and statist. But more important, the competitive dynamic of capitalism has also made it such that local entrepreneurs find the creation and maintenance of increasingly strong state structures to be their major organizational strategy to compete in the market. Finally, the operation of both capitalist accumulation and the state system combine to form the third basic feature of the modern world-system: the core-periphery division of labor. This feature represents the basic structure of stratification of the world-system, organizing, more than any other feature, the basic inequalities of territory, commodities, political power, and wealth.

Since these three features are the basic structures of the world-system, then much of the dynamics of development involves the processes which maintain and transform these three features. Studies within the world-system perspective are distinctive in their attempt to explain any particular phenomenon in terms of the operation of all three features of the system.

CYCLES OF THE WORLD-SYSTEM

Understanding social systems involves more than analyzing the processes that maintain its basic structures. Most social systems are also characterized by a series of cyclical processes. In the world-system, three basic cyclical processes have been identified: long waves of economic growth and stagnation, long-term cycles of the distribution of power among core states between periods of rivalry and hegemony, and alterations in the core-periphery control structure between colonial control and informal control. Though these three cycles can be analytically separated, they seem to be empirically correlated, such that periods of expansion culminate in the rise of a hegemonic core power and informal controls, while periods of economic stagnation lead to competition among core powers and more direct colonial-type controls.

These cycles have been of great interest in much of the research on the world-system and have been used to explain a number of different phenomena. For example, these cycles have been used to account for the cyclical pattern in international trade between periods of relatively free trade and periods of relatively high tariffs. Similarly, periods of economic stagnation have been seen as fundamental in allowing some countries to shift their position in the core-periphery division of labor. Such periods have also been seen to provide the condition for increased concentration of capital and consolidation.

The determination, measurement, and consequences of these three cycles is a second basic set of development dynamics in the world-system. Understanding these cycles is fundamental to understanding not only the functioning of the world-system but also the long-term developmental changes in the world-economy. This is because, as Wallerstein argues, the cycles of the system are what determine the third set of basic processes, the secular trends of the world-economy.

SECULAR TRENDS

If we study the modern world-system over the past four hundred years, we see a system that is basically the same in terms of the features we have already described. But the system is also different, in the sense that it has been characterized by a series of long-term systematic changes. These changes are the secular trends of the system, and, again, three trends are typically distinguished: the expansion of the size of the system; the interrelated increases in proletarianization, commodification, and capital concentration; and the increase in mechanization.

These secular trends represent the third basic set of developmental dynamics. The development of the world-economy is explained through analysis of their causes, measurement of the changes, and understanding of their causes. Indeed, it is the understanding of these trends which may be the most important set of development dynamics, for they would seem to necessarily involve the transformation of the world-system itself. This is because these secular trends all have finite limits. If the structural tensions within the world-economy have been periodically allayed by increases in these trends, and the trends themselves are approaching their inherent limits, then we can expect that the institutionalized competition within the world-economy will be transformed into conflict. Political resistance to this system will increase, and eventually there will be a fundamental transformation of our modern world-system.

THIS VOLUME

The structural features, cycles, and secular trends represent the basic development dynamics of the world-system. The papers in this volume share a concern with understanding the past, present, and future of this system. As concrete studies, they cannot be grouped into analyses of any one set of development dynamics. Rather, the reader should try to see how these studies advance the understanding of the whole range of processes of development of the world-economy.

Most of the empirical analyses of the development of the world-economy have come from studies of a particular country within one of its three structural zones: the core, semiperiphery, or periphery. Parts I and II present such studies. The first two papers analyze development in peripheral areas; both are distinguished by their simultaneous attention to the specifics of the individual case and to the general processes of peripherial development.

The paper by Michel-Rolph Trouillot calls to our attention the often-ignored coffee revolution in the eighteenth-century French colony of Saint-Domingue. He leads us to an understanding of why coffee production flourished amid the better-documented sugar boom of the island. His analysis starts at the level of the world-economy as a whole and moves step by step to the point of production, the *caféteries*. As the demand for coffee increased in the European core areas during the eighteenth-century, dominant groups there moved to control its production. This process led to the geographic relocation of coffee production from its initial locus in external arenas of the world-economy to the outer (peripheral) areas in the Indian Ocean and then to the Caribbean. This process was so successful that, by the latter part of the century, coffee from Saint-Domingue was being reexported by France to its former suppliers in the external arenas of the world-economy. But why was France the core country to take control of coffee production? Here Trouillot's analysis tells us that we must move to the level of understanding the competition among core states. Dutch influence was declining and the British were in the process of controlling production and trade in tea. France could then seize the opportunity to control coffee production. Why, then, did Saint-Domingue emerge as the leading coffee producer? Coffee had ecological characteristics that allowed it to be grown even on an island dominated by sugar. More important was the class of producers. These people were of two groups, the *gens de couleur* of the island and the white newcomers. Both groups were marginal to the dominant sugar complex, and coffee production was their opportunity. Trouillot's analysis, then, integrates the broad patterns of the expanding world-economy to expropriate production of profitable commodities from external arenas to the analysis of how this process allowed a marginal group of people in the colony of Saint-Domingue to seize the opportunity for their own advantage.

   The paper by Kostis Papadantonakis analyzes the process of peripheralization, the process by which an area outside the world-economy is incorporated. His case is Greece, but his concern is the general process. The Ottoman Empire existed side by side with the European world-economy until the middle of the nineteenth century, when it was peripheralized. The focus of his paper is on the political process of the shift from external arena to periphery. His argument is that this process required the shift from a weak political authority to a much stronger one, a process he conceptualizes as "inverted mercantilism." The analysis is important for those who assume that the expansion of the world-economy was a process of core action over an inert area or merely a process of economic reorganization. Rather, he isolates as crucial the creation of a political apparatus which redirected the flow of economic surplus. This analysis is especially useful in highlighting how the creation of the Greek state was itself a function of class dynamics within Greece which resulted in a reorganization of its indigenous class structure to fit its new role as a periphery in the European world-economy. This analysis links the formation of national states, the organization of peripheral class structures, and the flow of commodities to provide a theoretical account of peripheralization which can be used as a basis for further studies.

Both the Trouillot and Papadantonakis papers also underscore the necessity of sensitizing analyses of peripheral development to the ways in which groups in these areas both collude and resist and seize opportunities as the world-economy has expanded.

The papers in Part II continue the analysis of particular case studies of development by focusing on three semiperipheral states: Mexico, Brazil, and Iran. Richard Tardanico's paper, "Perspectives on Revolutionary Mexico: The Regimes of Obregón and Calles," is part of his continuing work on the Mexican Revolution. The problem that guides this work is the issue of the mobility of countries within the world-economy. Mexico was peripheralized during the initial expansion of the European world-economy in the sixteenth century. During the twentieth century, Mexico has shifted its position to that of a semiperipheral state. By what process did this shift occur? Tardanico argues that the Mexican Revolution was crucial in creating a significantly stronger state apparatus. In this way, his analysis echoes that of Papadantonakis on Greece. Movement in the world-economy, whether from external arena to periphery, from periphery to semiperiphery, or from semiperiphery to the core, requires a relatively sudden political transformation in conjunction with longer-run economic shifts. Tardanico's analysis is concerned with the particular dynamics of this political transformation. He explains how the Mexican Revolution allowed Mexico to take advantage of economic shifts in the world-economy to gain a larger share of the world economic surplus for itself and to outstrip other peripheral areas. But while the Mexican Revolution allowed Mexico to shift upward in the world-economy, it did not produce a situation of autonomous development. Rather, the economic consequences of the revolution were to reorganize its economic activities to simultaneously increase its advantages over other peripheral areas in Latin America while at the same time strengthening its dependence on the United States, the emerging hegemonic power in the world-economy. Tardanico, then, illustrates two important dynamics. First, he details the conditions under which the state machinery in peripheral areas can be strengthened to allow an area to shift into the semipheriphery; and second, he shows how this shift further integrates and strengthens the ongoing patterns of development of the world-economy.

Walter Goldfrank's paper, "Dependent Development and Third World Fascism: Two Views of Brazil," follows these same themes to evaluate two works on contemporary Brazil. His paper contrasts the analysis of Brazil in Noam Chomsky and E. S. Herman's work, "The Political Economy of Human Rights," with Peter Evans' "Dependent Development." Chomsky and Herman focus on what Goldfrank sees as one aspect of the *essence* of Brazilian development—brutal repression undertaken with the support of the United States. Evans' work, by contrast, focuses both on what Goldfrank terms *essence* and *variation* in his study of the triple alliance of multinational firms, local capital, and state actors as the institutional crux of semiperipheral Brazil. The essence is the workings of dependent development; while the variation is the awareness of Brazil as an area which has shifted from the periphery to the semiperiphery and now faces a critical problem in the success of its strategy of development. Goldfrank insightfully analyzes these works to demonstrate how a proper conceptualization of world development is necessary for understanding any particular case and to point out strategies for analysis.

Nesar Ahmad's paper concludes this section with an analysis of the agrarian crisis in Iran which preceded the recent fall of Reza

Shah Pahlavi. Ahmad studies the process of agricultural and land reform. He details in Iran a recurrent process in peripheral areas: (1) the rationalization of the rural areas through land reform, as a mechanism to lay the institutional conditions for the expansion of agriculture (The most important consequence of this movement, Ahmad argues, was the creation of a class of agrarian producers willing to participate in the world-economy.); (2) the introduction of commercialization, mechanization, and technical assistance for production; (3) the direct participation of multinational agribusiness in the production and distribution of agricultural commodities. Ahmad follows the impact of this process on the crisis which led to the fall of the Shah through a decline in the production of food staples, through inflation, and through the loss of land by the peasants and their subsequent migration from the rural areas.

The papers in Parts III and IV consider the analysis of general processes of the development of the capitalist world-system. Chapters 6 and 7 consider the general processes of state formation. James Lunday ("Political Regionalism and Struggles for State Hegemony") brings out an important theoretical strategy for explaining the relationships among states, dominant economic classes, and development. Most analyses of the dynamics of political transformation focus on the control of state institutions, studying the relationships of economic interests to these institutions. But Lunday points out that such an approach often misses the high degree of political decentralization or political regionalism or federalism on which central states are often built. Economic actors will attempt to use whatever political structures are available to further their interests. As a consequence, he argues, struggles for state hegemony often take the form of struggles over political regionalism and not directly over the central state. Explaining which economic interests eventually come to dominate the central state, then, requires an analysis based on the relationship of economic interests to more local political units. In Brazil, for example, São Paulo had been the power base of the Old Republic because of its role as the major producer of coffee for export. But it also became the major power base of the new regime under Vargas because of its role as the major center of manufacturing. As a consequence, the classical pattern of conflicting interests between agrarian exporters and emergent industrialists took place within a single political region, the state of São Paulo. In the nineteenth-century United States, by contrast, the dominant agricultural exports were located in the South, while the emergent industrial interests were located in the North; with each group having control over its own local political structures, the several states. Hence, the same conflicts took place between different political units, rather than within one unit as had occurred in Brazil. Lunday then links the different patterns of national center-formation and political transformation to these different patterns of the political ecology of economic interests.

The paper by Francisco Ramirez and George Thomas tackles the development of the international state system as a whole. They start with the observation that the development of the capitalist world-economy has also been the development of the state system. Not only has the world-economy organized the globe into a series of nation-states; but these states also have become stronger in relation to their national populations, and statist ideologies have come to the foreground. These authors seek to analyze the conditions which have led to such long-term secular trends. The strategy they use is to critically analyze and organize a large set of quantitative, cross-national studies of the relationships among economic dependence, political organization, and economic development. They work through these studies by stages, extracting empirical findings and organizing a theoretical explanation. They distinguish between the classic idea of economic dependence and what they term "embeddedness" in the world-economy. They find that dependence has led to a lessening of the fiscal power of states, but also to the growth of centralized regimes. Embeddedness—the degree of activity in the world-economy regardless of power-dependence relations—has led to an increase in the fiscal power of states and also to an increase in the growth of centralized regimes. Ramirez and Thomas' analyses clarify the seemingly paradoxical nature of the state system: The world-economy as a system of competing states leads to greater statist organization as a consequence of the increased density of interaction among states; but as a system of stratification it also leads to a relative weakening of dependent states. Hence, all states become stronger and more centralized in relation to their own populations; while at the same time the relative strength remains among states from core to periphery.

Part IV moves to analyses of systemic patterns of the world-economy as a whole. The chapter by Dale Johnson, which is drawn from his larger, forthcoming study, deals with the problem of theoretically and empirically understanding the class structure of the world-economy. The theoretical problem he poses is the following: The long-term processes of capitalist development create an increasingly bipolar class structure of bourgeois and proletarian; yet in all particular social instances, a number of intermediate classes are present. How are we to understand their presence? Many analysts answer this question by claiming that the existence of a variety of forms of the middle class is proof that capitalist development does not lead to bipolarization. Other analysts claim that these middle classes represent vestiges of old classes which are continuing to disappear, or claim that such classes exist but are not part of the patterned development of capitalism. Johnson's answer, however, seems much more theoretically and empirically useful. He argues that the constant appearance of intermediate classes, though they take many diverse forms, is the consequence of the process of bipolarization. The intermediate classes are one expression of the process of class polarization. Each intermediate class is specific to its historical and geographical location; but each one is also transitory. The constant process of bipolarization also creates these transitory intermediate classes. Johnson's analysis finds the mechanism for the creation of these classes in the general process of capital accumulation; but he also underscores the necessity for a theoretical framework that understands capital accumulation as a process of class formation.

The second paper in this section, Albert Bergesen's "Long Economic Waves and the Size of Industrial Enterprise," represents another piece of research in his program to understand the relationship between the cyclical patterns of the world-economy and its secular trends. One of these trends is the increasing size of the capitalist firm. He distinguishes two sources of increase in size: expansion through increasing the volume of business and expansion through merger or consolidation. He argues that these two patterns alternate with each other, and that their alternation can be tied to the cycles of expansion and contraction in the world-economy. During periods of economic expansion, firms grow by expanding their volume of business and organizational framework. During periods of economic contraction, firms grow through merger and consolidation. Bergesen then presents his historical periodization of this process and speculates on the future form of the capitalist firm.

The chapters in Part V are not studies of the world-economy per se, but represent attempts to integrate two bodies of social science analysis into work on the world-system. The basic idea of each of these papers is to use the world-system perspective to help understand their two specific problems and to utilize the work in these areas to aid in analyzing the development of the world-economy.

The paper by Roberta Spalter-Roth and Eileen Zeitz deals with the production and reproduction of labor. These issues have been extensively studied by Marxist sociologists, but they have not been systematically introduced into a systematic, historical analysis of capitalism. Spalter-Roth and Zeitz argue that the issues of women's work and sex role stratification have most often been conceptualized as mechanisms of maintaining a reserve army of labor, of reducing the costs of the reproduction of labor, or as a last area of primitive accumulation. Sex role stratification is, then, functionally equivalent to phenomena such as African migrant labor reserves, illegal immigration, or the informal sector. But they argue that a complete theoretical analysis of these issues must see sexual stratification as a constituent antagonism within capitalist development, not just as a functional equivalent of other phenomena. Just as the world-system understands that uneven development is the concrete manifestation of layer upon layer of bipolar antagonisms between geographic regions, between states, between city and country, between status groups; so also should . sexual stratification be seen as one of these basic bipolar oppositions.

The paper by Sally Ward draws from the traditional area of community studies. She employs hypotheses utilized in work on the world-economy to see if they can explain the degree of inequality within local communities. Using the basic ideas of dominance-dependence relations and external control, she predicts inequality within communities and finds that external control, but not dominance, leads to greater inequality. In trying to understand these findings, she focuses on the fact that the degree of permeability of the political boundaries of communities is much greater than that of state structures. Ward's findings are useful not only for understanding communities but also for calling attention to taking account of the uneven degree of permeability of political boundaries in all studies of development.

The final paper in this volume presents an overview of the latest theoretical and empirical work of Terence Hopkins and Immanuel Wallerstein from their ongoing program on the structural transformations of the world-economy. They present the ways in which they are rethinking and reconceptualizing the basic processes of the development of the world-economy. This ongoing theoretical work is presented as part of their empirical analyses of the process of incorporation of areas into the world-economy. They discuss, in turn, each of the basic ideas employed by the papers in this volume and other work: the axial division of labor, the state system, peripheralization, bipolarization, uneven development, and the like. But as they go over seemingly old ground in the light of recent empirical work, they are constantly reconceptualizing, trying to fit the pieces together in different ways to lead to greater understanding. Their paper is an accumulation of past work and a tearing down and reconstruction of that work.

As such, the final chapter serves as a guide to the collective enterprise of those whose concern is to understand the dynamics of development. The important guidelines are to continue the detailed empirical studies using the theoretical concepts and ideas developed in past work, but to continue to creatively transform that theoretical perspective in order to reach a fuller understanding of our modern world.

REFERENCES

CHASE-DUNN, C. and R. RUBINSON (1977) "Toward a structural perspective on the world-system." Politics and Society 7: 453–476.
HOPKINS, T. and I. WALLERSTEIN (1977) "Patterns of development of the modern world-system." Review 1: 111–146.

PART 1

DEVELOPMENT IN
PERIPHERAL AREAS

Chapter 1

PERIPHERAL VIBRATIONS: THE CASE OF SAINT-DOMINGUE'S COFFEE REVOLUTION

Michel-Rolph Trouillot
Johns Hopkins University

In his recent book, *Le Temps du Monde,* the third and last volume of *Civilisation Matérielle, Economie et Capitalisme,* Fernand Braudel repeatedly warns us that privileged attention to economic factors can result in schematic oversimplification. But, says Braudel (1979b: 9), we can at least "exorcize the difficulties" of an approach which remains valid in its general perspective. This paper strives toward some kind of "exorcism" in analyses of peripheral formations.

If I were not afraid to say at once both too much and too little, I would simply assert that my argument comes back to the need for a dialectical understanding of world-economies. The complex in-

AUTHOR'S NOTE: I wish to thank Sidney W. Mintz and Katherine Verdery for their helpful comments and suggestions on an earlier version of this paper.

teraction between core and periphery defies not only the current lack of perspective of most microlevel studies but also the simplicity of mechanical generalizations. The notion of periphery rests on the assumption of some overarching unity; yet it also requires the acknowledgment of a differentiation which manifests itself through space. But if that space itself is in movement, how do we grasp the differential momentum carried by geopolitical characteristics, by particular social organizational and historical developments (and their social significance), in an analysis premised on the global relevance of world-historical forces?

A second dialectic seems to me inseparable from that of core and periphery relations and is what Marx, in the *Grundrisse* (1973), called the contradictory "unity" of production and consumption. Advocates and critics of "dependency" and "world-system" theories have forcefully argued from both sides of "the internal production-external exchange problem" (Frank 1978: 15). But the contradictory unity between production and consumption sketched by Marx (1973: 99ff) suggests that a dichotomous perception of those two processes may very well impair, rather than enhance, our understanding of peripheral particulars. More attention to the manner in which the production and consumption of particular commodities affected each other, more empirical studies of their combined effects in historically defined economic arenas, might shed new light on the determinations and limits inherent to each of these processes. The aim should be to understand in what manner and to what extent each, *when seen against the background of the other,* affects social relations in the periphery.[1]

My third and last point pertains to what Braudel called the reintroduction of social and cultural factors into economic analysis.[2] Those who never intended to ignore the social might simply want to reaffirm that peripheral dynamics ultimately rest upon particular human beings, who claim, accurately or not, an understanding of their situation, to the despair of social scientists.

These points are not new, but they are relevant to a discussion of peripheral dynamics on the one hand and to the study of a much-neglected episode of Caribbean history on the other: the "Coffee Revolution" of the second half of the eighteenth century in the French colony of Saint-Domingue.[3] The data from which these questions flow have been incorporated and discussed in a lengthier paper, from which I will draw here as needed.[4]

Historians usually associate the name Saint-Domingue with the cultivation of sugarcane; and the overwhelming importance of coffee in the export market of contemporary Haiti appears to be an unforeseen consequence of the Haitian Revolution. To be sure, not long after the formal cession of the colony by Spain in 1697 French metropolitan policy systematically encouraged large-scale sugarcane cultivation in that western third of Hispaniola. Opportunities created by the expanding European market for sucrose attracted Caribbean planters and metropolitan merchants. By 1789, Saint-Domingue's exports had far surpassed the century-old sugar production of Martinique and were almost equal in volume to those of all the British Caribbean islands together. But the characterization of eighteenth-century Saint-Domingue as *l'Isle à Sucre par excellence* rests on an oversight. Even while the French colony was becoming the world's largest sugar producer, between the 1760s and 1789, the volume of its coffee exports quadrupled. During the same period, values from these exports sextupled, and by 1789, while sugar there continued to grow in importance, Saint-Domingue became the main coffee supplier of the western world-economy. Figures eloquently document the speed of that development. The number of trees climbed from 22 million in 1750 to more than 300 million in 1789. Total exports were estimated at 7 million pounds in 1755, 40 million in 1774, and 77 million in 1790. Values from these exports rose from an annual average of 12 million colonial *livres* in 1767 to 48.8 million in 1783–1784, and 71.5 million in 1787–1789, which was almost equal to the 75 million *livres* that the colony received for its sugar. By 1789, Saint-Domingue was producing almost 60 percent of all the coffee sold in the western world-economy.

That development exemplifies the convergence in one time and at one locus of peripheral particulars and world-historical forces.

Its understanding requires an approach that takes into account not only these two fields of forces in sum but their specific, processual interaction. I suggest that such a grasp can be aimed at within the framework of a progression which would take us from the level of the system at large—that is, the European world-economy— down to the smaller local level of analysis (that is, the unit of production). In the latter case, this means the *caféteries*, or *caféières*, as they were called in eighteenth-century Saint-Domingue.

A full demonstration of the procedure would require more time than I can take; I will limit myself to a few brief illustrations. Taken at the larger level of the system, Saint-Domingue's "Coffee Revolution" appears to have been the terminal in a process which was to put the means of production of a crop, coffee, newly introduced and growing in popularity within the world-economy, under firm control of particular European dominant groups. As consumption increased in Europe and North America, production moved from the external arenas of the system to the outer peripheries of the Indian Ocean, then to the Caribbean islands and to the continental dependencies of the circum-Caribbean. Let me retrace the sequence, as outlined in the larger paper, in order to make my second point: the need to examine the contradictory unity of production and consumption.

Base-line (1580–1650).

Coffee drinking, spreading through the Near East, reaches Venice, the Netherlands, England and France, but it remains the fancy of a few wealthy aristocrats. The limited trade is divided between European (Dutch) and non-European (Lebanese Jews, Turks) merchants, but production is seated in an external arena of the European world-economy (Arabia).

First Step (End of the seventeenth century–First quarter of the eighteenth century).

Substantial production persists in Arabia, while growing production within the system is largely confined to the Indian Ocean dependencies (Ceylon, Java, Bourbon, Mauritius). Only the Dutch initiate export-oriented production in a Caribbean colony (Surinam); but French, British and Portuguese entrepreneurs also try to acclimatize the plant in their American dependencies. Consumption spreads in the courts of Europe, and the drink is praised by members of the leisure classes, while mercantile interest groups (e.g., the Dutch East India Company, the French Compagnie des Indes and some newly-created Marseille merchant houses) strive to seize control of trade and distribution. One must emphasize that different processes are simultaneously set in motion during this first crucial stage:

a) demand is being created;

b) control over the trade is being secured by European merchants;

c) the locus of production is moving from areas where the core has no control over the means of production, to areas within the European world-economy;

d) the structures are being tuned up for the expansion of production in more tightly-controlled peripheries.

Second Step (Second quarter of the eighteenth century).

Production increases in the Caribbean (Martinique and, especially, Surinam) while the use of coffee spreads quantitatively among specific categories in European core societies: merchants, nobles, clerics, intellectuals. But demand is also being created among the lower classes. Thousands of *cafés* open in major European urban centers, and coffee appears for the first time on the wholesale list of commodities in some North American cities. By 1734, imports from the Caribbean exceed both those from the Levant and those from the Indian Ocean dependencies in Marseille, then the turnstile of the Mediterranean French trade. By 1750, the locus of production has definitely moved from the Indian Ocean to the Caribbean—which is to say, *to peripheral areas geopolitically more integrated within the world-economy, where control of and access to the means of production are more tightly secured.*[5]

Third Step (1750's–1789).

Thereafter, consumption spreads, both quantitatively and socially, within the core, and the use of coffee becomes effectively "pop-

ular" among the laboring classes of many European countries and
even in some North American urban centers. At this stage, the
ever-growing production of the Caribbean peripheries exceeds the
demands of the core itself. This surplus production of the inner
peripheries then impinges upon production in the external arenas
and outer peripheries. Moreover, it contributes to the increasing
integration of these former leading producers in the world-
economy. Indeed, less than a hundred and fifty years after the
Dutch had started massive distribution of Arabian coffee in the
West, the direction of the trade between Europe and the Near East
had changed and, by 1774, Marseille alone was re-exporting more
than 2 million pounds of coffee a year to its former suppliers in the
Levant! [Trouillot, 1979].

As gross as it is, this sketch suggests the rewards of a progression beginning at the widest level of analysis.[6] The inclusion of the
early experiments in coffee cultivation in Saint-Domingue within a
general movement toward specific peripheral areas raises questions about the differential control of the market by segments of the
core and the effects of their trading activities on particular peripheries. Why Saint-Domingue? And since Saint-Domingue itself
was a French colony where coffee production escalated with metropolitan encouragement, why France? Such questions require
that we move from the level of the system at large to the level of
colonial networks and look more closely at the competition between diverse European core states and at the contradictions within
some of them. Let me say quickly that after the Peace of Paris
(1763), in part because of the English tea trade, in part because of
Dutch economic decline, French merchants encountered relatively
less competition in the expanding coffee trade. This brings us—
too quickly, perhaps—to a third level of analysis, the French
colonial network in the particular conjuncture of the mid-1760s.
Let us underline especially the fact that the continuing expansion
of *sugar* indirectly contributed to the coffee boom. It is well
known that Voltaire expressed the feeling of many when, referring
to the loss of Québec, he rejoiced at the choice of the Crown, who

had given up "a few acres of snow" in order to keep the major Caribbean dependencies, the sugar islands of Martinique, Guadeloupe, and, above all, Saint-Domingue. At the issue of the Seven Years' War, that island had become one of the most promising colonies in a much smaller empire, a major attraction for both migrants and investors.

The perspective being thus set from the point of view of the system at large to that of the narrower, intermediate levels, we can legitimately move down to the level where peripheral dynamics take definite and concrete shape, where the world-historical and the local fields of forces unite and clash—and thereby create, on the ground, the particular conjuncture which human beings can perceive, seize, and act upon.

The preeminence of sugar meant that whatever crop would succeed in eighteenth-century Saint-Domingue would have to find itself a new niche: an ecological and social space within which sugar could not expand. Coffee presented that counterpoint. It liked the moisture and higher rainfall of the highlands and needed little water and little processing. Its production was not time-restricted (at least, not as much as sugar). These differences, in turn, lowered significantly the minimum capital required to start a *caféterie*. If one adds to the relatively high expenditures for buildings, tools, materials, and a huge labor force that a socially imposed economy of scale forced on the sugar planter, it is safe to suggest that, in eighteenth-century Saint-Domingue, one could start a *caféterie* with one-sixth or less the capital required for a sugar plantation. But these possibilities, as set at the point of encounter of contradictory fields of forces, required local initiative, human beings acting, forcing the opportunities, and seizing their time. In eighteenth-century Saint-Domingue, who was willing to make that choice, and why?

This brings us to my third major point, the sociocultural dimensions of peripheral dynamics. The counterpoint that coffee presented to sugar in Saint-Domingue can be looked at from different complementary angles: an opposition between two groups of planters, between two views of colonialism, between two subcultures, between center and periphery within the island itself. But the relevance of all these oppositions takes root in the differential commitment of the two groups of planters to capital and plantation slavery. This fundamental difference enhanced the minor ones and contributed to the fact that, *in sum,* they represented a threat to the local social, racial, political, and economic orders.

The record shows that coffee first flourished, at least two decades before the boom, in the hills surrounding the major sugar parishes. In this early phase, the owners were most often whites of moderate resources: junior managers of the sugar plantations, low-ranking functionaries, craftsmen, and professionals. But at the first decline in prices (and perhaps before), these pioneers sold their highland properties, most often to free blacks. And indeed, record of the coffee explosion of the late 1760s and 1770s shows that it occurred most strikingly in parishes dominated by *gens de couleur* (as the free blacks were called in Saint-Domingue) and/or parishes erected after the Peace of Paris (1763) and heavily populated by migrants recently arrived from France or from other colonies.

It seems to me that there is much more at work in this transfer than simply land speculation or new sources of investment capital. If a difference can be established between the first and second generation of coffee growers, it is that those of the second generation (both *gens de couleur* and newcomers) were marginals—economically, socially, and politically—to the sugar socioeconomic complex. To be sure, the first coffee planters did not belong to the higher levels of Saint-Domingue's social hierarchy. But it is highly probable that most of them could aspire to better positions within the sugar complex. These were people tied to "the sugar structure" and dissatisfied with it—yet they were bound to survive if the structure itself was to survive. Their rather hesitant involvement with coffee I believe was limited by their ambivalence vis-à-vis the sugar socioeconomic complex. Because they probably thought they had a chance for mobility within that complex, they refused to venture too far from it. Only people who clearly lacked such aspirations as well as a concrete and material basis for having them could assume on a more stable basis the risks of coffee and, eventually, its profits.

Colonial society was structured by poles of diverse kinds: economic, occupational, phenotypical, legal, even spatial. There were enslaved and free people, there were blacks and whites, there were towns and plantations. The *gens de couleur* never belonged; neither black nor white, neither slave nor free, dislodged from the towns and the big plantations, seeking a niche where their legal "freedom" could be experienced and exercised outside the confinement of the colonial regime, they occupied the hills and mountains where their provision grounds gave them their first chance for economic independence. They used the panic resulting from the first price declines to consolidate their control in the mountains. By 1755, their growth was already a cause of concern for the administrators; by 1775, that growth was irreversible—what made the difference was coffee.

Analysis of the available figures for population and production (see Moreau de Saint-Méry 1958 [1797]) shows that after 1775 all the parishes where freedmen outnumbered whites were primarily coffee-producing parishes. (In the colony as a whole whites outnumbered freedmen in the official censuses, though the margin kept shrinking, especially in the second half of the century. One suspects that, on the eve of the Haitian Revolution, the number of free blacks may have equalled the number of whites.) But when one compares diachronically the reported figures of population and production, it appears that no parishes were dominated by free blacks before the Coffee Revolution. Their demographic takeover in those secluded parishes actually parallels the expansion of coffee.

Thousands of whites of moderate resources reached the colony after the Peace of Paris; most of them also jumped on the coffee bandwagon. They also were marginal people; marginals in France itself, members of the petty-nobility *("la petite noblesse")* low-ranking professionals, craftsmen, and soldiers, pushed out of rural France by economic hardship and the complacency of the Crown. They had come with hopes of glory and fortune, like those who had preceded them after the treaties of Utrecht (1713) and of Aix-la-Chapelle (1748), when cessation of military confrontations with England had allowed massive migrations to the French Caribbean possessions. Many of these newcomers belonged to the same socioeconomic strata as the earliest generation of coffee growers. But they did not share the ambivalence of their predecessors: After the Peace of Paris, there simply was no more room for them to find a secure place within the sugar socioeconomic complex. The agricultural saturation of the alluvial lowlands, rapidly rising population density, and the concentration of the plantations themselves in fewer hands foreclosed further expansion in this direction. Sugar's sweet road to wealth was closed. With its relatively modest needs for land, slaves, and materials, coffee soon became the second last chance of the newcomers. They were marginal in France; they became marginal in the colony. They invaded highlands of which the administrators themselves did not know the existence. Isolated on their holdings with as few as twenty slaves, with almost no contact with other whites (and often no hope or desire to entertain such relations), they accommodated their dreams to the world they were living in. They married their slaves and legitimized their children. And, in desperation if not of necessity, they established with their free black neighbors ties which potentially threatened the colonial social order.

From the point of view of those who ran Saint-Domingue, both *gens de couleur* and these white newcomers were outsiders. They were treated as outsiders; they reacted as outsiders. The economic counterpoint that coffee afforded sugar matched the social challenge that these marginals presented to France and to the sugar plantocracy. First, the free blacks' accession to economic power, at first modest, produced contradictory effects. On one hand, urban poor whites, sugar planters, and administrators systematically intensified the racist legal apparatus. On the other hand, many alliances were formed and maintained among blacks and whites in the hinterland. Second, these alliances across color lines of two groups marginal to the sugar complex seem to have gradually resulted in clear social challenges.

Before the Coffee Revolution, sugar was not only the major source of revenues; it was the very principle around which life was organized. Towns were created because of its proximity. Time was marked by its harvest, and status was linked to its possession. Sugar was noble; sugarcane planters had become noblemen. But by the late 1760s, the success of many coffee growers threatened not only the *sucriers'* economic preeminence but the sociopolitical order which rested on that wealth. Having completely transformed hitherto neglected areas of the colony, with no hope to visit or to return permanently to France, coffee growers proclaimed themselves the "true sons" of the island and asked—sometimes violently—a greater share in policy-making. Some ultimately challenged French power itself during and after the so-called "white revolt" of 1769. Many more engaged in smuggling by shipping coffee to North America, especially since their rapid expansion on frontier zones protected them from an already weakened state apparatus.

The consequences of the Coffee Revolution again exemplify the complexity of core and periphery relations. At the level of the system at large, Saint-Domingue's boom furthered the integration of the world economy. It reinforced, for instance, the already important ties between the Caribbean and the emerging United States, the new citizens of which had turned to coffee in the early 1770s, partly in the course of a more global reaction against tea and Britain. By reversing the trade between Europe (particularly Marseille) and the Levant, it accelerated the dependence of Near and Middle Eastern areas to European distribution. The Levantine and intra-European trades also strengthened France's position among the core states. But within Saint-Domingue itself, the Coffee Revolution ultimately weakened France's control over the colony.[7]

That such points can be made about a Caribbean colony at the peak of its sugar-and-slave career seems to me extremely significant. While one need not dwell here on all the peculiarities of the Antilles' integration in the European world-economy (Mintz 1966, 1974, 1977; Frank 1978: 120–129) it may be necessary to remind the reader that these islands were in fact Europe's earliest and—for a long time—most "dependent" colonies; colonies in the most complete sense, especially after the Amerindian genocide: populated, organized, shaped from the outside in accordance with the mercantilist dream of remote social entities which would exist—as Colbert put it—"only by and for the metropolis." From guests to hosts, from tools to buildings, from export crops to provisions and plantation to plantation, these were cloned societies, manufactured—as it seems—overnight for the sole benefit of capital. Here more than anywhere else, in the absence of indigenous polities and cultures, one would expect only mechanical responses to world-historical forces, circumscribed by the external and homogeneous imposition of a total dependency. That such was not the case in any of the Antilles—that in Saint-Domingue itself systemic imputs, clashing with particular developments, skewed in unforeseen directions—attests to the resonance of peripheral vibrations and underscores the need for a nuanced understanding of the interaction that they reveal.

NOTES

1. Tomich (1976: 7–8) quotes some of these thought-provoking passages from the *Grundrisse,* and also points to the necessity of treating "capitalist market and relations of production as a *unity.*" But to the extent that such relations are premised on the system itself, and that relations of domination are also taken into account, it might be appropriate to state that, in particular circumstances, *social* relations of production (though not necessarily the labor process) can be ultimately determined by processes of exchange and distribution. Marx's full text seems to allow for such a possibility, and I have suggested elsewhere that such a determination seems at work in the case of Haiti (Trouillot, 1980).

2. It is clear that Braudel speaks of "reintroduction" only because he sees the initial separation between economic and sociocultural frameworks ("cadres") as methodologically inevitable. But "society" *lato sensu* remains for him "the ensemble of ensembles" (see 1979a: 48–55, 540–544; 1979b: 407–410 and especially 409).

3. The term "Saint-Domingue" refers to the French colony which occupied the western third of the Caribbean island of Hispaniola. The term "Haiti" refers only to the independent nation that this colony became after the slave revolution of 1791–1804.

4. This paper is substantially based on a study of the "Coffee Revolution," presented at the Johns Hopkins Seminar in Atlantic History and Culture, "Motion in the System: Coffee, Color and Slavery in Eighteenth Century Saint-Domingue" (Trouillot, 1979). The original references to most factual statements and a more detailed analysis of the empirical evidences are included in that much larger version. I apologize to the reader for drawing, at times extensively, from a previous work, but this was unavoidable. The aim of this version is to expand theoretical views and methodological insights derived from the original work.

5. The fact that the Dutch East India Company never achieved total supervision of coffee cultivation in the Netherland Indies during the seventeenth and early eighteenth centuries, and at times could impose the crop only as a tax to be collected by native officials, evidences partly the differential control of the means of production (and of the labor force) in the outer and inner peripheries (see Leirissa, 1978; Wertheim, 1959). I am grateful to Suzanne Siskel for these references.

6. Of course, such a point of departure may not always be easily definable; and a "bottom-up" approach may fit more handily some disciplinary conventions. Using a "bottom-up" approach, Marilyn Silverman (1979) has produced a stimulating analysis of class formation in rural Guyana, in which she articulates macro- and micro-processes by focusing on middlemen as agents of mediation. Without denying the efficacy of a downward progression from the larger levels to more circumscribed ensembles, she suggests that anthropologists, having a "worm's eye view of society," might find an upward movement more manageable (1979: 469). As a student of anthropology, I sense no fundamental incompatibility between a downward progression and specific micro-analyses. Indeed, such a progression seems amenable to Silverman's paper, which "begins with the premise that West Indian economies are dependent" (1979: 467). I suggest that it might be necessary for those engaged in research activities such as fieldwork or the untangling of specific historical events to distinguish between the order of discovery and the order of exposition. In the particular case of Saint-Domingue's Coffee Revolu-

tion, the downward progression seems to ensure the incorporation of the larger processes in the analysis and, moreover, to facilitate the discovery of legitimately defined (and/or viable) units of study at lower, more intermediate levels.

7. For reasons of space, the progression is not carried down, in this particular paper, to the level of the unit of production. But the swift development of coffee cultivation seems to have introduced qualitative changes in the daily practice of slavery on the plantations, and may have influenced, in yet unclear ways, the emerging Creole culture (Trouillot, 1979). The possible impact of the coffee explosion on the slave rebellion of 1791 has yet to be examined.

REFERENCES

BRAUDEL, F. (1979a) Civilisation Matérielle, Economie et Capital-isme, XVe–XVIIIe Siècle. Tome 2. Les Jeux de L'Echange. Paris: Armand Colin.

————(1979b) Civilisation Matérielle, Economie et Capitalisme, XVe–XVIIIe Siècle. Tome 3. Le Temps du Monde. Paris: Armand Colin.

FRANK, A.G. (1978). World Accumulation, 1492–1789. New York: Monthly Review Press.

LEIRISSA, R.Z. (1978) "The Dutch trading monopolies," in H. Soeba-dio and C.-A. du Marchie Savaas (eds.) Dynamics of Indonesian History. Amsterdam: North Holland.

MARX, K. (1973) Grundrisse. New York: Vintage Books.

MINTZ, S.W. (1966) "The Caribbean as a socio-cultural area." Cahiers d'Histoire Mondiale IX: 916–941.

————(1974) Caribbean Transformations. Chicago: AVC.

————(1977) "The so-called world-system: local initiative and local response." Dialectical Anthropology III (4): 253–270.

MOREAU de SAINT-MÉRY, M.L.E. (1958[1797]) Description Topo-graphique, Physique, Civile, Politique et Historique de la Partie Fran-çaise de l'Isle Saint-Domingue. 3 vols. Paris: Société de l'Histoire des Colonies Françaises et Librairie Larose.

SILVERMAN M. (1979) "Dependency, mediation, and class formation in rural Guyana." American Ethnologist VI (3): 466–490.

TOMICH, D. (1976) "Some further reflections on class and class conflict in the world-economy." Fernand Braudel Center, Working Papers, Seminar I.

TROUILLOT, M.-R. (1979) "Motion in the system: coffee, color and slavery in eighteenth century Saint-Domingue." (unpublished)

———(1980) "Review of M. Lundahl, Peasants and Poverty: A Study of Haiti." Journal of Peasant Studies VIII (1): 112–116.

WERTHEIM, W. F. (1959) Indonesian Society in Transition. A Study of Social Change. The Hague and Bandung: W. van Hoeve.

Chapter 2

THE STATE AS
INSTRUMENT OF INDUCTION
TO THE PERIPHERY:
THE CASE OF GREECE

Kostis Papadantonakis
Essex Community College

First, I would argue that Greece is *not* in the semiperiphery![1] It may have belonged there long before Greek Independence was achieved through the Revolution of 1821–1828, in the sense that the Ottoman Empire, against which the Greeks revolted, was semiperipheral with respect to the European world-economy in the seventeenth through nineteenth centuries. But the process through which the Ottoman Empire (meaning the entire Eastern Mediterra-

---

AUTHOR'S NOTE: My thanks to Chandler Morse and Linda Zeidman for their thorough criticisms in the earlier stages of this paper's preparation; to the many discussants, following the reading of a (herein revised) version at the conference; and to Terence Hopkins and Immanuel Wallerstein, who were kind enough to include responses to certain issues raised above in their own presentations on the second day of the conference.

nean basin) was ultimately assimilated into the periphery of the world-system entailed the disintegration of the empire and its replacement by a number of nation-states. Modern Greece was first of this number, preceding Serbia (which gained autonomy at the same time but became independent some fifty years later), Egypt, Rumania, Bulgaria, and others—including Turkey, which acquired the character of a national state only after the turn of the century, when the liquidation of the Ottoman power was almost complete.

This poses an ideological contradiction, in that the very act of national liberation from the eastern multinational empire was also a decisive step toward the peripheralization of that entire empire to the West (and, incidentally, toward the national subordination of Greece to the neocolonial rule of Western imperialism).

As the Greek territories expanded in the course of national liberation struggles, in the first century following independence, the new nation's budding ruling class tried to solve this contradiction—at least in rhetoric—by promoting their own imperialistic ideology of *Meghali Idea:* "Greece shall straddle the Five Seas and the Two Continents!" What this "grand ideal" envisioned was nothing short of the resurrection of the Byzantine Empire as the successor of the Turks' rule over the entire Eastern Mediterranean basin.[2]

Had this been accomplished, we could well be talking today of Greek subimperialism; we could be thinking of Greece as a semi-peripheral entity, possibly even a young core formation. Fortunately for the almost-subjects of this latter-day Hellenic Empire, all that has survived from *Meghali Idea* is the rhetoric of Greece as the outpost of Western civilization protecting Europe's flanks from "oriental barbarism," much as Greeks and Turks alike supposedly protect NATO's southeast flank from the "communist menace" today. For, by the nature of its creation, the Greek ruling class developed little stomach for taking on the role of a rival to its core-based masters. Such a posture would have entailed trading the function of the Europeans' *agent liquidateur* for that of an anti-European *agent nationalitaire*—a unifier of peoples, a creator of oriental nationalism on the scale of the Balkans, Anatolia, and the Middle East, or at least over some of these subregions of the Eastern Mediterranean basin. As it happened, the more consolidated the statehood of the new Greek nation became, the more parochial the Greek ruling class and the firmer its entrenchment proceeded as a class of marginalized capitalists in the periphery of the European- and later American-dominated world-economy.

GENERALIZATIONS

Indeed, I shall be arguing that the development of a strong national state (in the narrow sense of the state as the coercive-administrative apparatus confronting the broader national arena of Greek civil society)[3] was instrumental in effecting Greece's induction to the periphery. The case of Greece demonstrates what I believe to be demonstrable again and again for many parts of the world which progressed in the seventeenth, eighteenth, and nineteenth centuries from semiperipheral to peripheral status. The passage from the former, looser, and somewhat ambiguous form of dependency (Wallerstein, 1979a, 1979b; Winckler, 1979) to the latter's well-determined position in the world division of labor has entailed a reversal—I should say, an *abrupt* reversal—from a weak state to a strong state.

As a first approximation, "weak" means that the state is subordinate to civil society with respect to the setting of economic goals and the determination of directions and limits to the development of economic and social institutions, while "strong" implies the predominance of the state over civil society in these respects. Ultimately, the question is as to where we locate the focus of social antagonisms, as they develop to the point when we may begin to talk of the existence of class polarity: Is this a process which primarily devolves out of the forces of the society and the economy at large—that is, of civil society? That would be the case of a weak state. Or is it a process fomented by the deliberate policies and general functioning of the state? (A strong state, in that event.)[4]

We have examples of weak states and strong states, thus defined, in the history of the core's formation.[5] The classical economic debate between mercantilism and liberalism is itself an example of the choice between strong and weak statism, consciously considered by the ruling classes of the core.[6] Finally, when we consider the core nations of our time, it is possible to speak of states, or at least statist trends such as that toward European integration,[7] becoming weaker or stronger, relatively to the pertinent civil society of the core.[8] It should be clear, moreover, that such varied examples show weakness no less than strength in the configuration "state and civil society" as having an equally salutory effect on the economic development and preservation of core-capitalism.

As regards the periphery of the world-economy, it is likewise possible to identify weak states and strong states, except that here both types have the negative effect of entrenching and perpetuating underdevelopment and subordination to the core. Thus, we may look at various colonial administrations as either weak or strong state formations, depending on whether their historic role was to allow a free hand in the actions of colonizers and of those among the colonized, whom we could label *compradores* (sellouts), or, by contrast, to force the hand of both colonial and indigenous elements away from contesting the peripheral status of the colony in question. Similarly, we have instances of formerly sovereign states in the semiperiphery and periphery that are weak or strong at different moments in their history of induction to the world-economy.

It is my contention that, in order to experience the passage from the external arena to the periphery, Greece and a host of similar countries had to undergo a passage from a patently weak state to a strong one. To draw a historical parallel (for there is more than irony in the symmetry of periphery to core in this case), I will be referring to the rise and functioning of a strong peripheral state as the phenomenon of "inverted mercantilism."

Inverted mercantilism, whether practiced by a colonial state or by one that boasts sovereignty, as in Greece, is the policy of rationalization of dependency; that is, of induction to and functioning within the periphery of the world-economy by using state intervention to tie the interests of the indigenous ruling class to the entrenchment of domination by the core. As such, it has the by-product of entrenching and perpetuating underdevelopment, by contrast to mercantilism proper, as it historically functioned in effecting the induction to or preserving the functioning within the core of erstwhile semiperipheral areas of the world-system.

PARTICULARITIES

How necessary was this inverted mercantilism in the peripheralization of Greece? In what ways did the state affect (and, more specifically, in what ways did it *alter*) the course of economic and social formation evolving in the relevant civil society before and after the induction of Greece to the periphery? Finally, what has been the role of the Greek state in fomenting the class polarities which define and (partially) determine modern Greek political life?

To begin with, we must establish which was the relevant socio-economic space in which Greece's preindependence civil society was located. In my mind, there is little doubt but that we should be talking of the entire Eastern Mediterranean basin—for that was the area which European mercantilism penetrated and eventually fragmented, in reducing the Ottoman Empire to semiperipheral status during the two centuries that preceded the Greek Revolution.

Many scholars opt for a narrow definition, considering only the Balkans and Anatolia as the relevant area, on the grounds that it was there that the Greek element was to be found in its heaviest concentration within the empire (Psiroukis, 1973; Kremmydas, 1976). This is fine, if one is interested in establishing the origins of the modern Greek nation. But it is not such introspective (not to say chauvinistic) historiography that interests us here. In retrospect, of course, it is easy to argue that the Ottoman Empire was little more than an agglomeration of more or less separately articulated national entities, distinct by religion, language, historical origin, and even consciousness, long before the nineteenth century. National historiography has done a lot to document, or conjure documentation for, such differences, which in any event became tangible from the end of the eighteenth century on.

Yet a noteworthy minority (from Stavrianos [1944, 1958] to Braudel [1949] and on to what threatens to become a majority in our day!) have approached the Ottoman Empire as something more than a multinational entity. Exactly what that is naturally varies. In my view it is not adequate to confine such an approach to the obvious coherency of the Balkan and broader Eastern Mediterranean area as an economic space, replete with its own "variegated methods of labor control" (Wallerstein, 1974: 38) in the context of its internal division of labor by region and/or product. There ought to be an additional, speculative element as a guide to historical research. This has to do with the Ottoman state and the role it failed to play in the face of mounting pressure and increasing penetration by the European capitalists and their Ottoman cohorts.[9]

STATE AND CIVIL SOCIETY
IN THE LATE OTTOMAN EMPIRE

By the standards set earlier in my argument, the Ottoman state was weak. More precisely, it had been strong in the fifteenth and sixteenth centuries, but thereafter the very characteristics which had made it a force of unification and cohesion in the early period turned more and more into liabilities by the end of the sixteenth century—and certainly by the second half of the seventeenth. I refer to much more than the success of Turkish conquests in the period of cohesion, for there were additional reasons why the economics of the Empire were relatively inwardly oriented at the time (Stavrianos, 1958: 81–136, 137, 887–889). By contrast, in the later period economic activity was forced to reorient itself outwardly, toward international trade.[10] The result was growing antagonism between private economic power and state power, an antagonism felt doubly as a strain that pushed against the cornerstones against which the empire was founded.

The first source of strain was the religious and ethnic divisions which coincided with the rift between private and state power. The Ottoman world-economy was that of a multinational empire. Its division of labor run along ethnic lines, with commercial and seafaring tasks becoming allotted to Greeks, by and large, as of the end of the eighteenth century. As the westerly reorientation of trade increased the controlling influence of these tasks, those who performed them formed the nucleus of a commercial capitalist class, strategically deployed to command all other *capitalist-leaning* elements within Ottoman civil society.[11]

On the other hand, military and administrative functions falling on the side of the progressively emerging watershed that was the domain of the state were also subject to an ethnic division of labor, reinforced by the not-so-rigid religious line separating Moslems from the rest. Ironically, here too, Greeks had a multiplicity of roles as their preserve by the turn of the century. These included nonmilitary central administrative posts, the bulk of foreign affairs, the administration of certain frontier-line provinces in the Balkans, and the central administration of Anatolian and Balkan Christians through the Orthodox clerical network. In the end, when the growing rift between state and civil society acquired religious and ethnic lines of demarcation as central features of its ideological expression, the Greeks dominating civil society either prevailed or appeared to have done so upon stateside Greeks— enough, at all events, to cause the Porte to dismantle a good deal of its statist human capital in the process of purging itself of its Greek functionaries.

The second strain, generated by the antagonism between creeping capitalism and the state, was felt upon the basic productive structures of the Ottoman economy. As the state's control over civil society waned, the position of peasant agriculture (by far the largest productive sector in the economy) was transformed from one of relative political stability to one of highly destabilizing explosiveness. Before this transformation, the state both received the lion's share of the surplus product (or at least determined its allocation) and regulated the rate of its extraction. After European penetration had been well on its way, the international market-oriented commercial interests came to control the realization of the surplus product—and thus indirectly determined (and largely profited from) its allocation as well as the rate of exploitation of the peasantry. The result was unmitigated deterioration in the peasants' standard of living, accompanied by the inevitable repression—a repression whose political character was ideologically masked by religious and ethnic bigotry, to be sure.[12]

In the view of some scholars (Kremmydas, 1976; Asdrachas, 1978), the extent of this transformation—particularly in the social relations of production and distribution—was just short of a timely transition to capitalist agriculture. Indeed, there is clear evidence that the shift to commercial cultures of exportables involved the mobilization not only of traditionally obligated peasant labor but also of privately owned slave-labor and seasonally employed wage-labor as well (Kremmydas, 1976: 49–55). Regardless of how close such a transformation might have been (a point of moot teleology, in any event), there is little question that what was precipitating it was the impetus of European penetration.

Similar arguments, purporting to show (and not without good documentation: Maximos, 1945; Kordatos, 1930) that certain areas of nonagricultural production were right at the crack of capitalist dawn, again leave little doubt that the development of such indigenous capitalism was stimulated by the growing penetration

of the empire from without. Thus, we have evidence of shipbuild-
ing, soap and textile manufacturing, and the production of other
exportables under social relations reminiscent of the final stages of
decay in western guilds and indeed, at times identical to early
capitalist manufactories and cottage industry arrangements, as
they occurred in the West.

In both cases, what is important has less to do with the extent of
creeping capitalism and more with the sources and consequences
of such a movement. First, European penetration until the second
decade of the nineteenth century was *not* underdeveloping or in
any sense peripheralizing of the Ottoman economy. It is true that
the capitalist manufacturing potential depicted above crashed under the combined weight of the post-Napoleonic depression
(1813–1820) and the flooding of eastern markets by British industrial products (Moskoff, 1972). However, there is no comparable
reversal in the case of agricultural development; such a reversal
comes later, in the wake of *national* policies deliberately pursued
by many of the Balkan and Middle Eastern states that emerge from
the empire. Second, underdevelopment and peripheralization,
first in the form of blocking the rise of industry and then in the
arrestation of capitalist development in agriculture, seem to have
been decided only as the course of a truly decisive battle for state
power was brought to its resolve.

That the outcome of this battle was the fragmentation of the
empire is in my view what really makes it decisive. For fragmentation meant much more than diminution in size. In effect, it made it
possible to deflect a social revolution, wherein a configuration of
classes had allied to wrest state power from a decaying class-
alliance unable to stem the historic tide that unmistakably
threatened the Ottoman world qua multinational empire. By functioning as the central authority in a multinational empire, the Porte
managed at once to preserve the Ottoman social order for a while
and to forego the chance for what in retrospect we could regard as
the course of "modernization." As the peasants of region after
region rose in revolt, supported and prompted by much of what

might have otherwise evolved into an Ottoman bourgeoisie, the state proved strong enough to resist them and weak enough to have no recourse but divestiture of the offending province.

Had the Greek, Serbian, and other revolutions been crushed, had Egyptian seditiousness not been seduced by the West, or had the Greek and other elements of the central state apparatus which were purged in the wake of 1821 been capable of asserting themselves in control of that apparatus, then the Ottoman Empire would have likely emerged as a formidable part of the semiperiphery in the final years of the nineteenth century. As it is, there are very clearly understood reasons why this did not happen. And consequently, by the end of that century, the peripheralization of the Eastern Mediterranean basin was almost complete.

CLASS POLARITIES AND
THE NEW GREEK STATE

The 1820s saw revolts by Albanians, Moldavians, Serbians, Rumanians, Armenians, as well as Greeks against the Porte. At the southern tip of the Balkan peninsula, the inability of the Turkish and Egyptian armadas to wrestle control of the littoral provinces of Moreas and Rumeli from the Greek privateers (and eventually from the combined fleets of the European powers) proved decisive. By 1828, with Russia's intrusion stopped by the British at Adrianople, the Porte was forced to recognize Greek independence. What had started as a generalized peasant revolution thus came to an end with minimal territorial losses for the empire, entailing one of its more mountainous and least fertile agricultural regions.

In the "liberated" area, moreover, the peasant revolution fared no better. Since it was thanks to foreign intervention that independence had been assured, the new nation had from the start the de facto status of a protectorate of the Great Powers (England, France, Austria, Russia). In total contrast to the revolutionary

process, where the rising masses conquered legitimacy in proportion to their former class subordination and consequent militancy,
a hierarchical chain was implied in the new postrevolutionary
order that placed at the top those who were most remote from the
revolution. These were, first, the leading Greek families of merchant houses located outside the Ottoman Empire; they were cosmopolitan elements of the core bourgeoisie, whose strength lay in
their ability to function as go-betweens, effecting the contact of
national elements of the core bourgeoisie (such as British or
French capitalists) with indigenous merchants of the Ottoman and
Russian Empires.

Second were those who constituted the next link in the chain of
contact described above. These were Greek merchants in the European semi-periphery (Trieste, Vienna, Odessa) and in the leading
commercial centers of the Ottoman Empire (Istanbul, Smyrna,
Alexandria, Saloniki). Along with these go-between commercial
elements were the leading members of large expatriate and Ottoman urban communities of Greeks who constituted an intelligentsia of sorts, at once alienated from their surrounding social formations and integrated in the as yet somewhat mythical society of
Greece proper.

In Greek society, finally, there was a distinguishable "upper
class" of warlord-landlords (though most of the landlords of the
region had been Turks and were expelled in the revolution) and
privateer merchants. Along with them were a large number of
nonnative Greeks, who had participated in the revolution or appeared on the scene shortly after its end, and who can best be
described as a declassé intelligentsia. In comparison to the Greeks
outside Greece described above, these "upper-class" strata were
situated in an ambiguous position. On the one hand, they were
precariously parochial, representing the "middle strata," as it
were, in the chain linking Greece as one (minor) part of the Eastern
Mediterranean basin to the core. On the other hand, they were
potentially secure in that they had a territorial base which the
cosmopolitan Greeks outside Greece could never hope to attain—a

factor that acquired growing significance in step with the rising
tide of nationalism in Europe and the Middle East. The first of
these contrasts placed the domestic elements in a subordinate position to the outsiders; the second placed them in the position of
rivals. Inevitably, such a formulation of positional choice leads to
the kindred observation that the first alternative (subordination)
would coincide with a peripheral status for Greece in the European
world-economy, while the second would imply at the minimum
an attempt to remove Greece from the periphery (semiperipheral
status).

In reality, there was little choice. The major polarity in Greek
society was between what I earlier called "the rising masses" and
the order implied by the country's status as a protectorate. Those
who had been the fodder for the revolutionary war were, of course,
the peasants, whose political demands had an urgency derived not
from the failure but the success of the new capitalist-leaning orientation in agriculture. This new orientation had entailed higher rates
of exploitation as the combined result of adverse market forces and
reduced state protection from private encroachment on the traditional limits of peasant obligations. In the absence of a sizable
domestic market for cash crops, little could be done about the
mounting pressures from the world market forces, short of wholesale retreat to a demonetized economy, as had been the case two
centuries earlier.[13] And in the absence of an effective replacement
for the old *anticapitalist* state of the Ottoman Empire, little could
be hoped for relief from capitalist encroachment on the rights of
peasants, short of the latter's complete elimination of the former.

In fact, the political aims of the Greek Revolution, insofar as
one can venture to ascertain what the peasantry fought for (Stamatopoulos, 1957–1973; Kordatos, 1946; Katsoulis, 1974), were for
direct control of the land (against landlords and tax-collectors),
presumably to the end of assuring the comfortable subsistence of
village communities (not commerce). Early in the revolutionary
war, the peasants lost most of their conscious leadership, focusing
on these demands, in the course of a concurrently fought civil war

against the warlords and their declassé allies. Thereafter, what might have started as a conscious revolutionary aspiration remained as a strong undercurrent. Indeed, it is not an exaggeration to say that the history of the one hundred years following Greek Independence (1828–1934) is that of containment of this revolutionary undercurrent (Zevgos, 1946). By the time a land reform was implemented, in the 1930s, the Greek peasant question had fallen to a secondary place, eclipsed by the confrontation between the state and the working class.

To sum up, the dominant class polarity of the nineteenth century was not between the cosmopolitan Greek capitalists and the domestic upper strata, but rather between all of these and the peasantry. Usually allied with the peasants were also the displaced wage workers and craftsmen of the soon-bankrupt Greek manufacturing units, along with the frequently idling crews of the sizable Greek merchant marine. It is this polarized confrontation between the new nation's classes that its freshly mounted state apparatus was *intended* to mediate. As the virtual protectorate of the Europeans, Greece had little choice but to accept such intentional arrangements. In this sense, the victory of European imperialism in establishing and thereafter controlling the historic Greek state signified the defeat of the Greek Revolution, both as the social movement in the early nineteenth-century Ottoman Balkans and as the social undercurrent of the class struggle in modern Greece.

Protracted into the second century of Greece's independent existence (1930s to the present), this class struggle has been complicated by the problematic character of the Greek state: a state at once mediating the external polarity of core-periphery relations and the internal polarity of the frustrated peasant revolution, followed by that of workers versus capitalists.[14] It is the result of the historic inability of the Greek people to overthrow this state that peripheral dependence and underdevelopment were first entrenched (roughly) between 1828 and 1909) and thereafter rationalized more or less as the dictates of the core's imperialism required.[15]

INVERTED MERCANTILISM
AND PERIPHERALIZATION

The history of such developments as are mentioned above is too long and complicated to recount here (Tsoukalas, 1969; Stavrianos, 1958), but the following generalizations are worth venturing to complete my argument.

First, contrary to the prerevolutionary period, the gap between state and civil society had all but disappeared in the wake of the revolution. Those who had power in civil society were at the helm of the state. Yet the contradiction between private economic power and state power had not been resolved. This contradiction had arisen in the broader arena of the Ottoman Empire; it contested the course of potential development in the entire Eastern Mediterranean basin, not merely in the minuscule portion that had just emerged as the Kingdom of Greece. The battle for control of the territories of the Sick Man of Europe had just begun. So long as it was to go on unresolved, the status of the Ottoman Empire was semiperipheral. And to be semiperipheral was to have a persistent hiatus between state and civil society, allowing the continued penetration of the latter and the subversion of the former from the West.

In Greece, too, this penetration was taking place, except that there it was not necessary to subvert the state. On the contrary, the rationalization of Greece's role in the division of labor within the world-economy of Europe was about to unfold as a process very much directed by the state. For the part of the Ottoman Empire that became Greece, the revolution entailed an abrupt reversal from a weak state, subject to foreign supplanting, to a strong state, subject to foreign control. The policies of that strong state (which I call "inverted mercantilism") succeeded in effecting the induction of Greece to the periphery over the remainder of the nineteenth century.

The systematic investigation of nineteenth-century Greek economic policy has yet to be carried out. Nevertheless, I sense a contemporary consensus in the making (Vergopoulos, 1975; Filias, 1974; Mouzelis, 1978) as regards the second set of generalizations: concerning the role of the state. First, it appears that it attacked both peasants and warlords with equanimity. It forestalled the mass demand for the distribution of the lands abandoned by the Turks to those who were propertyless, but it also prevented its appropriation by the warlords. This was conscious policy, dictated by the Great Powers, who were the guarantors of the Greek external debt; for the lands in question were considered collateral for the Greek state's bonds. Behind the Great Powers were leading financial centers of the West European core. But the holders of the bonds, floated by these financiers, were by and large cosmopolitan Greeks! In as much as these latter were influential in the shaping of Greek politics (partly through direct involvement and partly through the progressive cooptation of the declassé elements of Greece's upper strata), there is little wonder that the new nation complied to pressure from the Great Powers without much protestation.[16]

Second, the resultant control of Greek agriculture by the state enabled the latter to indicate a course of increasing agricultural specialization which rendered the country's production monocultural by the last quarter of the nineteenth century. When the bottom fell out of the market for Greek currants in the West, the stage was set for following the path of Ottoman Turkey by declaring bankruptcy and accepting an "International Control Commission" as the overseer and eventual (1901) manager of Greek fiscal matters. Thus, all public policy was ultimately reduced to direct external decision-making.

Third, by reducing the power of warlords and other localized elements of political strength, the state asserted a highly centralized network which facilitated the emergence of a cultural and eventually economic dualism within Greece. The political dependence of the countryside on the urban center of Athens seems to have functioned as an alternative mechanism for the emergence of middle layers in Greek society, consisting of dignitaries feeding on the relative splendor of the royal palace, the civil service, and military elite, the resourceful interlocutors with connections abroad, and the like. This adulterated bourgeoisification, as a leading Greek sociologist has called it (Filias, 1974), entailed a process of class formation which attracted the leading elements of a preexisting "petty bourgeoisie in-the-making" from the artisan, the small-town merchants and the ranks of kulak peasants. All these tended to flock into Athens, turning the city into an enclave of Europeanized ex-Ottoman subjects surrounded by a sea of over-taxed, overexploited peasants, ready to revolt once again in order to attain the revolutionary goals of 1821.

I would argue that what was occurring economically at the time was a double process—and this is a third cluster of generalizations. On one level, we have a continued process of disaccumulation in the provinces, complemented by the sustained influx of monetized surplus to Athens. This enabled Athens to grow in size and change in quality so that it could assume the characteristics of a westernized enclave, as noted above. On a second level, we have a process of continuing (and deliberately pursued) linkage-creation between the Greek periphery (the provinces) and abroad (the core of the world-economy), so that the Greek center (Athens) could attain satisfaction of its Europeanized tastes. Urban imports are thus traded for rural exports—and the principal beneficiaries of such trade activity are cosmopolitan Greeks who are experienced in such ventures from the trade of the Ottoman and Russian Empires.

By the turn of the century, this situation reached a dead end. Disaccumulation reduced the potential of the countryside for growth at the moment when parasitic consumption habituated Athens to a pattern of permanent external deficits, with respect to the European core. Having bled the countryside white, the city felt poor—and this not-so-feigned poverty of the city seems to have left no hope for supplying any developmental aspirations in the countryside. Underdevelopment in its classicial, Nurksean form (Nurkse, 1953) became a reality.[17]

The Greek state did not *wish* such underdevelopment. Yet it did attack those who wished to avert it—and it did so as a matter of conscious policy. As a final generalization, it is possible to sketch the class polarities referred to earlier against the scenery provided by the above observations. Those who were the enemies of the state can be juxtaposed to those for whom the state was a friend.

At one pole we have the peasants. It is not, however, that the state was harsh on the peasants; quite the contrary. At times it appeared outright sympathetic (Vergopoulos, 1975, 1978). Rather, the chief preoccupation of the state was to avoid a change in the status of the peasants. Can we argue with any conviction that a capitalist agriculture might have developed had state policy been different? I am not sure, but there *is* room to argue that it would have been problematic to subdue and destroy the loci of accumulation in the provinces without the multiple network of centralization wrought by the state. Without localized accumulation, primitive though the forms of this accumulation might have been, it would be unreasonable to expect to see the development of capitalist accumulation in the periphery of Athens.

At the other pole we have "the Greek ruling class" as it developed in the course of the first century of independence. Here again, it is not that the state was the conscious instrument of an identifiable social group from the start. Rather, the state was the rallying point around which such a grouping could be formed in the course of the century. Can we postulate some alternative ruling class in the absence of the historical Greek state? Here I think that what was said about the Ottoman Empire as a whole, before the Greek and other revolutions took place, suggests some answers. The Greek state became the rallying point of cosmopolitan Greeks, among others. It provided them with territoriality even as they continued in their function as go-betweens (Tsoukalas, 1977; Psiroukis, 1974) in the world-system at large. As seasoned capitalists, the cosmopolitans were formidable rivals to lesser actual or potential indigenous capitalist elements; as seasoned *compradores,* they were in a position to do unto Greece what they were eventually prevented from doing in other areas of the Eastern Mediterranean basin and Russia. The nationalistic developments abroad stopped them as capitalists at large; but in Greece nationalism meant their glorification. In the end, Greek capitalism emerged as a well-articulated class without an economy to go with it. That, too, is an aspect of Greek underdevelopment in the twentieth century. And I would argue that such a contradictory situation could not be sustained without a strong state apparatus.

CONCLUSIONS

I have tried to show that even in the midst of a course of spiraling economic weakness, of underdeveloping weakness, and even in the course of intensifying setbacks in a country's ability to determine its social and economic orientation, there is an element of strength that is required in order for this course to be successful. Some people regard peripheralization as the consequent of core-country action in an otherwise inert world. Others see it as the result of sheer economic activity undertaken by complying social classes, enlisting themselves somehow in the ranks of a rational division of labor on a worldwide scale.

While very accepting of the significance of such factors, I believe that it is a mistake to overlook the determining role of the political process in effecting this economic direction which places a country in a state of dependency and rationalized participation in the world division of labor. Such placement does not come naturally. The trends toward capitalist agriculture in the Ottoman Empire, for example, could be seen as more natural as they were multiplying in the era of semiperipheral dependence than, say, the trend toward economic dualism in Independent Greece.

It is not true that it suffices to do nothing for dependency to develop. It is hard work to break down a society's motion toward technical and institutional modernization. It is not sufficient to be slothful in order to become backward.

NOTES

1. Since this paper was read in the session of the conference devoted to the semiperipheral state and development, a heated discussion arose as to the meaning of the terms "periphery" and "semiperiphery" and as to whether Greece is part of the one or the other category of states in the world-system. As the Hopkins-Wallerstein session finally confirmed, it is a mistake to think of the core, the semiperiphery, and the periphery as unilinear elements in a progression of sorts within the world-system. The essential relationship is that between core and periphery, which constitutes a dialectical pair, so to speak. Semiperipheral are the entities which do not fit either pole of this dialectical relationship. My argument is that Greece fits in this polarity quite unambiguously.

2. This, at least, is the logical consequence of what at times appeared as little more than a nationalistic aspiration to unify all Greeks within one national state, while in certain authors' and orators' arguments the matter of national unity was clearly supplanted by that of national supremacy over all others.

3. Another semantic debate erupted here during the follow-up discussion of this paper. The distinction between state and civil society, rather familiar from Hegel's fundamental discussion of the State (1896: sections 182ff, 251ff) is meant here in the way Gramsci has amplified in his like-titled essay (1971: 210ff). Unlike the German idealist, the Italian Marxist employed the dialectical juxtaposition between the political society, which supplies the social space for locating the state, and the civil society, wherein he analyzes his concept of hegemony, in order to comprehend not the state but its revolutionary negation in the course of the class struggle. In this paper, "civil society" refers to the socioeconomic framework of particular (more or less private) power relations; to that aspect of the wielding and reproduction of power and ideology which is not the state.

4. Nothing in this definition of the state, especially the strong state, should be construed to imply a state-complex operating for itself, liberated, as it were, from the usual instrumental function of the state apparatus in the service of the objective interests of the ruling class. A strong state is merely one whose action is required in order to effect (or obstruct) social

change, in whosever interests such change may (or may not) be; by contrast, a weak state is merely one whose actions or inactions are less consequential, typically proving to be secondary to initiatives taken, and carried out one way or another in the nonstatist arena—that of civil society.

5. Without much conviction, I would think of the period of U.S. development from Hamilton to the ascendancy of Jackson as one of strong statism, coinciding with the removal of the new republic from the periphery. The period immediately preceding U.S. induction to the core (and in that sense, the era of transformation from semiperipheral to core status), from Jackson to the Civil War and to the crash of the Populist movement (from which point on imperialism becomes conscious policy at home and abroad), seems by contrast to be one marked by a weak state in the context of the above definitions.

6. A debate, to be sure, not over the question of bringing power to bear or not, but rather of whether power was to be exerted through the mechanisms of the state or through private mechanisms of comparable or greater effectiveness (Dowd, 1971).

7. The weakening of West European state apparatuses is feared by the authors of *"Le Marché Commun contre l'Europe"* on the grounds that "the more the Community institutions will gain power, the more they will exercise it to dismantle and cause to disappear whatever might inhibit the development of savage Capitalism" (Jaumont et al., 1973, my translation).

8. Undoubtedly, it is the internationalization of civil society at the core that dictates much of what is transpiring at the state level. The more what used to be *international* economic and social processes become *regional* processes (in the transnational sense of "region"), the more we have to revise our notions of what constitutes a strong state and what makes a weak one (Palloix, 1975).

9. See Stavrianos: "Another subject requiring serious research for an understanding of Ottoman decline is *the location of power* after the weakening of the sultans. . . . Closely related is the influence of various national groups at various periods. It appears that the Serbs and the Jews played a dominant role in imperial affairs to the seventeenth century and were replaced by the Greeks to 1821 and by the Bulgarians and Armenians for the remaining period" (1958: 889, my italics). The second question he raised is only incidentally touched upon here; nevertheless,

the centrality of Greeks in imperial affairs has a lot to do with the subsequent role of the Greek ruling class in the nineteenth century.

10. The main staple involved in this trade reorientation was wheat. But the forms this trade assumed are of greater interest to the discussion that follows: At first much of this trade was illegal (that is, contraband and even piracy, in the form of first capturing domestic-bound wheat shipments and then illegally exporting them to the West); later it was undertaken under direct European trade monopolies, in the context of special concessions *(capitulations)* by the Porte (Kremmydas, 1976: 118, 62–63). The failure of the Ottoman state to reverse the trend set by these concessions left little choice for indigenous commercial and seafaring interests: Either the erst-while pirates and contrabandists had to go out of business or they were to accede to the role of agents for the direct trade monopolies of external holders of capitulations.

11. I do not mean to ascribe to the term "capitalist-leaning" any teleological pretenses. Simply, I find it convenient as a shorthand reference to all the many loci of surplus appropriation and potential or actual accumulation in private or otherwise decentralized hands. Within the empire, such loci were many and diverse—their diversity being largely a function of the noncapitalist character of the Ottoman world-economy as a whole. It is not the scope of this paper to investigate the rise of such elements (to which I refer as "creeping capitalism" later on), although I am trying to shed light to their eventual arrestation.

12. This is hardly an exceptional development. It appears that the shift from state-determined ethnic, religious, or racial divisions of labor to market-determined specialization frequently tends to replace the relatively benign and undoubtedly equilibrating pluralism of statist multinationalism, multiracialism, and the like, by a more pernicious individualistic ideology of stratificational bigotry. Privatization breeds racism, as it certainly did for the Ottoman world.

13. Rather than thinking of such an alternative as retrogression, we could, of course, liken it to the Maoist policy of "walking on two legs," with agricultural production yielding a surplus sufficient to finance national industry. Naturally, such a policy would require the peasants to be very much in control of the state (though not necessarily by themselves), rather than attempting to retreat to some anarchic (and mythical) "natural economy."

14. In the nineteenth century, the Greek ruling class succeeded in placing emphasis on the external polarity (the "Grand Ideal") enough to

disorient the conscious popular forces and thus defuse the internal polarity. By contrast, the Communist leadership of the early 1940s managed to identify the two polarities and project them onto the popular consciousness as one: the anti-imperialist struggle *for* a socialist Greece.

15. Two critiques of Wallerstein's penchant for somewhat teleological historiography, one thorough (Brenner, 1977) and the other rather flippant (George, 1980), have sensitized me to the perils of ascribing intentionality to historical developments. Yet it seems to me that, precisely for that reason, we must be particularly sensitive to the role of the state in shaping the world-system; for the state, especially an *imposed* state, is uniquely intentional. After all, it is no accident that all conscious fighting of class struggles has sooner or later to be focused upon the capturing (or preservation) of state-power.

16. There were exceptions, to be sure. The naval blocades of the 1850s and 1860s by the French and British "protectors" were ostensibly carried out to safeguard foreign creditors. In all such cases, however, what was at issue was not Greece's willingness to honor its foreign indebtedness, but more substantive matters of internal political developments which were potentially disruptive of the nation's peripheral status.

17. Nurkse theorized, it will be recalled, that a "vicious circle of poverty" characterized by extremely low levels of surplus and consequently no room for significant investment (which would be required to ensure growth in future surplus) frequently tends to perpetuate an "underdevelopment equilibrium" as the secular trend.

REFERENCES

ASDRACHAS, S. (1978) Μηχανισμοί της αγροτικής οικονομίας στην Τουρκοκρατία (ΙΕ΄–ΙΣΤ΄ ΑΙ) (Mechanisms of the Agricultural Economy under the Turks, XV-XVI Centuries).Athens: Themelio.

BRAUDEL, F. (1966) La Méditerranée et le monde méditerranéen à l'époque de Philippe II. 2 vols. Paris: Librairie Armand Colin.

BRENNER, R. (1977) "The origins of capitalist development: a critique of neo-Smithian Marxism." New Left Review 104: 25–92.

DOWD, D. F. (1971) The State, Power, and the Industrial Revolution, 1750–1914, Union for Radical Political Economics Occasional Paper No. 4. New York.

FILIAS, V. (1974) Κοινωνία και εξουσία στην Ελλάδα. Η νόθα αστικοποίηση, 1800–1864. (Society and Authority in Greece: The Adulterated Bourgeoisification, 1800–1864). Athens: Synchrona Keimena.

GEORGE, C. H. (1980) "The origins of capitalism: a Marxist epitome & a critique of Immanuel Wallerstein's modern world-system." Marxist Perspectives 3, 2: 70–100.

GRAMSCI, A. (1971) Selections from the Prison Notebooks, Q. Hoare and G. N. Smith (eds.). New York: International Publishers.

HEGEL, G. F. (1821) Philosophy of Right (S. W. Dyde, trans. [1896]). London: George Bell & Sons.

JAUMONT, B., D. LENÈGRE, and M. ROCARD (1973) Le Marché Commun contre l' Europe. Paris: Seuil.

KATSOULIS, G. D. (1974) Οικονομική ιστορία της Ελληνικής Επαναστάσεως (Economic History of the Greek Revolution). Athens: Difros.

KORDATOS, Y. (1930) Εισαγωγή εις την ιστορίαν της ελληνικής κεφαλαιοκρατίας (Introduction to the History of Greek Capitalism). Athens: Panepistimiako Vivliopolio Alex. N. Kolovou.

—— (1946) Η κοινωνική σημασία της Ελληνικής Επαναστάσεώς του 1821 (The Social Significance of the Greek Revolution of 1821). Athens: 4th Edition.

KREMMYDAS, V. (1976) Εισαγωγή στην ιστορία της νεοελληνικής κοινωνίας, 1700–1821 (Introduction to the History of Greek Society, 1700–1821). Athens: Exantas.

MAXIMOS, S. (1945) Η αυγή του ελληνικού καπιταλισμού. Τουρκοκρατία, 1685–1789 (The Dawn of Greek Capitalism. Turkish Rule, 1685–1789). Athens: Politiki Vivliothiki A. Karavia.

MOSKOFF, K. (1972) Η εθνική και κοινωνική συνείδηση στην Ελλάδα, 1830–1909. Ιδεολογία του μεταπρατικού χώρου (National and Social Consciousness in Greece, 1830–1909. Ideology of Comprador Space). Thessaloniki: Nea Poria.

MOUZELIS, N. (1978) Νεοελληνική κοινωνία. Όψεις υπανάπτυξης (Modern Greek Society. Aspects of Underdevelopment). Athens: Exantas.

NURKSE, R. (1953) Problems of Capital Formation in Underdeveloped Countries. New York: Oxford University Press.

PALLOIX, C. (1975) L'internationalization du capital; éléments critiques. Paris: Maspero.

PSIROUKIS, N. (1973) Ιστορικός χώρος και Ελλάδα (Historical Space and Greece). Athens: Epikairotita.

_____ (1974) Το νεοελληνικό παροικιακό φαινόμενο (The Modern Greek Colonizing Phenomenon). Athens: Epikairotita.

STAMATOPOULOS, T. (1957–1973) Ο εσωτερικός αγώνας πριν και κατά την επανάσταση του 1821 (The Internal Struggle before and during the Revolution of 1821). 4 vols. Athens: various editions.

STAVRIANOS, L. S. (1944) Balkan Federation. A History of the Movement toward Balkan Unity in Modern Times. Smith College Studies in History, vol. 27. Northhampton, MA: Department of History, Smith College.

_____ (1958) The Balkans since 1453. New York: Holt, Rinehart and Winston.

TSOUKALAS, K. (1977) Εξαρτηση και αναπαραγωγή. Ο κοινωνικός ρόλος των εκπαιδευτικών μηχανισμών στην Ελλάδα, 1830–1922 (Dependence and Reproduction. The Social Role of Educational Mechanisms in Greece, 1830–1922). Athens: Themelio.

_____ (1969) The Greek Tragedy. Baltimore: Penguin Books.

VERGOPOULOS, K. (1978) Κράτος και οικονομική πολιτική στον 19ο Αιώνα (State and Economic Policy in the XIXth Century). Athens: Exantas.

_____ (1975) Το αγροτικό ζήτημα στην Ελλάδα. Το πρόβλημα της κοινωνικής ενσωμάτωσης της γεωργίας (The Agrarian Question In Greece. The Problem of Agriculture's Social Incorporation). Athens: Exantas.

WALLERSTEIN, I. (1974) The Modern World-System. Capitalist Agriculture and the Origins of the European World-Economy in the Sixteenth Century. New York: Academic Press.

_____ (1979a) The Capitalist World-Economy. New York: Cambridge University Press.

_____ (1979b) "Underdevelopment and Phase-B: effect of the seventeenth-century stagnation on core and periphery of the European world-economy," in W. L. Goldfrank (ed.) The World-System of Capitalism: Past and Present. Beverly Hills, CA: Sage.

WINCKLER, E. A. (1979) "China's world-system: social theory and political practice in the 1970's," in W. L. Goldfrank (ed.) The World-System of Capitalism: Past and Present. Bevery Hills, CA: Sage.

ZEVGOS, Y. (1946) Σύντομη μελέτη της νεοελληνικής ιστορίας (A Concise Essay of Modern Greek History). Athens: P. Nassiotis.

PART 2

DEVELOPMENT IN
SEMIPERIPHERAL STATES

Chapter 3

PERSPECTIVES ON
REVOLUTIONARY MEXICO:
THE REGIMES OF
OBREGÓN AND CALLES

Richard Tardanico
Tulane University

What is—or *was*—the Mexican revolution? This question has commanded the serious attention of Mexicanists during the last decade or so, a period of Mexican history marked not only by a crisis of capital accumulation but also by mounting popular protest and government repression (for example, see González Casanova and Florescano, 1979). Efforts to reassess the sociohistorical nature of the revolution are politically crucial at this juncture. For even as governmental policies increasingly favor foreign capital at the expense of the country's masses, Mexican regimes have wielded official interpretations of the revolution to legitimize their claims to, and exercise of, state power. It thus behooves critics of the Mexican state to reexamine the revolution and its relationship to present modes of political domination.

This climate has nurtured a growing body of literature concerned with several politically and intellectually challenging questions: Is the revolution an ongoing phenomenon or a thing of the past? Does it represent a sharp break with, or a veiled continuation of, the Porfirian era (1876–1911) of Mexican history? Should we regard the revolution as one coherent transformation or as a melange of tenuously connected sociopolitical forces and historical accidents? Is the essence of the revolution captured by any one label, or combination of labels, such as "nationalist," "bourgeois," "agrarian," "popular," "democratic," "corporatist," and so on? And what political ends are served by our answers to these questions?[1]

This paper shares these concerns. It focuses on the crucial state-making activities of the regimes of Alvaro Obregón (1920–1924) and Plutarco Elías Calles (1924–1928), and presents several hypotheses about their undertakings in light of recent perspectives on capitalism as a world-historical system. What follows begins by discussing some competing interpretations of the campaigns of Obregón and Calles to erect a new-regime state. It then addresses some issues raised by these approaches and concludes by suggesting an alternative conceptual framework.

MEXICO, 1920–1928:
SOME COMPETING PERSPECTIVES

According to David C. Bailey (1978: 67–69) and Gilbert M. Joseph (1979: 46–47), revisionist ideas about twentieth-century Mexico must be viewed in the context of the pro-revolution scholarship published in the 1920s and '30s. This included the influential work of Frank Tannenbaum (1929, 1933), who portrayed the revolution as fundamentally a mass upheaval, or rather a number of independent regional mass upheavals, against the dictatorship of Porfirio Díaz and its underlying amalgam of feudal legacies and foreign-dominated capitalism. It was, in Tannenbaum's words, "the common people, the peasants, the Indians, the city laborers" who essentially made the revolution (1933: 115). Indeed, the political contributions of its urban-based leadership, he claimed, were decidedly inferior to those of the lower classes. That is, in the absence of an intelligentsia capable of formulating any grand plan of action, the goals of the revolution were defined by the popular sectors themselves during the course of their struggles between 1910 and 1917. And to the extent such goals had been attained, it was primarily by virtue of mass movements, above all those of the countryside[2] (Tannenbaum, 1933: chap. 11).

Tannenbaum (1933: chap. 16) asserted that the revolution would ultimately be judged by its impact on the hacienda system. He observed, however, that as a result of the resistance of the traditional upper stratum and foreign interests, as well as the sociocultural and political gulf between government officials and the rural poor, large estates generally remained untouched. Meanwhile, external capital posed the main obstacle to urban labor reforms, though organized workers had won major concessions as a by-product of agrarian rebellions and the New Regime's efforts to regulate transnational business firms (Tannenbaum, 1933: chap. 19). Its serious limitations notwithstanding, Tannenbaum regarded the revolution as a sharp and ongoing repudiation of Mexico's colonial and Porfirian legacies. For, in his view, the essence of the revolution remained intact: the promise of social justice and dignity for the popular classes and for the Mexican nation as a whole in its dealings with industrialized countries (Tannenbaum, 1933: 180–183, 259–262, 307–308).

Just as Tannenbaum's populist interpretation captured the profound hopes awakened by the revolution, so, too, do more recent perspectives emphasize its bitter consequences. The Marxist approach of Adolfo Gilly (1972, 1979) is particularly intriguing in the way it grapples with the past and potential future revolutionary gains of the masses, on one hand, and the harsh realities of their present situation, on the other. Like Tannenbaum, Gilly (1979: 21–22) stresses that while the revolution comprised both bourgeois and popular movements, its basic force was a massive *cam-*

pesino struggle for land. Gilly's analysis, however, is explicitly concerned with the circumstances that promoted and hindered the realization of lower-class revolutionary goals. The fundamental question, he argues, is this: To what extent were Mexico's under-classes organizationally and ideologically independent of the state and dominant classes?

The importance of this question lies in Gilly's assertion that where the combined and uneven development of capitalism inter-sected with such independence among the masses, the result was a deep, sustained revolutionary uprising. This was the case in south-central Mexico, where, under the leadership of Emiliano Zapata, *campesinos* presented the most radical and enduring challenge not only to the Porfirian state but also to the bourgeoisie's revolution-ary factions (Gilly, 1972: chaps. 3, 8; 1979: 30–37). Nevertheless, in the absence of an organizationally and ideologically mature proletariat, the tradition-bound Zapatistas were eventually forced into a tactical alliance with the radical and ultimately victorious petty bourgeoisie.[3] The consequence, according to Gilly (1972: 402–405; 1979: 50–53), was not the defeat of the lower classes but rather the "interruption" of the revolution in 1920. By this he means that despite the triumph of bourgeois-democratic forces, what the masses gained in political consciousness and experience survives as a very real contribution to the making of socialist revolution in Mexico's future.

Gilly's attention, then, is not restricted to Mexico's past. On the contrary, his fundamental objective is socialist revolution in Mex-ico,[4] and this end, he writes, cannot be attained without a clear understanding of the nation's class history (1979: 52–53). It is in this context that the notion of an "interrupted revolution" assumes importance. For the official view is that, unleashed in 1910, the revolution is a continuing process, moving unevenly but gradually toward the goals of social justice and national capitalist develop-ment (see Díaz Ordaz, 1976; Echeverría Alvarez, 1976). In sharp contrast is Gilly's position that while the petty bourgeoisie seized state power in 1920, the New Regime could not undermine the incipient anticapitalism of the masses. He therefore concludes that, lacking a firm social base and historical legitimacy among the popular classes, the bourgeoisie that emerged from the revolution has striven to coopt the masses by portraying their interests and struggles as synonymous with its own (Gilly, 1972: 396–399, 401–404).

What does this mean with respect to the state-making campaigns of Obregón and Calles during the 1920s? It follows from Gilly's perspective not only that the state established during the 1920s was bourgeois but that its governments were *postrevolutionary*. Within this framework, he analyzes the administrations of Obregón and Calles as "bonapartist" regimes; that is, as regimes situated above a postrevolutionary stalemate among conflicting classes and class sectors but nonetheless acting to promote the development of a national bourgeoisie (Gilly, 1972: 338–349; 1979: 47–50.) In this setting Obregón and Calles resorted to a policy of limited reforms and nationalist rhetoric both to thwart the independent organization of the lower classes and to rally them against U.S. imperialism as well as what remained of the defeated Porfirian oligarchy. In spite of major tactical concessions to the United States, this policy enabled the bonapartist governments of the 1920s to stabilize the bourgeois state that has ruled Mexico ever since. Their success in doing so, Gilly contends, was based on the revolutionary heritage of the class faction in control of the state; it could therefore effectively manipulate revolutionary symbols and aspirations to impose bourgeois domination upon the masses (1979: 49–50; see also 1972: chap. 9).

Another important Marxist analysis is that of Arnaldo Córdova (1972, 1973, 1979), who challenges the idea that the revolution marked a clear, abrupt break with Porfirian state and society. Though he does not deny the fundamental contributions of the revolution, Córdova argues that just as significant are the institutional continuities between the old and new regimes. Their basic commonality, he writes, was that both the Porfiriato and the revolution were part of the same historical process: the consolidation and development of a national capitalist economy. From Córdova's perspective, what underlay Mexico's capitalist development was the centralization of political authority under Porfirio Díaz as well as the governments of the New Regime. The result was the Mexican state of today, which, he contends, is unique within Latin America in its ability to regulate conflicting forces and protect its capitalist underpinnings (Córdova, 1972: 13–16; 1979: 55–56, 60–61).

But Córdova, again, does not overlook the institutional divergencies between the Porfiriato and the New Regime. The key difference, he claims, lies in the relationship of the new-regime state to the masses. In this respect, Córdova (1972: 19–23, chap. 4) observes that, once consolidated, the revolutionized state was much more centralized and institutionalized than its oligarchic predecessor. He explains this transformation as having been based on the national project initiated by the bourgeois revolutionary clique under the leadership of Obregón and Calles. The members of this faction were generally middle class in background and bourgeois in their aspirations but tied to no particular ideology; therefore, Córdova argues, they were politically inclined to act on behalf of the Mexican bourgeoisie as a whole (1973: chap. 5; 1979: 84–86). In the context of a dependent economy and intense, *campesino*-based pressures from below, such action took the form of a mass-inclusionary political program. This program was significant in that it acknowledged the emergence of the popular classes as an authentic source of power in destroying the Porfirian state and in creating and consolidating the New Regime. The political leverage of the masses was limited, nonetheless, by their disunity and underdeveloped class-consciousness. Thus, far from indicating true political autonomy on the part of the underclasses, the populist measures of the Obregón and Calles governments served as an effective weapon to control the masses and stabilize the new-regime state (Córdova, 1972: 20–23, chap. 2; 1973: chaps. 3, 5–6).

Not surprisingly, then, Córdova (1972: chap. 2) considers Mexico's to have been a bourgeois-political rather than a social revolution. This means that, rather than abolishing private property, the revolution simply undermined the oligarchic political structure of the Old Regime which blocked the development of a national bourgeoisie. In regarding the revolution as fundamentally political, Córdova (1972: 50–54) maintains that by institutionally buttressing the New Regime, the establishment of a central political party in 1928–1929 more or less signaled the start of the post-revolutionary era.[5] He is much more negative, however, in his evaluation of the economic accomplishments of the new-regime governments during the 1920s. The Calles administration, to be sure, was particularly active in building the nation's economic infrastructure. Córdova (1973: 292–306, 379–401; 1979: 75–79) emphasizes, however, that the prerevolutionary class structure remained intact and that foreign capital actually strengthened its hold over the Mexican economy. He concludes, nevertheless, that the populist tactics of Obregón and Calles were politically crucial. For, by giving the state the false image of belonging to no single class, such tactics protected Mexican capitalism from radical challenges (Córdova, 1979: 89).

Jean Meyer's (1973, 1976a, 1976b) account of state-building under Obregón and Calles is perhaps best labeled as independent and critical, or as history "written from below." This intellectual and political posture is compellingly displayed in his critiques of both official and Marxist interpretations for masking what to him were the revolution's defining characteristics: numerous distinct lower- and middle-class movements and the imposition of a highly centralized authoritarian state upon the masses (Meyer, 1973: 7, 9–10, part II, chap. 5; 1976a: 713, 719). Like Córdova, Meyer (for example, 1973: 265–268) treats the Mexican case as an example of political revolution. His analysis further converges with Córdova's insofar as, while recognizing the ideological and institutional distinctiveness of the revolution, both scholars regard it as having continued the state- and economy-developing tasks of the Porfiriato, and as having ended with the consolidation of the new-regime state.[6] In fact, Meyer (1973: 267; 1976b: chaps. 1–2) goes even further by discussing the historical continuity between the Bourbon reforms of colonial Mexico and political centralization in the nineteenth and twentieth centuries. But the uniqueness of Meyer's position revolves around his criticism of those who characterize the revolution as "bourgeois-democratic," "anti-imperialist," "agrarian," "popular," and the like. Such views, he asserts, overlook the basic heterogeneity and contradictions of the revolution, not to mention the importance of historical accident in deciding its outcome. They result, he says, in rigid, overly deterministic interpretations which exaggerate the interests of one group or another in "making" the revolution (Meyer, 1973: 267; 1976a: 712–713, 715–717).

What indeed emerges most clearly from Meyer's analysis is the bewildering complexity of domestic and external forces that impinged upon the regimes of Obregón and Calles. He argues that in response to these forces, petty-bourgeois revolutionaries used a variety of tools—cultural nationalism, tactical concessions, and naked repression—to modernize the Porfirian system and in large part create Mexico's authoritarian state of today (Meyer, 1973: part II, chap. 5; 1976b: 17–25, 31). The irony of this historical portrait is that despite their expressed contempt for Mexico's colonial and Porfirian legacies, state makers responded to national and world conditions during the 1920s by doing more to conserve than to change preexisting institutions. Thus, foreign capital was placated, regional inequalities were exacerbated, and, underlying it all, the Old Regime's agrarian institutions were only marginally reformed (Meyer, 1973: part I, chap. 2, 264). The more fortunate of the masses did make some gains in the form of land distribution and labor reforms. But for the overwhelming majority, the only real change was that a more powerful state was erected against them. In Meyer's words, "What happened in Mexico is of no particular theoretical interest" (1973: 268). This conclusion is predicated on his belief that the Mexican revolution, like all revolutions to date, created a state that would serve above all the purpose of forestalling future revolutionary threats.

TOWARD AN ALTERNATIVE INTERPRETATION

Seminal works that they are, the contributions just reviewed give rise to countless questions of historical and theoretical interest. Some of the most challenging ones—for example, those pertaining to the causes of both the Mexican revolution and revolutions in general—are beyond the scope of this essay.[7] In what follows I shall tease out several issues relating to state-formation under Obregón and Calles and suggest an alternative framework based on recent approaches to the study of capitalism as a world-historical system.

Among the most important questions emerging from the literature reviewed are those that concern the extent to which the New Regime created during the 1920s merely perpetuated colonial and Porfirian legacies or promoted fundamental change. For instance, Córdova and Meyer underscore the fact that, far from making progress toward the revolutionary bourgeoisie's goal of a more independent national economy, the nascent state's policies actually reinforced Mexico's dependence on foreign capital. Neither Córdova nor Meyer ignores the efforts of the new-regime governments to regulate and tax transnational firms. They emphasize, though, that a combination of political-economic exigencies and emergent interests within the state's machinery minimized the enforcement of constitutional provisions for nationalist action and social reform. The result, according to Meyer, was that during the 1920s the revolution simply reoriented Mexico's dependence from Europe to the United States. Gilly concurs with this assessment in noting, among other things, that a common interest against the Mexican lower classes facilitated the rapprochement between the Calles regime and the U.S. government in 1927–1928. Tannenbaum, of course, did not write in the context of the Mexican and world crises of the 1960s and '70s, and hence lacked the hindsight that underlies the revisionist historiography. But in spite of his praise for the accommodation between the U.S. government and the Calles administration, Tannenbaum underlined the role of external opposition as a powerful obstacle to social reforms. It is generally acknowledged that the Porfirian elite had been shorn of its political, if not economic, power, a factor which played a key role in the subsequent course of Mexican development.[8] Still, what is emphasized is that as of the late 1920s the revolution had basically maintained Mexico's preexisting institutions and subservient relationship to foreign capital.

In order to evaluate this position from an alternative perspective, I will first present an overview of state-making under Obregón and Calles. Of initial importance are the old-regime structures that confronted the incipient state's managers. In the late nineteenth-century setting of an expanding and deepening world economy, foreign interests transformed Mexico into a dynamic, regionalized exporter of a diversity of primary products. Foreign capital flowed especially into the key economic sectors— infrastructure, mining, and oil—leaving agriculture mostly to the Mexicans and participating jointly with the latter in the backward manufacturing sector.[9] What left Mexico all the more economically and geopolitically vulnerable was the growing leverage of U.S. business and governmental interests not only during the Porfiriato but also during the revolutionary strife of 1910–1917 and the decade after World War I (R. F. Smith, 1972; Goldfrank, 1975, 1979).

The embryonic New Regime, then, was thoroughly subordinate to U.S. governmental and capital interests. It was also plagued by economic destruction and the politically disunified resistance of lower-class insurgents, military and civilian bosses, and remnants of the Porfirian elite. Furthermore, in spite of their nationalist rhetoric, the revolutionary coalition's military-political and economic cliques were oriented more to regional interests than to the construction of a strong national state (Tardanico, 1980a).

Following a coup against the government of Venustiano Carranza (1917–1920), the regimes of Obregón and Calles worked pragmatically to prevent a U.S.-backed counterrevolution and to strengthen the state apparatus. This meant a policy of broadening the state's domestic base by coopting the leaders of strategic mass organizations, while concurrently mixing tactical concessions to foreign interests with often bold but not reckless measures to reduce their autonomy. Nationalist measures included increased taxes on oil and mining firms as well as general regulatory legislation, acts which raised the threat of expropriation. These were accompanied by mass-incorporating policies, such as programs of cultural unification, limited agrarian and labor reforms, the appointment of selected lower-class leaders to political office, and the founding of the central political party (Carr, 1974; Vaughan, 1975; Warman, 1976). Populistic nationalism helped to centralize power at the expense of not only domestic opposition but also foreign interests. The regimes countered this strategy, however, with a variety of actions to attract and protect transnational capital. Among these were tax exemptions, promises of organized labor's cooperation, external debt agreements, and assurances that foreign-owned properties would not be expropriated (L. Meyer, 1972; R. F. Smith, 1972).

In sum, the administrations of Obregón and Calles strove to strengthen the state's authority over external capital, even as they made substantial concessions to forestall counterrevolutionary threats and secure foreign investments. Integral to this pragmatic course of action were the populistic measures implemented by the regimes. For these measures improved their ability either to deploy lower-class groups against foreign and domestic resistance or to control them so as to forge tactical alliances with political rivals. In addition to stabilizing the New Regime, this mode of political domination allowed Obregón and Calles to concentrate more on rationalizing the state's machinery and developing the economy's infrastructure. Important as these gains were, the leverage of U.S. interests combined with continued domestic unrest and an accommodation between the revolutionary elite and the old-regime upper class to preclude anything more than minimal economic advances (Tardanico, 1980a, 1980b).

So, as the revisionists emphasize, Mexico's economic dependence *was* deepened and its state *was* becoming more authoritarian. These facts are indeed deplorable; yet, taken by themselves, they are neither surprising nor theoretically interesting. But in viewing the governments of Obregón and Calles from the standpoint of the subsequent course of Mexican history—as Gilly, Córdova, and Meyer do—it is clear that what happened during the 1920s *is* of theoretical interest. For the important question is this: How and to what extent did Mexico's path of state-formation during the 1920s contribute to its resurgent populistic nationalism during the Great Depression and its import-substitution development during World War II? In other words, what was the relationship of governmental policy under Obregón and Calles to the subsequent improvement of Mexico's relative standing in the capitalist world system?

The fundamental issue, then, is the interrelationship of Mexican state-making and the world-historical development of capitalism. This issue revolves around the expansion of the world-system's semiperipheral stratum during the mid-twentieth century, and why Mexico—among a select group of poor countries—moved into the semiperiphery while the vast majority of peripheral countries fell behind. This perspective underscores the dynamic interaction of class struggles, interstate competition, and capital accumulation on a world scale (Amin, 1976; Hopkins and Wallerstein, 1977). Hence, it does not merely underline the constraints these forces impose upon peripheral states, but also directs attention to the limited opportunities they create for such states to advance within the changing world order.[10] The emphasis, then, is on the relationship of past, present, and future transformations at the interdependent levels of class, state, and the world political economy.

With respect to the regimes of Obregón and Calles, two theoretical questions arise. First, under what domestic and global conditions can peripheral states be substantially strengthened? Second, under what conditions, to what extent, and how can strengthened state power be used to transform the relationships of peripheral countries to the world capitalist system?

In regard to the first question, by 1928–1929 Mexico's new-regime state was more centralized and institutionalized than had been the oligarchic state of the Porfiriato. This difference, to repeat, was based on the populistic nationalism of the Obregón and Calles governments. But their political accomplishments depended on several factors: divisions throughout the Mexican class structure; interests within the United States that deterred its government from backing a counterrevolution; the Obregón-Calles faction's use of the state both for personal gain and for national development; and, finally, the assassination of Obregón in 1928, in the context of which Calles founded the central party (Tardanico, 1980b).

In regard to the second question, by 1928 Mexico was bound as tightly as ever to foreign interests. Indeed, despite strengthened state power, old-regime legacies and the postwar political and economic leverage of the United States stood directly in the path of populistic nationalism. But more important is how the policies of Obregón and Calles contributed to later economic and political gains. These contributions were more politico-organizational than economic in nature. They centered, in fact, on the creation of the populistic regime structure discussed above. As already mentioned, this mode of political domination enabled the state's leadership to direct selected mass organizations against *caudillos* and propertied interests, or to control such organizations in order to promote political stability and economic recovery. Thus, the policy of limited populism underlay the New Regime's capacity to combine pragmatically nationalist and collaborationist policies of development according to domestic and world conditions. This capacity was just as important in the 1920s as it would be during later periods of Mexican history, today included. For, in the face of U.S. economic and geopolitical expansionism, political centralism not only better enabled Obregón and Calles to take nationalist action whenever the opportunity arose, but enabled them to deal with U.S. threats by protecting that country's interests and thereby attracting its capital.

The clientelistic route, of course, was the one most commonly taken. It imposed heavy burdens upon the lower classes and possibly upon the local bourgeoisie as well. Nonetheless, in correctly underscoring its deleterious consequences, what the revisionists miss is the way clientelism, as well as nationalism, helped to strengthen the new-regime state.[11] This point is not an obvious one; yet, if the hypothesis is correct, the clientelistic advances of peripheral states are made not at the expense of core interests—as are nationalist gains—but rather at the expense of other peripheral states less successful in securing core investments.

How, then, might collaborationism have served to strengthen the Mexican state and contribute to its advancement within the world political economy? A priority of the new-regime governments was to strengthen the state's fiscal base, and its revenues did increase substantially during the 1920s. Nevertheless, the state's extractive power remained minimal. Thus, the growth of federal income did little more than keep pace with GNP and was largely a function of the prosperity of foreign enterprises operating in Mexico (Tardanico, 1980a, 1980b). This does not mean that the revenue-generating policies of the Obregón and Calles regimes were unimportant; they were indeed important, but mainly insofar as they enabled the Mexican state to keep pace with the growth of world surplus during the 1920s at the relative expense of those peripheral states that lagged behind. In this respect, institution-building advances enabled the Calles administration to channel a larger portion of the state's growing revenue into public works and banking programs. Perhaps more important, they combined with bureaucratic and military reforms and the founding of the central party to create a growing body of technocrats and political officials. Hence, government policies not only augmented the state's organizational powers and, to a lesser degree, reinforced its economic underpinnings. They also boosted the number of middle and lower bureaucrats and politicians whose upward mobility depended on the consolidation of a more independent national state and economy.[12] At the same time, public works projects hastened the growth of small-scale industrialists and merchants, whose aspirations, nonetheless, were blocked by old-regime legacies. As had occurred with the bureaucrats and politicians, these economic interests emerged as a key nationalist force during the Great Depression, when the government of Lázaro Cárdenas acted vigorously to strengthen the central party, to internalize control over the economy, and to redistribute wealth (see Wionczek, 1964; Medín, 1977). By virtue of this institutional transformation, Mexico's regimes of World War II through the early 1950s were able to use both nationalist and clientelistic policies to lift the country into the world economy's expanding semiperiphery.

The final segment of this essay has not addressed the gamut of issues raised by Tannenbaum and the revisionists. Instead, it has suggested some hypotheses pertaining to the interrelationship of Mexican state-building during the 1920s and the development of capitalism on a world scale. It should be clear that I am in basic agreement with those who conclude that the new-regime state erected by Obregón and Calles was more centralized than was the Porfirian state. I likewise agree that Mexico's lower classes remained, for the most part, as oppressed as ever, and that the Mexican state and economy continued to be thoroughly subordinate to foreign interests. But we must explore beyond these conclusions. From the perspective of capitalism's world-historical development, the fundamental question is this: How and to what extent did the new-regime policies during the 1920s contribute to the advancement of Mexico—along with a select group of other peripheral countries—to the semiperiphery in the mid-twentieth century?

NOTES

1. See especially Ross (1976), Bailey (1978), Gilly et al. (1979), Brading (1980), and Carr (1980).

2. The centers of rural lower-class rebellion were the south-central state of Morelos and the northern state of Chihuahua. In Morelos, Emi-

liano Zapata led a *campesino* movement for land reform and village autonomy. In Chihuahua, Pancho Villa headed a revolt which comprised a more heterogeneous, mobile work force and stood for a vaguely defined program of social reform. The most important faction of Mexico's nascent, geographically splintered urban-industrial labor force was the Casa del Obrero Mundial, an anarcho-syndicalist organization centered in Mexico City. Its leadership, however, was coopted by the Constitutionalists, the victorious revolutionary movement whose following ranged from the petty bourgeoisie to some upper-class interests.

The Constitutionalists were committed to a pragmatic brand of nationalism and to varying degrees of political and social reform. Their populist wing was headed by Alvaro Obregón, a middle-class farmer from the northwestern state of Sonora. The other wing's leader was Venustiano Carranza, a *hacendado* from the northern state of Coahuila, who was more inclined to liberal-bourgeois reform. Although the Obregónistas dominated the Constitutional Congress of 1916–1917, Carranza served as president from 1917 until a coup brought Obregón to power in 1920.

On the revolution's lower-class forces, see especially Womack (1968), Carr (1974), Waterbury (1975), and Katz (1979). On the Constitutionalists, see Cumberland (1972), Carr (1973), P. H. Smith (1973), and Richmond (1979).

3. This was the wing of the Constitutionalists led by Obregón. Gilly (1972: 337–338) observes that the Carrancista wing was unwilling to enter into a coalition with the masses, preferring to seek political support among the seriously weakened old-regime interests.

4. A Trotskyite, Gilly contends that socialist revolutionary forces in Mexico are part of a world-historical revolutionary process.

5. Córdova (1972: 54) observes, though, that the regime of Lázaro Cárdenas (1934–1940) fully consolidated the new-regime state by reorganizing the party and transforming it into a more mass-incorporating institution.

6. Meyer (1973: 263–264) considers the orderly presidential succession of 1940 to have marked the end of the revolution.

7. On the causes of revolutions in general, see Skocpol (1979). On the causes of the Mexican revolution in particular, see Goldfrank (1979).

8. Manuel Aguilar Mora (1979: 119–121) criticizes Córdova for having underplayed the political losses sustained by the old-regime upper class.

9. Of relevance is the fact that the Porfirian state was minimally centralized and incapable of challenging transnational and domestic upper-class interests. That the Porfirian regime survived as long as it did was a function of export development, disunified opposition, and Díaz's remarkable political skills.On the Porfirian state, see Wolf and Hansen (1967: 178–179), Córdova (1972: chap. 1), Goldfrank (1975), and Leal (1975).

10. See especially Wallerstein (1979: 73), who argues that "it is not possible theoretically for all states to 'develop' simultaneously. The so-called 'widening gap' is not an anomaly but a continuing basic mechanism of the operation of the world-economy. Of course, *some* countries can 'develop'. But the some that rise are at the expense of others that decline."

11. Wallerstein (1979: 76–81) notes that nationalism is generally a more viable path during periods of world depression or military conflict in the core, when the latter's leverage over the periphery is weakened. In contrast, collaborationism is often the only viable option of peripheral governments during times of expanding world production and trade.

12. On the political role of state bureaucrats in comparative perspective, see Trimberger (1978).

An important point is that by the late 1920s upper-level government officials had been incorporated into Mexico's propertied elite, and thus they were less inclined to implement nationalist and popular reforms.

REFERENCES

AMIN, S. (1976) Unequal Development. New York: Monthly Review Press.

BAILEY, D. C. (1978) "Revisionism and the recent historiography of the Mexican Revolution." Hispanic American Historical Review 58, 1: 62–79.

BRADING, D. (1980) Caudillo and Peasant in the Mexican Revolution. London: Cambridge University Press.

CARR, B. (1973) "Las Peculiaridades del Norte Mexicano, 1880–1927: Ensayo de Interpretación." Historia Mexicana 22 (January–March): 320–346.

_____ (1974) "Labour and politics in Mexico, 1910–1929." Ph.D. dissertation, Oxford University. (unpublished)

_____ (1980) "Recent regional studies of the Mexican Revolution." Latin American Research Review 15, 1: 3–14.

CÓRDOVA, A. (1972) La Formación del Poder Político en México. Mexico: Serie Popular Era.

_____ (1973) La Ideología de la Revolución Mexicana: La Formación del Nuevo Régimen. Mexico: Ediciones Era.

_____ (1979) "México. Revolución Burguesa y Política de Masas," pp. 55–90 in A. Gilly, A. Córdova, A. Bartra, M. A. Mora, and E. Semo. Interpretaciones de la Revolución Mexicana. Mexico: Editorial Nueva Imagen.

CUMBERLAND, C. (1972) Mexican Revolution: The Constitutionalist Years. Austin: University of Texas Press.

DÍAZ ORDAZ, G. (1976) "A presidential reply," pp. 263–272 in S. R. Ross (ed.) Is the Mexican Revolution Dead? Philadelphia: Temple University Press.

ECHEVERRÍA ALVAREZ, L. (1976) "Our revolution has not ended," pp. 289–307 in S. R. Ross (ed.) Is the Mexican Revolution Dead? Philadelphia: Temple University Press.

GILLY, A. (1972) La Revolución Interrumpida. Mexico: Ediciones "El Caballito."

_____ (1979) "La Guerra de Clases en la Revolución Mexicana (Revolución Permanente y Auto-Organización de las Masas)," pp. 21–54 in A. Gilly, A. Córdova, A. Bartra, M. A. Mora, and E. Semo, Interpretaciones de la Revolución Mexicana. Mexico: Editorial Nueva Imagen.

_____ A. CÓRDOVA, A. BARTRA, M. A. MORA, and E. SEMO (1979) Interpretaciones de la Revolución Mexicana. Mexico: Editorial Nueva Imagen.

GOLDFRANK, W. L. (1975) "World system, state structure, and the onset of the Mexican Revolution." Politics and Society 5, 4: 417–439.

_____ (1979) "Theories of revolution and revolution without theory: Mexico." Theory and Society 7 (January–March): 135–165.

GONZÁLEZ CASANOVA, P. and E. FLORESCANO [eds.] (1979) México, Hoy. Mexico: Siglo Veintiuno Editores.

HOPKINS, T. K. and I. WALLERSTEIN (1977) "Patterns of development of the world-system." Review 1 (Fall): 111–146.

JOSEPH, G. M. (1979) "Mexico's 'popular revolution': mobilization and myth in Yucatán, 1910–1940." Latin American Perspectives 6 (Summer): 46–65.

KATZ, F. (1979) "Villa: reform governor of Chihuahua," pp. 25–46 in G. Wolfskill and D. W. Richmond (eds.) Essays on the Mexican Revolution: Revisionist Views of the Leaders. Austin: University of Texas Press.

LEAL, J. F. (1975) "El Estado y el Bloque en el Poder en México: 1867–1914." Latin American Perspectives 2 (Summer): 34–47.

MEDÍN, T. (1977) Ideología y Praxis Politica de Lázaro Cárdenas. Mexico: Siglo Veintiuno Editores.

MEYER, J. (1973) La Revolución Mejicana, 1910–1940. Barcelona: DOPESA.

────── (1976a) "Periodización y Ideología," pp. 711–722 in J. W. Wilkie, M. C. Meyer, E. Monzón de Wilkie (eds.) Contemporary Mexico. Berkeley: University of California Press.

────── (1976b) The Cristero Rebellion: The Mexican People Between Church and State, 1926–1929 (R. Southern, trans.). London: Cambridge University Press.

MEYER, L. (1972) México y los Estados Unidos en el Conflicto Petrolero (1917–1942). Mexico: El Colegio de México.

MORA, M. A. (1979) "Estado y Revolución en el Proceso Mexicano," pp. 109–134 in A. Gilly, A. Córdova, A. Bartra, M. A. Mora, and E. Semo, Interpretaciones de la Revolución Mexicana. Mexico: Editorial Nueva Imagen.

RICHMOND, D. W. (1979) "Carranza: the authoritarian populist as national president," pp. 47–80 in G. Wolfskill and D. W. Richmond (eds.) Essays on the Mexican Revolution: Revisionist Views of the Leaders. Austin: University of Texas Press.

ROSS, S. R. [ed.] (1976) Is the Mexican Revolution Dead? Philadelphia: Temple University Press.

SKOCPOL, T. (1979) States and Social Revolutions: A Comparative Analysis of France, Russian, and China. London: Cambridge University Press.

SMITH, P. H. (1973) "La Política dentro de la Revolución: El Congreso Constituyente de 1916–1917." Historia Mexicana 22 (January–March): 363–396.

SMITH, R. F. (1972) The United States and Revolutionary Nationalism in Mexico, 1916–1932. Chicago: University of Chicago Press.

TANNENBAUM, F. (1929) The Mexican Agrarian Revolution. New York: Macmillan.

—— (1933) Peace by Revolution: Mexico After 1910. New York: Columbia University Press.

TARDANICO, R. (1980a) "Revolutionary nationalism and state-building in Mexico, 1917–1924." Politics and Society 10: 1:35–62.

—— (1980b) "State-making in the periphery and the limits of nationalism: Mexico, 1924–1928." Presented at the annual meeting of the American Sociological Association, New York, August.

TRIMBERGER, E. K. (1978) Revolution From Above: Military Bureaucrats and Modernization in Japan, Turkey, Egypt, and Peru. New Brunswick, NJ: Transaction Books.

VAUGHAN, M. K. (1975) "Education and class struggle in the Mexican Revolution." Latin American Pespectives 2 (Summer): 17–33.

WALLERSTEIN, I. (1979) "Dependence in an interdependent world: the limited possibilities of transformation within the capitalist world-economy," pp. 66–94 in I. Wallerstein, The Capitalist World-Economy. London: Cambridge University Press.

WARMAN, A. (1976) Y Venimos a Contradecir: Los Campesinos de Morelos y el Estado Nacional. Mexico: Ediciones de la Casa Chata.

WATERBURY, R. (1975) "Non-revolutionary peasants: Oaxaca compared to Morelos in the Mexican Revolution." Comparative Studies in Society and History 17 (October): 410–442.

WIONCZEK, M. S. (1964) "Electric power: the uneasy partnership," pp. 19–110 in R. Vernon (ed.) Public Policy and Private Enterprise in Mexico. Cambridge: Harvard University Press.

WOLF, E. R. and E. C. HANSEN (1967) "Caudillo politics: a structural analysis." Comparative Studies in Society and History 9 (January): 168–179.

WOMACK, J., Jr. (1968) Zapata and the Mexican Revolution. New York: Vintage Books.

Chapter 4

ESSENCE AND VARIATION: APPROACHES TO THE STUDY OF CONTEMPORARY BRAZIL

Walter Goldfrank
University of California, Santa Cruz

Whither Brazil, and whither the analysis of Brazil? Routinely mentioned now in conventional media and social science as the most advanced and promising of the so-called "emerging nations," Brazil's trajectory in the last fifteen years has been held up as an example of what capitalism can do, for better and for worse. Some observers focus on the astonishing economic growth rate, some on the deepening of the accumulation process, some on the state's role in that process, some on the new expansion into the Amazon, some on the continuing wretchedness of the northeast. Some focus on the widening gap between rich and poor, some on military and police repression and the reemergence of civilian politics, some on the expanded Brazilian role in world politics and trade. No work that I know of has captured all of these aspects in what seem the right proportions, and I am not about to attempt such a synthesis here.

Rather, I consider two new (and contrasting) treatments of the Brazilian situation, focused on different aspects to be sure, but each in its own way calling into question the practice of conceiving of Brazil as a model for other Third World countries. The first volume of Chomsky and Herman's *The Political Economy of Human Rights,* entitled *The Washington Connection and Third World Fascism* (1979a), is more valuable politically than as social science, and its portrayal of Brazil as an example of "Third World fascism" or "client fascism" is one reason for that rather low opinion. Evans's *Dependent Development* (1979), subtitled *The Alliance of Multinational, State, and Local Capital in Brazil,* works out some of the institutional economic arrangements that distinguish Brazil and a handful of other semiperipheral countries from the relatively weaker and poorer periphery. He is thus much clearer both about the limitations of his theoretical model in accounting for Brazil's dependent development and about the limitations of Brazilian actuality as a model for other countries.

Before I discuss these works in some detail, two general issues require comment. These are (1) the two usages of the term "model," and (2) the dual purpose of social science. As suggested above, the term "model" is used in two distinct ways in macrosociology. On one hand, "model" refers to concrete examples in the phenomenal world, examples which might be followed by others: the Prussian road, the Soviet model, the Chinese model, and so forth. On the other hand, "model" refers to abstract depictions (usually partial) of that phenomenal world. Insofar as the Brazilian experience since 1964 has been an *empirical* model, it has been a failure. Over the past seven years, the Pinochet regime in Chile has attempted to recreate the so-called "Brazilian miracle" by combining terrifying repression and open invitations to multinational capital. The result has been far short of miraculous, even from the regime's standpoint: industrial stagnation, dynamism only in the primary export sector, exodus of skilled and professional workers, and low levels of foreign investment. The story in Uruguay since 1971 is much the same. A model that cannot be copied is not a model but a phantasm.

As for abstract depictions of Brazilian development, "model" in the second sense, quite a number have gained currency in the last decade, all of them capturing aspects of that development. O'Donnell's "bureaucratic authoritarianism," Schmitter's "corporatism," Fernandes's "bourgeois autocracy," Cardoso's "associated dependent development," Marini's "sub-imperialism," all contribute to a sophisticated picture. But whereas Chomsky and Herman add only "the Washington connection" to O'Donnell by their focus on repression, Evans enriches the Cardoso/Fernandes depiction in two ways. First, he fleshes out the structure—the triple alliance—through which multinational firms, Brazilian enterprises, and state agencies antagonistically cooperate. Second, by moving a good part of the way toward applying Wallerstein's concept of "semi-peripheral states" in his concluding comparisons of Brazil with Mexico and with Nigeria (although, unaccountably, not with Argentina), he specifies and delimits the applicability of his own model of the triple alliance.

This leads to the second general point: namely, what seem to me the two intellectual tasks of social science. The first task is to identify essences; to name, define, and characterize material and social relationships. The second is to explain variation. Most social science necessarily does some of each, although routine social science, in Kuhn's sense, simply assumes, through its use of terms and concepts, that the essences have already been properly identified. Conversely, most ideological struggle among social scientists focuses precisely on questions of essence rather than variation (for example, status versus class, norms versus material structures). Stinchcombe (1975, 1978) thinks that identifying essences is either ritual totemism or irrelevant baggage and that explaining variation is all that matters, all that distinguishes strong social science from weak. But in my view the two tasks are connected, because the better one's identification of essences, the more likely one is to be able to account for variation. This is particularly true for routine social scientists. And insofar as social science is inescapably political, getting the names right is half the battle.

Chomsky and Herman's book is limited by the fact that they are not interested in variation, but only in documenting an important essence of contemporary Third World reality—namely, brutal repression with U.S. aid, connivance, and misrepresentation. Evans, by contrast, cares *both* about an essence—industrial development—*and* about variation—*more* or *less* industrial development in different countries and at different times. This interest in explaining variation is what enables him to define so clearly the configuration he finds in Brazil's economic institutions.

THIRD WORLD FASCISM

Chomsky and Herman's basic thesis in their first volume is that "under frequent U.S. sponsorship, the neo-fascist National Security State and other forms of authoritarian rule have become the dominant mode of government in the Third World" (1979: vol. I, 8).[1] An essence is posited, with two aspects: terrorism by the state in the form of torture and genocide, and a massive U.S. presence in promoting, supplying, condoning, and downplaying or misrepresenting that terrorism. Numerous instances of this essence are then described: East Pakistan, Burundi, Paraguay, Brazil, East Timor, Indonesia, Thailand, the Philippines, the Dominican Republic, Chile, Argentina, Guatemala, Nicaragua, and the various Indochinese countries.

There is a basic truth here, a monstrously important truth, usefully catalogued and righteously denounced. In the post-World War II period the United States has been the major purveyor of terror in the world; in Chomsky and Herman's language, *"Washington has become the torture and political murder capital of the world"* (p. 16, italics in original). This is amply documented by Michael Klare, whose indispensable labors the authors amply draw upon. Furthermore, no satisfactory holistic account of the recent Brazilian trajectory is possible if it slights the use of repressive violence against the left and the use of genocidal violence against the indigenous population. Nor would such an account be complete without exploring Brazil's role as what Chomsky and Herman call the "torture-aid subcontractor" for Latin America. (Evans, in fact, slides over these issues.) Finally, there is no gainsaying the fact that state-initiated repressive violence *"has a functional relationship to investment climate"* (p. 54, italics in original). Insofar as there is any economics in Chomsky and Herman's "political economy of human rights," this is it.

However, if one is interested in variation as well as essence, Chomsky and Herman are not particularly helpful. They organize much of their book around a distinction between "benign" and "constructive" terror, the difference presumably being Washington's degree of approval. "Benign" and "constructive" terror contrast with "bloodbaths" and other heinous forms of Communist terror which so preoccupy American officials and journalists. Chomsky the linguist quite properly turns on its head the everyday usage of a term reserved for the Palestinians and Vietnamese. But there is no consistent analytical thread here: Both anti-communism and the desire for investment and trade opportunities motivate the United States in supporting and/or justifying all this benign and constructive violence, and the authors attempt neither to connect different sorts of U.S. interests to different kinds and amounts of terror, nor to connect these latter to different political and economic outcomes. One could plausibly assert, for example, that it was in large measure the relative *absence* of U.S. economic interests that led to the wanton devastation of Laos and Cambodia. One could add to such an account Franz Schurmann's (1974) subtle analysis of bureaucratic trade-offs: the unrestricted Air Force and Navy bombers had a green light denied them over the more politically sensitive (and semiperipheral) Vietnamese terrain. Perhaps you can bomb only the periphery back to the stone age.

Because they are interested in essences rather than variation, Chomsky and Herman's rendering of Brazilian "subfascism" is superficial and, in places, misleading. To start with, they place such emphasis on the U.S. role in subverting Brazilian democracy in the early 1960s that they slight the activity of the Brazilian right in general and the military in particular. This gives an impression of U.S. imperialist omnipotence, when in fact the Brazilians have used the United States as much as the other way around, if not more. Second, the characterization of Brazil's "denationalized client fascist elite" as "devoid of any economic ideas of their own," as engaged in "dogmatic adherence to free enterprise," as "economically illiterate" (p. 25), is simply farfetched. Diemists and Mobutuites, perhaps; Brazilian generals and technocrats, hardly. Or again, to say that those generals are "visionless creatures of U.S. imperial policy aping their masters" (p. 103) is to miss the consciously nationalist self-strengthening activities that go back to the late thirties, activities that would enable the Brazilian government to tell President Carter in 1978 to peddle his human rights pieties elsewhere. Third, there is no dynamism in Chomsky and Herman's model, no tension or contradiction, but rather superabundant moralizing. They speak of an "expanding empire of violence" (p. 9) when events in Iran and Nicaragua—not to mention Zimbabwe or the U.S. defeat in Indochina—suggest that there are strong counterforces at work in the world. Not the least of those forces exist at the present time in Brazil, where, from the standpoint of capital, the conjuncturally specific job of repressive violence (and I am not one of those who thinks it greatly inappropriate to call it fascist) has quite possibly been done. In fact, the time may be ripe for further openings toward a more democratic politics as one way out of the current stagnation.

Finally, Chomsky and Herman have written a painful political tract about "the sun and its planets" (frontispiece), the United States and its clients. The book's strength as an outraged correcting of the official and journalistic rhetoric is at the same time its weakness as social science: It largely remains at the level of discourse used by the authors' political opponents. It names and defines an essence all too frequently missing from current social science analysis of the Third World. But in so doing, it fails even to suggest reasons for the variations in "fascism," as exemplified in its failure to provide more than an extremely rudimentary model for comprehending Brazil.

DEPENDENT DEVELOPMENT

Evans's *Dependent Development* is by contrast attuned both to essence and to variation. It thereby provides a useful model, not of Brazil as a whole, but of the organization of the three major economic actors: multinational firms, local capital, and state actors. An introductory discussion of dependency theory from Baran and Furtado to Amin and O'Donnell introduces that trio theoretically, recapitulating the idea that military rule is necessary for the repression of the previously mobilized and organized urban working class, which repression is, in turn, necessary for moving beyond easy import substitution to heavy industrialization. A long second chapter discusses the transition from periphery to semiperiphery— or, in Evans's language, from "classic dependence" to "dependent development." Then follow several case studies of the competition and bargaining among the three fractions of capital in various sectors: the multinationals and the national bourgeoisie in pharmaceuticals and textiles; the multinationals and the state in research and development; all three in steel, petrochemicals, and metals. A final chapter attempts to put the whole model in perspective, in part by comparing Brazil to Mexico and to Nigeria.

Two questions thus animate Evans's book: What are the origins and limits of dependent development, and what are the institutional mechanisms through which it works? To take the second question first, Evans shows convincingly that "the global rationality of the multinationals" detracts "from their natural [sic] contribution to local accumulation" but that this "contradiction" is "resolvable by bargaining" (p. 276), bargaining which cumulates

over time. The outcomes of such bargaining vary "by industry and
by issue" (p. 277), but local capital—the famous national
bourgeoisie—is by no means dead, having decided advantages "in
situations where integration with the local social structure [is] the
key to business success" (p. 281). "The weakest of the three partners" (p. 280), local capital has yet shown considerable vitality and
entrepreneurship. As for the state, its central role in promoting
accumulation is amply documented, but the case studies also show
that because state enterprise managers share conventional corporate ideology, their activities are not always consistent with overall
state policy. The case studies, and especially Evans's discussion of
their implications (pp. 275–290), will repay careful attention,
including his penultimate warning that the "vulnerability" of Brazilian accumulation to "disruptions in the international economy
constitutes the most obvious limitation of the triple alliance"
(p. 290).

Evans's answer to the first question, the origins and limits of
dependent development, makes an important contribution by specifying the applicability of his triple alliance model to semiperipheral countries. Here I find Evans caught halfway between
the conventional "developmentalist" perspectives that still hold
sway in most studies of "national" industrialization (Marxist or
otherwise) and the emerging world-systems perspective. To judge
from the organization of the book, he began his work as a developmentalist and came to see the conceptual advantage of the semiperiphery as he was finishing it. This is highlighted in his concluding comparison of Brazil with Mexico, where the parallels are
great, and with Nigeria, where the petroleum boom has paid for an
increasingly strong state now in the process of orchestrating a
triple alliance.

Although he is not so explicit about it, Evans's account of Brazil's transition from periphery ("classic dependence") to semiperiphery ("dependent development") also exemplifies the advantages of a world-systemic view, especially as his data contradict
the "developmentalist" theoretical statement with which he begins:
"Classic dependence . . . created forces of production and social

groups that eventually transformed it into a very different kind of political economy" (p. 56). The linchpin of his argument about the transition is the shift from Great Britain to the United States as the major source of foreign capital (p. 76): U.S. capital was never much invested in Brazilian primary exports and went heavily into industry. Furthermore, U.S.-German rivalry before and during World War II gave the Vargas government leverage to gain financing for state-owned steel works (pp. 88–89); and, both rivalry *with* and imitation *of* Argentina (Evans somewhat downplays this aspect) pushed the Brazilian military to pressure for both steel and petroleum production by the state (p. 90). To this one may add such better-known facts as the world depression-induced spur to import substitution, the World War II boom, and the outward push of U.S. capital. Thus, it is incorrect for Evans to claim that classic dependence was a "self-transforming" system (p. 94): His analysis shows quite clearly that Brazil was and is part of a larger, truly self-transforming system, the capitalist world-system.

This brings me back to the present, to the limits of the current arrangements in Brazil, to the questions of essence and variation, of Brazil as a model, and of models of Brazil. Evans is quite clear that dependent development has reached a critical point, especially given the world economic slowdown, with capital and intermediate goods imports rising faster than exports, thus creating mounting indebtedness. He usefully points to the three Brazilian strategies of export expansion, all of which in combination will help somewhat: renewed classic dependence through primary exports,[2] subimperialism through exports of manufactured goods to the periphery, and export platform manufacturing for the core. The competitive success of these exports requires that Brazilian wages be kept low; yet to increase the size of the Brazilian national market would require that *some* workers' wages be raised. Unfortunately, Evans does not explore the political possibilities through which this structural contradiction will or will not be overcome; he merely concludes that for dependent development to continue, core capitalists will have to keep up *their* end of the multinational alliance against the potential resistance of neoprotectionists and endangered workers.

Evans's "triple alliance" model, then, is a helpfully accurate representation of Brazil, in part because his interest in variation as well as essence leads him to see Brazil itself as a model for only a few Third World semiperipheral states rather than as an instance of some fascist essence. Perfectly aware that accumulation has thus far required exclusion of the mass of the population from welfare and politics, Evans, like Chomsky and Herman, has perhaps underestimated the chances for greater political and material inclusion of parts of the working class. For the members of the triple alliance there are obvious risks in such a change, hence the hesitancy with which democratic openings have been broached in the last few years. Unfortunately, Evans so concentrates on economic institutions that one cannot learn from his book how united or cohesive the Brazilian bourgeoisie really is, how likely it is to try to combine internal with export expansion. As Dos Santos put it recently, "The art of making concessions reveals the political capacity of a class, or at least of its most aware sectors" (1980: 37). How far will they dare go? Will the rightwing sectors attempt a coup? Successfully? We simply get no help on this score, let alone any appraisal of the likely parameters of popular power.

To summarize, Chomsky and Herman call attention to numerous examples of repressive and genocidal states in the Third World, all supported in one way or another by the United States. The absence of a political dialectic, the lack of any serious economic analysis, and their innocence of comparative method greatly detract from the scientific value of their work, which is, just the same, a political compilation which must not be ignored. Evans's sociological analysis of economic institutions in Brazilian industry and his comparisons of Brazil to other semiperipheral states make a scientific contribution with political lessons for those who wholesale this or that model of revolution as promiscuously as conventional social scientists wholesale this or that model of modernization, dependence, or class struggle. One wishes for more research like his, but with more explicit attention to the political aspects of world capitalism as well.

NOTES

1. Their second volume, *After the Cataclysm* (1979b), attempts to show the way U.S. officials and journalists have tried to reconstruct "imperial ideology" by misrepresenting the realities of postwar Indochina, including the refugee situation. Although occasionally marred by intemperate and misguided swipes at journalists, it is a laudable intervention in U.S. politics guaranteed a minuscule audience by the sorry history of its nonpublication by Warner (1979: vol. I, xiv–xvii).

2. Here he misses the role of highly capitalized agribusiness firms in new farm exports, not quite the same thing as "classic dependence."

REFERENCES

CHOMSKY, N. and E. S. HERMAN (1979a) The Washington Connection and Third World Fascism. The Political Economy of Human Rights, Vol. I. Boston: South End Press.

——— (1979b) After the Cataclysm. The Political Economy of Human Rights, Vol. II. Boston: South End Press.

DOS SANTOS, T. (1980) "Economic crisis and democratic transition in Brazil." Contemporary Marxism 1: 31–42.

EVANS, P. (1979) Dependent Development. Princeton: Princeton University Press.

SCHURMANN, F. (1974) The Logic of World Power. New York: Pantheon.

STINCHCOMBE, A. (1975) "A structural analysis of sociology." American Sociologist 10: 57–64.

——— (1978) Theoretical Methods in Social History. New York: Academic Press.

Chapter 5

AGRARIAN CAUSES
OF THE IRANIAN CRISIS

Nesar Ahmad
Arlington, Massachusetts

THEORETICAL FRAMEWORK

Most students of Iranian politics would agree that the rapid transformations of the Iranian countryside, especially since the early sixties, has profoundly affected the course of recent political developments. Therefore, an adequate understanding of the nature of these transformations becomes important. Such an understanding can throw significant light on the national crises that preceded the fall of Reza Shah Pahlavi.

Let me begin with a reference to the fact that during the early sixties the Shah's attempt to implement land reform laws hastened the process of fundamental structural transformations in the countryside. But why did the reforms become such a crucial part of the state policies at the point in time that it did? What were the motivations behind such policies?

Robert Graham says "it [land reform] was a political maneuver by the Shah to win over the rural masses and curtail the power of the big landowners" (1979: 40). Is this an adequate explanation? If the Shah's intention was to create rural equality and thus win over the masses, successful implementation of his policies would have meant popularity for his regime and lessening of social tension in the villages. In reality, however, as a direct consequence of the state agricultural policies, new forms of inequality emerged, class struggle intensified, and such events contributed significantly to the demise of the Shah's regime. Why did the reforms fail?

Fred Halliday provides a better framework within which this question can be answered (1979: 103–137). He places the Shah's measures in the context of class struggle. The Shah sought capitalist development, which required capitalization of rural Iran. A transformed countryside was expected to satisfy the growing needs for agricultural products by the manufacturing sector, as well as to expand the home market, creating increased demand by the rural sector for the products of the industrializing economy. But, says Halliday, as the Shah was about to introduce measures to capitalize Iranian agriculture, he encountered opposition from some of the landowners, who must have felt threatened by the prospect of surrendering their traditional social power by redistributing portions of their lands to the cultivating peasants. So the Shah turned to the rural masses and raised the slogan "land to the tiller." As the peasantry began to be aroused, the Shah, with its backing, enforced reforms, weakening the power of the large landowners. However, according to Halliday, the Shah's purpose was never to create equality. Hence, during the later phases of the reform the government policies seemed to reverse from the earlier declarations of returning land to the tiller. The later measures sought to reform the tenancy laws; and far from offering land to the peasant, the state began to take possession of large tracts of land as it created such corporate structures as farm corporations and agribusinesses. This direct intervention in production, according to Halliday, was a consequence of the state's eagerness to promote capitalist enterprises. From this perspective, the Shah's agricultural policies were a success: They created a class of rural bourgeoisie and one of rural proletariat; they introduced commodity relations and cash economy.

Halliday's interpretation clarifies a number of rather puzzling events. It explains, where Robert Graham's account does not, how the Shah's attempt to befriend the rural masses was merely a tactical move to drum up support for his policies. It also explains why the reforms did not eliminate the landowning class, and enables us to see why the reforms intensified class struggle rather than subduing it.

However, Halliday's interpretation has not gone unchallenged. Mustafa Afkia,[1] in his study (in progress) of rural Iran, finds that the predominant relations of production in the Iranian hinterland continue to be precapitalist. An overwhelming number of the peasantry, he claims, continue to live on subsistence farming; hence, we cannot say that there is a significant number of rural proletariat in Iran.

How can we resolve this controversy? By appealing to empirical evidence? Not quite, because Afkia's assertion regarding the presence of subsistence farming is empirically valid. And Halliday is not wrong when he says that capitalism significantly penetrated Iranian agriculture as a result of the Shah's policies.

What is required here is a conceptual clarification. In my opinion what should determine the extent of capitalization of an economy is the extent of integration of that economy within the world economy. If linking rural producers with the world market is a criterion of capitalization, the process of capitalization did advance in the Iranian villages, notwithstanding the absence of a large agricultural proletariat.

If this integration was desired by the Shah, his policies were successful. However, if his intention was to generate capitalist development in Iran by creating a home market, as Halliday has suggested (1979: 130–132), then his measures failed hopelessly.

The Shah may have been interested in generating economic development, but, in the more immediate sense, the ruling elite in Iran had sought to line their pockets. Expanding import and export trade enriched the royal coffer, and the small elite profited. The meager allocation to agriculture (Katouzian, 1974: 231–232) by the reformist regime of the Shah points to the relative indifference toward efforts to expand rural demands for consumer and manufactured goods.

However, when these demands increased as a by-product of the limited degree of agricultural mechanization, generous credit policies toward the larger landowners (Katouzian, 1978: 349), and creation of a small but enterprising middle peasantry (Hooglund, 1975: 141), this only led to the boosting of import rather than to the establishment of manufacturing industries. This occurred irrespective of the will of Iranian policy makers. The constraints to significant industrialization were structural. As Samir Amin points out, it is as a consequence of the ties with the world market that the capital goods sector often tends not to expand in the periphery: "In the formations of 'central' capitalism the predominant income is capitalist profit, whereas in those of peripheral capitalism it is often the rent drawn by the landowners, the class that predominantly benefits from integration in the international market" (Amin, 1974: 84).

Unlike the entrepreneurs in the central formations, the landowners' dependence on international markets through the sale of agricultural commodities discourages investment in industrial and capital goods, depressing the demand for labor power—hence the chronic crisis of overproduction in the periphery. The flow of oil revenue in Iran could only exacerbate this crisis of overproduction.

AGRICULTURAL TRANSFORMATIONS: A CLOSE LOOK

The agricultural transformations in Iran were represented by a series of changes which sought to lay the groundwork for multinational agribusiness takeover of its rural sector on a large scale. This is what constitutes the linking of the Iranian producers with the world market.

Economist Oddvar Aresvik, whose study of Iranian agriculture was financed by the International Maize and Wheat Center in Mexico (a Rockefeller-funded organization) designed to promote "Green Revolution," called Iran "agriculturally a sleeping giant" (Aresvik, 1976: viii). If the Shah had survived, the giant would have awakened in the eighties, only to be subdued by international agribusiness.

Let me now state the framework, which I deem proper for the study of Iranian agriculture.

In his essay "The Rural Economy in Modern World-System," Immanuel Wallerstein (1979: 119–131), criticizing the concept of "dual economy," points out rather "the dual mode of involvement" of the world economy as the cornerstone of the capitalist system:

> The slowly developing, slowly eroding, marginal, largely subsistence sector of the world economy, within which live the largest part of the world's rural populations . . . do not pose a problem to the world economy. These areas are and have been from the beginning one of its major solutions [Wallerstein, 1979: 123].

These areas, as Wallerstein points out, provide the avenues for expansion.

Since the second world war, the demand for agricultural commodities in the core countries has increased, providing tremendous boosts to the expansion of both "plantation systems" and agricultural industries in the periphery.

This recent expansion has followed three different phases. The first phase has marked a step toward rationalizing the rural sector or laying the groundwork for the actual expansion. In concrete terms, this has meant the promulgation of land reform, the outcome of which has tended to be the creation of an enterprising class willing to participate in the world-economy. Measures such as exemptions of lands, producing cash crops and those under "self-cultivation," from being redistributed, has encouraged commercialization of land. Further incentives have been provided to these landlords by the offer of easy credits and other subsidies. The second phase is what is usually characterized as the Green Revolution. The introduction of artificial seeds, with its own requirements (mechanization, use of fertilizer and pesticides, and so on) has resulted in the penetration of agribusiness in what used to be the subsistence economies of the Third World. The last phase has been the direct participation of the MNCs in the production and the distribution processes. Chronologically, this kind of expansion occurred first in Latin America and then in Asia and Africa.

The results of the massive penetration of agribusiness have been the upsetting—sometimes to a considerable extent—of the subsistence economies, landlessness, expansion of shantytowns, and food crises. These subsistence regions, no longer able to provide for themselves, are even more dependent on the few grain-producing nations for food. Politically, the crisis has manifested itself through resistance-repression cycles. Iran provides an illustration of this.

The First Phase

The Land Reform Laws in Iran were promulgated in the sixties. But these state actions were the result of an ongoing process of the integration of the Iranian economy into the world-economy. The consolidation of the state's authority was a condition for such an integration, and at least one motivation for the implementation of land reforms was to extend the authority of the state to the countryside (Katouzian, 1974: 224).

The logic of integration also required creating conditions which would enable the landowning interests to diversify and thus facilitate their transition into commercial producers for the world market.

In the early fifties, when the nationalist Prime Minister Mohammed Mossadegh was seriously challenging the Shah's authority, the latter took steps to distribute "crown lands" among the peasantry (Katouzian, 1974: 223). This was a clever move on the part of the monarch. On one hand, it was intended to pacify the populist and socialist forces; on the other, the compensation from the sale of land to the state for redistribution enabled the royal family to diversify its personal fortune. Out of these compensations, the family set up the Pahlavi Foundation, which became the personal investment channel for the Shah. Eventually, the foundation became the owner of such enterprises as Iran Air, the Tehran Sheraton Hotel, the Bank of Omran, and a part owner of General Motors of Iran (Business Week, 1974: 52).

This diversification of the landowning interest into the commercial and industrial sector in cooperation with international capital was a model that the state, through land reform measures, sought to thrust upon the landowners of Iran. Contrary to what some, like Halliday, would say, the goal was not the *embourgeoisment* of rural aristocracy to force the development of indigenous capitalism, but the facilitation of the association of internal sources of capital with external entrepreneurs.

The state had yet another motivation for land reforms—to stabilize the monarchical rule. And this motivation fit perfectly with the strategic goals of the hegemonic power, the United States. It is a fact that the clientile regime of the Shah was nudged to take steps toward stabilization by the United States. At the end of the fifties, Senator John F. Kennedy led a Senate delegation to Iran. By 1961, the Senator had become President of the U.S. And, as Eric Hooglund points out, "Under the administration of President Kennedy, the U.S. actively encouraged economic and social programs, especially land reform" (1975: 81n).

Between 1955 and 1962 (the period of Second Seven Year National Plan), the state began investing in "development projects." About 80 percent of the oil revenues went into such expenditures (Katouzian, 1978: 352). A good portion of this amount was spent

on the construction of hydro-electric dams (1978: 352). At least in
the short run, such large-scale projects proved counterproductive.
The state diverted resources to projects with long gestation periods. However, the World Bank's participation in such projects
clearly points out their significance in bringing Iran closer to world
economy (Katouzian, 1978: 360).

The Shah's "open door" policy toward import to meet the requirements of such projects, as well as to satisfy the rising demands for consumption demands, led to a serious balance of pay-
ment crisis and to a three-year recession period (1959–1962). The
Shah attempted to stem the tide of political crisis which followed
the economic crunch by undertaking reformist measures, including land reforms.

Land Reforms

The first stage of the reform was spearheaded by the liberal
Prime Minister Ali Amini and the radical intellectual Arsanjani,
whom Amini had appointed as Minister for Agriculture. The law
required all landlords to sell their holdings in excess of one village.
The state resold the purchased lands to the *Nasaqdars* (sharecroppers). Of a total of 2.4 million, 750,000 sharecroppers received
land (Hooglund, 1975: 114). The speed of the reform measures'
implementation caused alarm among the absentee landowning
class. The Shah apparently thought it unwise to continue to alien-
ate this class, and forced Amini and Arsanjani to resign. Their
resignations brought an end to the first stage of the reform
(Hooglund, 1975: 94–95).

The second stage of the reform began in January 1963; however, its provisions were further watered down in 1964 (Halliday,
1979: 111). These provisions sought to legitimize absentee land-
ownership and were directed more to the regularization than to the
elimination of sharecropping. They offered an option to the landlord to contract written thirty-year rental agreements between
peasants and owners.

The immediate outcome of this reversal in government policy was the outbreak of rural violence. "In several districts," reports Hooglund, "owners had to enlist the aid of the gendamerie to compel recalcitrant tenants to pay rents and to quell various disturbances" (1975: 106). The unrest led the government to promulgate the third phase of the reform laws in 1969. The new laws provided peasants with the opportunity to purchase directly from the owners of the land they rented. Since the government itself would not pursue the implementation, the success of this stage was rather limited.

By 1972, about 67% of the *Nasaqdars* became owners of their land. On the surface this was an impressive outcome, but a close examination of the various reform laws and their modes of implementation reveals that far from simplifying and equalizing the rural stratification system, these laws yielded very complex results.

In the process of implementing the land reform laws, a large bureaucratic structure was created, one effect of which was to subsume the landowning class under this bureaucracy. However, state intervention in rural life did not reduce either their income or their high status within the village structure. For the landlords were able to retain the best lands, while they redistributed primarily the barren portions of their holdings. Moreover, they became the chief recipients of various susidies from the state. And "many of the peasants who did get plots of land under the reform received it in amounts that were too small to be viable. Sixty-eight percent received plots of under 5 hectares, whilst the minimum viable outside the north is 7 hectares per family" (Halliday, 1979: 112).

The cooperatives that were set up under the provisions of the land reform favored the rich peasants, who held larger shares than the poor peasants; and the large agricultural corporations joined the rich landowners with the state in profitable partnership.

A significant impact of the land reforms was differentiation within the peasantry; the redistribution of land to the middle strata of rich peasantry created a buffer class between the large landowners and the poor peasants, as well as the huge number of landless peasants.

Differentiation of the Peasantry

In Iran, prior to land reform, the sharecroppers worked mostly in collectives, called *Bonehs*. These were production teams. The purpose in organizing these teams was efficient utilization of human labor. Each *Boneh* was supervised by a peasant called *Sarboneh*, who commanded social status and whose job became hereditary, as landlords often chose sons to replace fathers.

In addition, from ancient times, Iranian villages had a village headman or *Kadkhuda*. Originally, the *Kadkhuda* may have been an elected representative (Hooglund, 1975: 27), but in recent times the *Kadkhuda* was chosen by the landlord and served his interests. Since 1936, the *Kadkhuda* is a state appointee, a bureaucrat, and serves as an intermediary between the villages and the state (Hooglund, 1975: 29).

The formulas adopted during the land reform favored the *Sarbonehs* and *Kadkhudas* over ordinary peasants. When the land reform officials adopted the principles of age and experience as farmers, the *Sarbonehs,* reputed to have the greatest expertise, qualified for more land; while the landlords, in many cases, intervened to ensure the *Kadkhuda* a greater share of the distributed land (Hooglund, 1975: 133).

As a result of the unequal distribution, of the two million peasants, a majority (about 68 percent) received small and fragmented plots, which rendered even a subsistence living impossible. About 27 percent obtained medium-sized acreages (5–10 hectares), while less than 8 percent received plots large enough (over 10 hectares) to pursue a relatively decent existence (Hooglund, 1975: 150).

So far I have talked about peasants who had the right to cultivate land before 1962. But these peasants constituted about 50 percent of all villagers. The rest were noncultivating peasants. Some of these villagers, known as *Khoshneshins* (those who sit happily), engaged in shopkeeping; some were blacksmiths, carpenters, barbers, and similar craftsmen. The rest were field laborers.

Since, according to the provisions of land reform laws, only cultivating peasants received lands, these provisions did not touch half the peasant population, the *Khoshneshins*. And yet the overall impact of the land reform laws was such that differentiation among the three groups of noncultivating peasants became more pronounced. While before the reforms the three groups had been unequal in status, after the reform the gaps broadened. The traders and entrepreneurs became richer, the agricultural laborers became poorer. "Through various policies such as high interest loans, food credits, and Salaf-Khari [advance purchase of crops]," says Hooglund "traditional middlemen keep a majority of the peasants perennially in debt and gain whatever surplus they produce above the absolute minimum requirements for subsistence" (1975: 153).

Moneylending boomed during the postreform period, as many poor ex-sharecroppers, cut off from their ties with the landlords, engaged in independent farming with insufficient resources and had to turn to the middlemen for loans to finance both basic consumption needs and expenses for farming. The rise in income of the middlemen as well as the rich peasants encouraged the import of manufactured consumer goods into rural society. These goods, in turn, adversely affected the sale of village craftsmen's handmade products.

The condition of field laborers also worsened as the reform measures went into effect. In reducing their costs, the new proprietors of land could not hire laborers, reducing employment opportunities. Large landowners resorted to mechanization, which further worsened the employment situation. Hooglund remarks: "agricultural laborers, and along with them the traditional village artisans and personal service workers . . . are emerging as a distinct class, a landless rural proletariat. This class consists of 1.4 million families whose common characteristic is a life marked by extreme poverty and persistent economic insecurity" (1975: 163).

The new disparities served two functions in consonance with the Shah's motivation for land reform. First, by creating a class of consumers (the rich peasants and the entrepreneurs), it linked them with the world market. Slowly, they began to depend on this market both for consumption and production (tractors, combines, fertilizers, and the like). Second, the newly emerging middle strata, though still supportive of the absentee landlords, became independent of their former masters. No longer a part of the *boneh* system, they became members of the rural cooperatives whose membership was enjoined upon them by the land reform law. Holding larger shares, they benefited from the cooperative credit programs disproportionately. The new situation, however, demanded their allegiance to the source of the credit they received: the state. With this influential group under its wing, the state was thus able to consolidate its authority in rural Iran.

Second Phase:
Agricultural Corporations

The state motivation for land reform found further fulfillment in the pursuit of its policies toward the formation of large, public agricultural corporations managed by a state-appointed director. These commercial farms embraced several villages, were mechanized, and produced cash crops. They were financed by both public and private sources (Hooglund, 1975: 111). Lands were appropriated from the peasants to set up these corporations. The peasants received allotments of shares according to the market value of the land, which was often insufficient. In many cases, the peasants became wage laborers with these corporations or sought employment elsewhere. Some former owners thought it demeaning to work as wage laborers in farms that had appropriated their own land, and (understandably) bore a grudge against the government policies.

The significance of these farm corporations from the perspective of Iran's entry into the world market was appreciable. Ahmad Ashraf reports that

by early 1976, the number of farm corporations rose to eighty-five units, encompassing 778 villages and hamlets with an area of 310 thousand hectares of which 140 thousand hectares was under annual cultivation. These corporations have 32.5 thousand shareholders and nearly $20 million in share capital. . . . The water supply of these 65 corporations increased from 51 to 87 thousand litres per second during the same period.

The use of tractors in farm corporations has risen from 20% of cultivated areas before the establishment to 100% in the agricultural year of 1974–1975. During the same period the utilization of combines has increased from 5% to 95% of the cultivated areas. A total number of 652 tractors and 95 combines and over 1600 other agricultural implements were distributed among these corporations [Ashraf, 1979: 9–10].

By emphasizing irrigation, the use of high-yielding, fertilizer-responsive seeds, pest control, and the use of tractors and other equipment, fodder production for livestock, the state was welcoming Green Revolution, which in turn meant greater dependence on international agribusiness firms, for they alone could supply the required inputs. It was through such sales that these firms entered the rural sector. This marked the second phase in the integration of Iranian agriculture into the world economy.

Third Phase

The third phase (that phase beyond supplying inputs) was the direct participation of these corporations in the production of agricultural commodities and the control of the export market.

Business Week reported on June 22, 1974:

the government had been building big dams and canal systems . . . to irrigate the arid plains of Khuzestan province. Honolulu based C. Brewster and Company is a minority partner with other Americans, Japanese and Iranian investors in a $12 million 42,000 acre diversified farming venture. . . . Brewster has been invited to invest in a $200 million in a mixed government and private sugar venture. . . .

Another sign of growing affluence is the plans of San Francisco's Foremost-McKesson, Inc. and Iranian partners, including companies in which two sisters of the Shah have interests to double the milk processing capacity of Pak Dairy in Teheran at a cost of $5 million. And World Airways Corporation of Oakland, California, is preparing to bid on a huge airlift of 250,000 pregnant cows that the Shah reportedly plans to import over the next five years [Business Week, 1974: 52].

According to Francis Fitzgerald:

Over the past few years, the government has leased hundreds of thousands of acres of production land to multinational agribusiness. In the Khuzestan region just above the oil fields, Shellcott, Hawaiian Agronomies and other multinationals have taken over huge tracts of newly irrigated land to develop with foreign technicians and modern farming machinery imported tax free [Fitzgerald, 1974: 78].

Thirty-eight thousand Iranians were displaced from about 140,000 acres of land in Khuzestan.

By the mid-seventies some of the foreign investors wound up their business, claiming lack of profitability in these agricultural enterprises (Graham, 1979: 114). As these investors (such as Citicorp, BankAmerica, Chase Investment Company and others) declared bankruptcy, the Iranian agricultural development bank stepped in, injected emergency funds, and rejuvenated these enterprises. However, this development should not be taken as a failure of Iranian agriculture's integration in the world market; rather, this reflects only a change in the mode of participation in Iranian agriculture by international agribusiness. For these international corporations continued to supply inputs to farm corporations after the state takeover.

IMPACT OF AGRICULTURAL POLICIES: PRELUDE TO CRISIS

Decline in Food Production and Inflation

The production of staple crops, wheat and barley, suffered during agricultural transformations. "In a period in which there has been a land reform," observes Katouzian, "booming market conditions, rapid increases in the application of technical inputs to agriculture, etc. . . . the average rate of productivity has been almost zero for wheat and negative for barley" (Katouzian, 1978: 364). The reason was the disproportionate investment of technical inputs in the 25 percent of arable land which produced cash crops— cotton, tobacco, pulses, oil seeds, fruits, vegetables and rice.

With no marked improvement in the supply of staple food, and with demands leaping due to disbursement of oil revenues among the urban elite as well as the rise of income among the middle sector of the peasantry, the prices of food skyrocketed. The state's efforts to import food and to subsidize food prices were no help to the rural masses. And as local rural crafts began to decline in the face of competition with manufactured goods, the peasants were deprived of their traditional affordable sources of supply for these consumption goods. Inflation hit them hard.

Dispossession and Migration

I have already mentioned the dispossession and the resultant unemployment of many peasants when lands were appropriated for farm corporations. Unemployment was also a consequence of the nationalization of pastures by the state. Traditionally, Iranians received their meat from the nomadic population. The Shah's regime nationalized the pasturelands, depriving the nomads of their grazing grounds, thus contributing to unemployment and to the

decline of meat production. Iran thus increasingly became dependent on multinational firms for meat. Thierry Brun and Rene
Dumont state the consequences of abandoning the natural resource
(pastureland) in these words:

> Sheep and goats are being replaced by cattle imported at great
> expense, which rely on massive imports of concentrated feeds
> based on soybeans or the wastes of food industries, a market
> dominated by a handful of multinational companies [Brun and
> Dumont, 1978: 18].

Impoverishment of a sizable portion of the village population
also occurred when the water supply, which was a free commodity
before the reform, was nationalized and mechanized. According
to Lambton (1979: 286), landowners sometimes received large
shares and also withheld the shares of the small peasants with the
intent of driving them out. The landowners could then mechanize
the land, thus making it exempt from the provision of the land
reform law.

Further, the drive to mechanization led to the use of motorized
water pumps and the sinking of deep wells. This caused the lower-
ing of water tables, decay of land previously flourishing and
cultivated by *qanat* water, the traditional irrigation canals. Lambton reported in 1964 that after land reform, *qanats* were allowed to
decay by landlords. The small farmers, who had depended on the
traditional source of water and who could not afford motorized
pumps to raise it, could not farm (Lambton, 1969: 243, 288–289).

The impoverished, dispossessed, unskilled, rural population
marched to the cities (at the rate of 380,000 a year between 1971
and 1976) only to join, in the urban slums, the army of the destitute
and the unemployed (Ashraf, 1979: 22). Industrial growth was not
fast enough to ensure a sufficiently high rate of absorption. It is no
wonder, then, that a good many of these destitutes gave expression
of their smoldering anger by joining the army of urban demonstra-

tors and thus played a significant role in toppling the Shah's regime (Hooglund, 1980: 3–6). Those landless and destitute peasants who had stayed behind in their villages became eager participants in occupying lands belonging to the large landowners during the revolutionary upheaval (Vicker, 1979: 1, 41; M. Hooglund, 1980: 7–12).

CONCLUSION:
THE FUNDAMENTAL WEAKNESS OF
THE IRANIAN STATE

It should be pointed out that the displacement of the peasantry, as a result of land reforms, was not in itself a critical factor in the political development. What was of significance, however, was insufficient employment opportunities as a result of the limited industrial development in Iran. The failure to bring about industrial development could be attributed to the state's inability to create a home market. Samir Amin (1974: 605) believes such a failure is not a surprise. In fact, it is this failure that defines Iran's peripheral status. However, in the world-system it is not uncommon to find peripheral states struggling to raise their status. In view of the active role of the Iranian state in efforts to bring about economic transformations, one may ask the following question: Did the Iranian ruling elite desire reintegration in the world market as a semiperipheral society rather than remaining in the periphery?

There were certain indications that the Iranian state sought such a path. The Shah's attempt to consolidate state power, encourage foreign investment and efforts to create and promote the regime's populist image despite the liberal use of highly repressive techniques, and to enhance the military might of the nation[2] point to the fact that the Iranian state did seek to improve its position in the world-system vis-à-vis other nations.

And yet the efforts culminated in mass uprising and the fall of the regime. What went wrong? Let me suggest a hypothesis: The primary failure to bring about cultural and ethnic integration foreclosed the possibility of strengthening the power of the Iranian state. And at least one reason why Iran failed to overcome its ethnic diversity was the very mode of colonization of the country. The dual control by Russia and Britain in the late nineteenth and the twentieth century of north and south, respectively, excluded the possibility of the creation of conditions which could lead to national consolidation (Avery, 1967: especially 179–209[3]; also see Kazemzadeh, 1968). The impact of the Bolshevik Revolution was, furthermore, to arouse patriotic and egalitarian feelings in the north, which were manifested in the desire to build regional Soviet republics, alienating further the ethnic groups from the center of the Iranian state (Avery, 1967: 211–221).

The impact of agricultural transformations in the sixties and seventies was to further intensify these regional, ethnic feelings. Some of the agricultural developments took place in those regions where centrifugal tendencies were most pronounced (for example, the Azerbaijan region). The impoverishment of the peasantry, a consequence of the modernization of agriculture, in my opinion facilitated an alliance between the dispossessed peasantry and the religious class against the Shah's regime. Temporary as the alliance was, it certainly turned out to be very powerful.

The alliance between the peasantry and the religious leaders, however, is facing severe strains as the intense postrevolutionary fervor has spurred the peasants to occupy the land of their former exploiters. Ahmad Ashraf (1979: 26) reports:

The prime example of class struggle in rural areas could be found in Gorgan Plain which has a high concentration of large scale capitalistic farms and quasi-plantation enterprises. The Turkoman tribes of the region, however, claim ownership of the Gorgan Plain. Leftist activists appeared on the scene and staged a struggle against the capitalist firms throughout the region. The reaction of the local landowners was severe and immediate. With the support of Islamic committees in the capital, they launched a full-scale war against the Turkomans and leftists, and eventually the armed forces were dispatched to the city of Gonbad to control the situation.

Similar incidents occurred in Kurdistan. Khomeini's Revolutionary Guards intervened on behalf of the landlords after extensive land takeover by the peasants, especially in Sanandaj-Marivan region. The struggle for self-determination by the culturally differentiated groups is, indeed, a manifestation of agrarian contradictions between the property owners and the dispossessed.

NOTES

1. Mustafa Afkia's work (his Ph.D. thesis for Aberdeen University, Scotland) is in progress. The thesis does not yet have a specific title. The main purpose of Afkia's work is to examine the significance of farm corporations in Iran. Thanks to Eric Hooglund for bringing this work to my attention.

2. For information on Iran's military and police deals, see Institute of Policy Studies (1979).

REFERENCES

AMIN, S. (1974) Accumulation on a World Scale: A Critique of the Theory of Underdevelopment. New York: Monthly Review Press.

ARESVIK, O. (1976) The Agricultural Development of Iran. New York: Praeger.

ASHRAF, A. (1979) "Rural stratification of Iran: recent developments." Presented at a Conference on Hierarchy and Stratification in the Contemporary Near and Middle East, Mount Kisco, New York, May.

AVERY, P. (1967) Modern Iran. London: Praeger.

Business Week (1974) "How Iran spends its newfound riches." June 22: 44–52.

BRUN, T. and R. DUMONT, (1978) "Iran: imperial pretensions and agricultural dependence." MERIP Reports 71 (October): 15–20.

FITZGERALD, F. (1974) "Giving the Shah everything he wants." *Harper's Magazine* (November): 55–82.

GRAHAM, R. (1979) Iran: The Illusion of Power. New York: St. Martin's Press.

HALLIDAY, F. (1979) Iran: Dictatorship and Development. New York and London: Penguin Books.

HOOGLUND, E. (1975) "The effects of the land reform program on rural Iran, 1962–1972." Ph.D. dissertation, Johns Hopkins University.

_____(1980) "Rural participation in the revolution." MERIP Reports 87 (May): 3–6.

HOOGLUND,M. (1980) "One village in the revolution." MERIP Reports 87 (May): 7–12.

Institute of Policy Studies (1979) Background Information on the Crisis in Iran. Washington, D.C.

KATOUZIAN, M. (1974) "Land reform in Iran, a case study in the political economy of social engineering." Journal of Peasant Studies I, 2 (January).

_____(1978) "Oil versus agriculture, a case of dual resource depletion in Iran." Journal of Peasant Studies 5, 3 (April).

KAZEMZADEH, F. (1968) Russia and Britain in Persia 1804–1914. New Haven: Yale University Press.

KEDDIE, N. (1972) "Stratification, social control and capitalism in Iranian villages: before and after land reform," in R. Antoun and I. Harik (eds.) Rural Politics and Social Change in the Middle East. Bloomington: Indiana University Press.

LAMBTON, A. (1969) The Persian Land Reform 1962–1966. London: Oxford University Press.

VICKER, K. (1979) "In a village in Iran, simplicity, piety, praise for Khomeini: Ayatollah's support is rooted in traditional way of life—and ouster of landlords." Wall Street Journal (November 22): 1, 41.

WALLERSTEIN, I. (1979) "The rural economy in the modern world-system," in I. Wallerstein (ed.) The Capitalist World Economy. London: Cambridge University Press.

PART 3

DEVELOPMENT AND STATE ORGANIZATION

Chapter 6

POLITICAL REGIONALISM AND STRUGGLES FOR STATE HEGEMONY

James E. Lunday
Johns Hopkins University

The world-system theoretical perspective has focused attention on the importance of the political organization of capitalist class interests in the world-economy. The work representing this perspective adds an important dimension to the classic Marxist focus on class struggle by moving toward a theoretical integration of the forms and dynamics of relations among fractions of capital in the world-economy with the forms and dynamics of class relations in states. The state has thus become pivotal to our understanding of capitalism as a world-system. The international system of states stands alongside the capital/labor relation and the world division of labor as a fundamental structural feature of the world-economy, and as one of the basic ways in which networks of social relations that constitute the world capitalist class are organized (Chase-Dunn and Rubinson, 1979; Hopkins, 1979; Wallerstein, 1974, 1979). As a consequence of this theoretical development, state formation has become a central analytical dimension of our study of the historical development of the capitalist world-economy.

Presently, social relations among states in the world-economy predominate in our thinking as those that matter. But, to limit ourselves to incorporating only those relations into our analyses of state formation may obscure a full explication of the configuration of forces involved in the development of the world-economy. There is reason to believe that it is a mistake to presuppose that only a full-blown (internationally recognized) state will figure significantly in the development of the world-economy. Given the instability of political boundaries over the history of the world-economy, the territorially based nationalistic tensions that mark many contemporary states, the political tensions associated with efforts to form transnational political institutions, as well as centralized national institutions, and the evidence that neither capitalists nor their political allies in one state hesitate for long to undermine the political unity of another state when economic and political interests are involved, it seems reasonable to propose that political entities other than states often figure significantly in the historical development of the world-economy. Analyses of state formation, then, should be attentive to the theoretical importance of all aspects of the political structure of the world-economy, not just the international system of states.

State formation in the world-economy is characterized by uneven development. One dimension of this uneven development is the variation across states in the level and structure of centralization of authority. Many states are organized into political regions which exercise varying degrees of autonomy and authority. Often these political units are only administrative units, as in the case of France. But in some states political regions are centers of considerable autonomy and authority over society (such as provinces of Canada and states in the United States). Federalism is one legal-institutional form that this political regionalism can take.

An essential feature of a state structured into political regions— and one important for the purposes of this paper—is that geopolitical divisions within the state are given some political importance and therefore define multiple and potentially contradictory lines of political (and sometimes military) authority and legitimacy for the population at large. Thus, it is relevant to ask whether and under what circumstances political regionalism plays a significant role in the struggles for state power that underlie state formation.

At this point in the development of the world-system theoretical perspective, differences among states in the world-economy have not been integrated into the theoretical specification of the structure of the world-economy.[1] Therefore, in our historical analyses of state formation, political regionalism is introduced as a factor in an ad hoc fashion, or in connection with the consideration of ethnic factors in various struggles over state power. However, if the guiding principle in our theoretical analyses of state formation is that the world-economy as a whole is the unit of analysis, then we need to be attentive to the full range of variation in the structures of political power that constitute the political structure of the world-economy. This suggests that we should begin to theoretically incorporate political regionalism into our specification of the international system of states and to employ the full variation in our analyses of state formation.

My concern with this issue grows out of an observation that patterns of state formation in Brazil during the period from 1930 to 1964 and in the antebellum United States seem to have been decisively shaped by regionally centered political activities and by the forms of struggle that mobilized resources and commitments at the level of political regions. Prior to 1930, the Brazilian state was composed of member states which exercised considerable autonomy and authority. The military was organized and controlled at the level of political regions (member states). The revolt of 1930 was a regionalist revolt, with the states of Rio Grande and Minas in alliance against São Paulo (Conniff, 1978).

During the 1930s under the Vargas regime, political regionalism was significantly reduced through the nationalization of the military and other centralizing measures (Skidmore, 1967). However, political regionalism seems to have continued to play a vital role in the ongoing struggles over the forms and control of state power. Just as São Paulo had been the power base of the Old Republic (pre-1930), because of its role as the major producer of coffee for export, it became the power base behind the Estado Nôvo of Vargas by the advent of World War II because of its role as the major center of manufacturing as well as coffee production.

With the exception of the early 1930s, a coalition of São Paulo interests seems to have dominated state formation, generating oppositional movements centered in other political regions. Thus, the political struggles over state power continued to take the form of regionally based political conflicts well into the post-World War II period. Even as late as the early 1960s, the United States used political regionalism in its efforts to undermine the Goulart regime. U.S. aid was channeled to the governments of friendly states (Skidmore, 1967: 323).

The key to the strategic role played by São Paulo in struggles for state power is the fact that the leading industrial sectors and the leading agricultural sector (coffee) were mainly situated in São Paulo. The fiscal underpinnings of the central state were thus concentrated in a single political region, which fact tended to relegate other political regions to peripheral roles in the state. Consequently, the search for political solutions to crises generated by shifts in the world-economy context, and which crises were different for the several sectors of the economy, was shaped by the unifying potential inherent in a common political region. Although the potential for a coalition was centered in a political region, the solution to the crises could be realized only through control of national policy-making and thus would require the subordination of other political regions to a São Paulo-dominated center coalition.[2]

The antebellum United States seems to have been a different case, since the U.S. economy was marked by regional specializations (cotton in the South, manufacturing in the Northeast, farming in the Midwest) that precluded the possiblity of forging a national coalition except in connection with federal institutions. However, if the antebellum period was one in which federal institutions (and their potential) were extremely limited, then a political region (state) may have been the only viable institutional locus for the formation of a center coalition. And this, of course, would mean that multiple and contradictory coalitions would emerge, engendering struggles for state power in any center coalition that might come to power.

My attempts to analyze state formation in Brazil and the United States suggest that neither the struggles over state power nor the outcomes of those struggles can be fully explained without taking into account the place of political regions in the larger configuration of relations that defined the locations and mobility options in the world-economy for those states. This suggests that treating certain political regions as parts of the political structure of the world-economy may be a useful step in our analyses of state formation. Currently, studies of state formation and national development do not do this, although they often suggest it (see, for example, Tardanico, this volume).

Although political regions are shown to be relevant to struggles for state power, studies of state formation and national development typically do not go beyond referring to particular political regions on a case-by-case basis. There is no attempt to specify the theoretical significance of that structure for the analytical concerns of those studies. Thus, it is not clear from those studies whether political regionalism is a theoretically important factor in the development of the world-economy.

In the next section I argue that the world-system logic of analysis that leads researchers to focus on relations among groups of capitalists in the world-economy that cut across the political boundaries of the system of states is also a logic that leads us to focus attention on political regionalism as a structural factor in struggles among those groups of capitalists for positions in the world-economy. Basically, my argument is that a political region, like the central state, can serve as an effective and necessary organizing device in the world-economy, so capitalists attempt to appropriate regional institutions to their ends where they find them and to create them where they do not exist but are required for their purposes. Consequently, political regionalism as a particular institutional structure of state power is both a manifestation and a determinant of struggles among groups of capitalists to dominate part of the political organization of capitalist class interests in the world-economy.

CENTER COALITION FORMATION
AND POLITICAL REGIONALISM

Given the uneven development of capitalism and the structural fractionalization of the world capitalist class, struggles for state power take the form of struggles among coalitions of capitalists in the world-economy (center coalitions). An analytical focus on center coalition formation is the key methodological factor in studies of state formation and national development. Moore's classic study of the social origins of dictatorship and democracy (1966) is an example of this type of analytical focus. Only recently have these studies begun to focus attention on the dynamic aspects of center coalition formation.

The world-system theoretical perspective has significantly enhanced the power of this type of analysis. By incorporating the effects of dynamic properties of the world-economy into analyses of center coalition formation, scholars are better able to explain the development of converging and diverging economic interests that underlie the formation of center coalitions. For example, Rubinson (1978) strengthens Moore's analysis by explaining the formation of important class alignments in nineteenth-century Germany and the United States with the interactions between the roles of capitalists in the world-economy and world-market trends and cycles. Rubinson's emphasis is on the dynamic properties of the world division of labor. In another direction, Skocpol (1979), Tardanico (this volume), Horowitz and Trimberger (1976), and others have introduced structural properties of the state into analyses of state formation. These studies give explicit weight to relatively autonomous state institutions and the activities of state personnel in shaping struggles over the formation of center coalitions and the institutionalization of state formation strategies. These analyses suggest that we need to pay closer attention to the full range of institutional structures in our analyses of center coalition formation. By implication, political regionalism may play a role in struggles for state power through its structural effects on the formation of center coalitions.

To link political regionalism to center coalition formation, we need to show when and how those political relations that demarcate political regions within a state play a theoretically significant role for capitalist class activities. The key to this analysis is a conceptualization of the role of state power in the world-economy. This conceptualization will allow us to specify a theoretical relationship between capitalist class activities and the institutions of political regions.

In the world-economy, state power is a critical resource for the capitalist class. Broadly speaking, state power in its various institutional forms plays a significant role in both the coordination of the world division of labor and in its transformation over time. Particular groups of capitalists attempt to use state power in their struggles to maintain or to alter their positions in the world division of labor at any particular time. Since these struggles are rooted in contradictions inherent in the development of the world-economy, they are endemic and pervasive. And since the political structure of the world-economy is a system of "sovereign" states, its development is often characterized by long and violent struggles for control of particular states. I refer to these as struggles for state hegemony.[3]

These struggles are for control of both existing state institutions and for the creation of new state institutions. State formation over any given period can thus be conceptualized as the configuration of struggles for state hegemony that constitute the interplay of social forces in the world-economy as a whole. And the political structure of the world-economy is the pattern of outcomes of those struggles at any point in time.

Neo-Marxist theories of the state in capitalism are relevant here. Many of these theories reject the notion that a stable and instrumental relationship between the capitalist class and the state can be assumed. Instrumentalist models attempt to explain the activities of the state by reference to the general interests of the capitalist class or to the specific economic interests of groups of capitalists. These models have been criticized for attributing too much power to the capitalists and too little power to the managers of the state and to the working class and other subordinate classes (Gold et al., 1975; Block, 1977). As a result, according to the critique, they are not very powerful tools for the analysis of historical cases.

In efforts to overcome the limitations of the instrumentalist models, Poulantzas and other neo-Marxists have adopted the concept of the "relative autonomy" of the state (Poulantzas, 1975, 1979). This concept is used to connote the idea that state activities do not directly reflect either the requisites for the reproduction of the capitalist system or the demands of the capitalist class or groups of capitalists (with historical exceptions). Rather, state activities are understood to emerge out of the interests institutionalized in the state, as well as out of the interests of capitalists. However, it can be said, without violating this proposition, that when they need to, capitalists approach state institutions instrumentally and that state institutions can become more or less effective instruments of specific capitalist class interests.[4]

We can explain this by making a distinction between state institutions and explicitly capitalist class (instrumental) institutions. Unlike instrumental institutions, the state can call upon two critical resources that give it a comparative advantage for capitalists, under certain historical conditions, over those instrumental institutions. First, the state tends to maintain a surplus of capacity to use force, over and above the capacity necessary to maintain its own existence against attackers or would-be attackers (both external and internal). Second and precisely because the state is not typically an unmediated instrument of the capitalist class, it can realize a portion of the surplus product at low cost through taxation. During periods of crisis these resources can be important to capitalist class interests.

Other institutions, such as trade associations, chambers of commerce, and international cartels, function as explicit instruments of capitalist class interests. State institutions, however, do not usually operate in such an explicit fashion—indeed, probably seldom do. But capitalists do attempt to appropriate institutions to their ends at certain times.

It can now be made clear why political regionalism needs to be incorporated into our analyses of center coalition formation. In many cases the institutions of a political region can stand in the same relationship to capitalists as can central state institutions, although they are more limited in their capacities as state institutions. However, it may not always be the case that they are more limited. In the antebellum United States the federal government was a pay-as-you-go operation, deriving its revenues from tariffs and land sales. Its army was extremely limited. By comparison, state governments taxed capital and incomes and borrowed extensively both domestically and from abroad. They also controlled their own militias. Brazil had a similar institutional structure in the 1930s. In these cases, at least, the institutions of a political region could stand in autonomous relationship to capitalists, providing state managers with significant bargaining powers vis-à-vis domestic and foreign capitalist class activities. They could thus be effectively appropriated as instruments of struggles for central state hegemony at critical historical moments.

Explaining the role of political regionalism in struggles for state hegemony requires a theoretical conceptualization of the historical circumstances in which political regions can be taken to have relatively autonomous locations and significant roles in the world-economy. This means that the theoretical importance of a political region can neither be derived from nor subsumed under another political entity. How to determine whether a political region has a relatively autonomous location in the world-economy is, of course, a problem.

Since the organization of political power in the world-economy (the international system of states) plays such a basic role in the development of the world-economy and in struggles among capitalists for profitable world-market positions, we need to be able to specify when a political region is a center of power in the world-economy. Hopkins (1979: 48) suggests a promising approach to this problem in arguing that what is decisive for the conception of a world-scale division of labor is "neither transport of goods nor exchange of 'values,' but instead whether the trade in question is or is not an integral segment of a larger complex of interrelated production processes." Pursuing this point, I suggest that a political region is relatively autonomous when its institutions can be mobilized by class actors to alter aspects of trade relations that are part of the world division of labor. Empirically, this would seem to include such institutional capacities as (1) directing investment, (2) providing protection from competition through the granting of monopolies and/or tariff protection, (3) waging war, (4) mobilizing capital through monetary policies and international debt, and (5) mobilizing and controlling labor. These are institutional capacities that have been used historically to alter sometimes directly, sometimes indirectly, sometimes incrementally, and sometimes radically, the configuration of world trade.

In a given historical situation, then, the institutions of a political region may suffice to alter or support a particular position in the world division of labor. A political region may serve as the institutional locus for the direct containment of class struggle and for the direct mobilization of popular support for national development strategies formulated by the regionally based capitalists and state managers. It can, therefore, serve as a political beachhead in a drive for upward mobility in the world-economy. It can also serve as a stronghold of resistance to the national development strategies being pushed from other political regions. This resistance may be from either opposing groups of capitalists and/or from subordinate classes.

In those cases we may expect to find intense struggles over the central state—provided, of course, that central state institutions are perceived to be appropriate instruments. But, and this is the point of this paper, this in no way means that political regions can be dismissed. In fact, the opposite may hold, if the case is, as I argue the case was in the antebellum United States and in Brazil in the 1930s, that the socioeconomic bases of state power in the world-economy are centered in one or a few political regions that are relatively autonomous.

Theoretically, then, it is useful to pay closer attention to the exploitability of the institutions of political regions *within* states, as usually defined, in our analyses of state formation, just as we now pay close attention to the exploitability of comparative advantages in production and/or trade in forming economic niches in the world division of labor.

POLITICAL REGIONALISM AND
CYCLES OF STATE FORMATION

State formation is an ongoing historical process and should not be conceived as a series of discrete events. However, for heuristic purposes both scholars and participants often focus on particular periods of political change as unusually important for the overall pattern of state formation. Such periods of rapid social and political change and/or regime changes that mark important departures in state formation are referred to here as "state formation events." These include social revolutions, military coups, and civil wars.

The line of analysis presented in this paper suggests that political regionalism will tend to become particularly important for state formation during those periods that lead up to and culminate in state formation events. Those periods are quite clearly periods of struggle for state hegemony. The relationship between political regionalism and state formation, then, is one that will vary in importance with the historical timing of state formation events and with their spatial distribution over the international system of states.

Because of the heightened interplay of the forces and contradictions of capitalism in the semiperiphery of the world-economy, state formation events tend to be concentrated in semiperipheral states. Those states are the centers of the most intensive competition among capitalists in the world-economy because they house both core and peripheral economic activities. These inherently contradictory positions in the world division of labor generate more or less continuous struggles over strategies of national development and state formation. Consequently, if political regions play significant roles in such struggles, those roles will tend to be most evident in the semiperiphery.

This theoretical specification of the loci of state formation events also has implications for specifying the periods during which the importance of political regions as instruments of center coalitions in struggles for state hegemony will tend to be clustered. Semi-peripheral states are characterized by heightened vulnerability to the effects of trends and cycles in the world-economy due to their simultaneous dependence on core-controlled capital and technology for industrial sectors and on core-dominated world-markets for export commodities (agricultural commodities, minerals, and light manufactures). Semiperipheral exports typically face extensive competition. Consequently, state formation events in the semiperiphery will tend to be clustered during periods of world economic slump. These are periods, according to Wallerstein (1979) and Chase-Dunn and Rubinson (1979), during which the disintegration of cohesion among core capitalists and core states weakens their institutional control over the semiperiphery, allowing a select few to make important advances toward core status in the world-economy. But taking advantage of the loosened core control of the world-economy requires effective state action both domestically and internationally. During the downturn of the economic cycles, the strategic importance of state hegemony is significantly enhanced because the state emerges even more decisively as the major factor standing between peripheral impoverishment or economic advancement. Similarly, during the period of the upswing, effective state action can take advantage of an expanding world-market to advance industrialization before core reorganization imposes new constraints on semiperipheral and peripheral states. The significance of political regionalism as a factor in state formation, then, will tend to be greatest in the semiperiphery during the troughs in the cyclical development of the capitalist world-economy.

CONCLUSION

This paper attempts to begin to theoretically incorporate political regionalism into our analyses of state formation in the world-economy. The need for such an effort is suggested by the seeming importance of political regions for state formation in pre-World War II Brazil and the antebellum United States, and by the theoretical emphasis in the world-system perspective on state formation as an integral part of the development of the world-economy. I have argued that our analyses of state formation should focus on the interplay between the political structure of the world-economy and the roles of capitalists in the world division of labor, and that in some cases the dynamic properties of that interplay will be centered in political regions within states.

This analysis questions the implicit assumption in most studies of state formation and national development that only central state institutions require serious theoretical attention, and suggests that important dimensions of the political structure of the world-economy are arbitrarily dismissed by too-close adherence to the conceptualization of that structure as a system of states. It would seem that, despite the "structuredness" of the world-economy and despite the seeming inevitability of core state control of the world-economy, the motivating forces may be considerably more fragmented and the possibilities for effective · .tical intervention more decentralized than the current attentiveness to nation-state boundaries allows us to appreciate.

NOTES

1. That is, with the exception of gross variations in state strength. Wallerstein argues that states in the core are stronger than states in the semiperiphery and periphery (1979). There is some debate over how state strength should be conceptualized.

2. A center coalition is a coalition of major sectors of the capitalist class and state managers. In it reside the viability and legitimacy of the state.

3. With the term "hegemony" I wish to convey the notion that the capitalist class may substantially define the parameters of state activities and substantially determine the direction of the state's development, but not in the form of direct political control. Rather, hegemony takes the form of a divison of labor between state managers and a coalition of capitalists (Block, 1977), the latter of which exercises substantial direct control over the means of production and thus over the conditions of existence for both the capitalist class and the state. In the world-economy, state hegemony constitutes political control (as well as substantial direct control) over a particular part of the world-scale appropriation of the surplus product.

4. The degree to which groups of capitalists attempt to appropriate state institutions to their ends and the degree to which they are successful are functions of (1) the historical circumstances that produce the need for certain capitalists to use the state, (2) the circumstances that generate contradictory forces within the capitalist class itself, (3) the amount of resistance from subordinate classes to the initiatives of the capitalist class, and (4) the structure of differential access to the resources of struggle available to sectors of the capitalist class and to subordinate classes.

REFERENCES

BLOCK, F. (1977) "The ruling class does not rule." Socialist Revolution 33 (May–June): 6–28.

CHASE-DUNN, C. K. and R. B. RUBINSON (1979) "Cycles, trends, and new departures in world-system development," in J. W. Meyer and M. T. Hannan (eds.) National Development and the World System: Educational, Economic, and Political Change, 1950–1970. Chicago: University of Chicago Press.

CONNIFF, M. L. (1978) "The Tenentes in power: a new perspective on the Brazilian Revolution of 1930." Journal of Latin American Studies (May): 61–82.

GOLD, D., C. Y. H. LO and E. O. WRIGHT (1975) "Recent developments in the Marxist theories of the state." Monthly Review 27 (September): 29–43; (October): 36–51.

HOPKINS, T. K. (1979) "The study of the capitalist world-economy: some introductory considerations," in W. Goldfrank (ed.) The World System of Capitalism: Past and Present. Beverly Hills, CA: Sage.

HOROWITZ, I. L. and E. K. TRIMBERGER (1976) "State power and military nationalism in Latin America." Comparative Politics 8 (January): 223–244.

MOORE, B., Jr. (1966) Social Origins of Dictatorship and Democracy. Boston: Beacon Press.

POULANTZAS, N. A. (1975) Political Power and Social Classes. London: New Left Books and Sheed and Ward.
——— (1979) State, Power, Socialism. New York: New Left Books/ Schocken.

RUBINSON, R. B. (1978) "Political transformation in Germany and the United States," in B. H. Kaplan (ed.) Social Change in the Capitalist World Economy. Beverly Hills, CA: Sage.

SKIDMORE, T. E. (1967) Politics in Brazil, 1930–1964: An Experiment in Democracy. London: Oxford University Press.

SKOCPOL, T. (1979) States and Social Revolutions: A Comparative Analysis of France, Russia, and China. New York: Cambridge University Press.

WALLERSTEIN, I. (1974) The Modern World-System: Capitalist Agriculture and the Origins of the European World Economy in the Sixteenth Century. New York: Academic Press.
_____ (1979) The Capitalist World-Economy. London: Cambridge
University Press.

Chapter 7

STRUCTURAL ANTECEDENTS AND CONSEQUENCES OF STATISM

Francisco O. Ramirez
San Francisco State University

George M. Thomas
Stanford University

INTRODUCTION

Within the world capitalist system, state organization and statist ideology have come to dominate societies. This global phenomenon has led to renewed interest in theories of the state within both Marxist and pluralist perspectives. This paper does not undertake an exegesis of current theories of the state.[1] Instead, we synthesize recent comparative research findings on the structural antecedents and consequences of expanded state authority and fiscal power. In

AUTHORS' NOTE: This paper was partially supported by funds from the Organizational Training Program of Stanford University (Grant No. HSMHA 2T32 MH 15149-03). We thank John Boli-Bennett, Walter Goldfrank, and John Meyer for helpful comments.

the course of developing this synthesis, we set forth an agenda for comparative studies of state structures that expands current models and more explicitly takes into account the contextual properties of the world political economy. Two main points emerge from these considerations: (1) It becomes apparent that economic dependence is dialectically related to state organization: Relations of dependence stifle national economic development, in part by diminishing the fiscal powers of the state; but dependence also creates the conditions under which nationalistic, mobilizing movements arise, centralizing authority within the state structure and undermining the effects of dependency. (2) In examining the concept of dependence we move from the idea that countries are solely dependent on other particular countries within the system to the idea that countries may be more or less embedded or incorporated into the world political economy as a whole.

The scope of our review of the literature will be restricted in two respects. First, we limit ourselves to empirical studies of two dimensions of state organization: the extent of the fiscal power of the state and the level of political centralism or absolutism characterizing the regime. This restriction leads us to ignore important research on other dimensions of state organization—for example, the degree to which the instruments of violence are effectively monopolized by the state. The dimensions we examine, however, have received major attention in a number of historical and comparative studies (Schumpeter, 1954; Moore, 1966; Huntington, 1968) and continue to be the object of more recent analyses (see the papers in Tilly, 1975, and in Meyer and Hannan, 1979).

A second restriction concerns the kinds of studies emphasized in our review. Although we refer to case studies and comparative historical analyses dealing with longer time periods, most of the research we examine in detail involves quantitative cross-national analyses for the Pax Americana period, 1950–1970. This restriction maximizes comparability across studies, a necessary condition for any serious effort at synthesis.

Theoretically, we are in fundamental agreement with the growing number of scholars who directly or indirectly postulate "the relative autonomy of the state" (Anderson, 1974; Block, 1977; Gold et al., 1975; Skocpol, 1979). However, we think it is inadequate to conceptualize the state as the organization of the interests of bureaucrats acting as a new class or status group. In exercising the extractive, administrative, policing, and defense activities of the state, a network of state officials and managers may indeed acquire enormous leverage within their own societies (Doggan, 1975; Lane, 1976). But what makes these functions, plus a whole range of public service and social justice activities, primarily the domain of the state? Clearly this has not been the case throughout most of human history, and, just as clearly, the state mode of political organization has never in the past dominated the whole world. To raise this question opens the door to the possibility that a theoretical explanation of the universality and legitimacy of state organization requires reference to the processes by which states and societies are linked to and shaped by the world political economy.

In pursuing this possibility, we begin with dependency theory because it attempts to view the relative position of a country in the world-system as a basic causal factor that influences its economy and its state. In the second section we expand the dependency model in order to account for the differential impact of relations of dependence on the fiscal power and centralized character of state organization. Both these dimensions of state power positively affect economic development and attenuate the negative influence of economic dependence. In the third section, we expand the concept of dependency itself, arguing that "dependence" on the world political economy as a whole is a key factor in the rise of statism and that this incorporation into the larger system works quite differently from solely economic dependence. These discussions highlight the paradoxical nature of centralism. We examine this fact by looking at statist effects on both repression and egalitarianism in the fourth section. We then conclude with some theoretical considerations of how the world political economy has created the era of statism.

It should be stressed that we do not equate world political economy with the totality of unequal exchanges of commodities, capital, and technological flows, though such exchanges take place and constitute an important foundation of the world political economy. The world-economy also includes systemic rulelike definitions of the appropriate agencies for articulating and transacting "societal interests," transnational standards for assessing transnational exchanges, and converging agreement on a world-view of social progress measured in economic development *and* egalitarian policy terms (Mazuri, 1976; Meyer, 1980). We develop this important point throughout the paper.

THE DEPENDENCY MODEL

The central intellectual theme underlying dependency theories is that the underdevelopment of the Third World is not a condition reflecting a set of internal sociocultural forces and traditions that hinder development. Rather, underdevelopment is a process of peripheralizing Third World economies (and societies) incorporated within the world capitalist division of labor. The logic of capitalist accumulation leads to the development of underdevelopment in the Third World. The main hypothesis is that a high level of inter-nation economic dependency stifles economic development. An extensive review of 19 quantitative cross-national studies shows that the long-run effects of investment and aid dependency on growth are indeed negative, but that the magnitude of the effects is stronger for the richer countries (Bornschier et al., 1978). This review also shows that there are short-run positive gains to be made by linking up to the world-system within a dependency relation, especially for the poorer countries. This main finding is consistent with the burden of evidence from case studies of Latin American (Bonilla and Girling, 1973) and African (Amin, 1974) countries. We do not assess any further evidence for

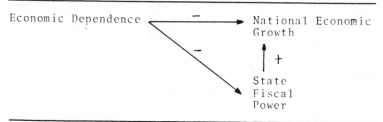

Figure 7.1: Economic Dependency Model of Statism

this issue, nor do we advance additional interpretations of it. We examine the processes through which degrees and kinds of dependencies may give rise to particular state structures, which may in turn have independent consequences for national economic development as well as for subsequent levels and effects of dependency.

Figure 7.1 shows that economic dependencies have direct negative effects on national economic growth and indirect negative effects mediated by the fiscal power of the state. Wallerstein (1974a) describes the emergence of strong states in the core areas and the development of relatively weaker ones in the periphery of the European world-economy in the sixteenth century. Pursuing this perspective, others have argued that a position of dominance in the world division of labor facilitates the development of strong state organization, which in turn is more likely than a weak one to successfully promote national economic development, either directly through some variant of state capitalism or indirectly via interventionist policies that promote the interests of nationally oriented capital over those of foreign capital and their local liaison elites.

Several indicators of economic dependence are commonly used to examine these hypotheses. One set attempts to measure the degree to which a country is in a dependent relation to another country. Export partner concentration, the proportion of total exports going to a country's largest exporting partner, gets at the number of external markets available to a country: The greater the concentration, the less the number of markets and the greater the dependence on the trading partner. Commodity diversity measures the degree to which a country can cultivate other external markets and diffuse internal capital growth across various sectors of the economy: The less the diversity, the greater the dependence. Taken together, these variables tap the degree to which a country is incorporated into the world political economy as a dependent collective actor relative to usually one other actor (see Galtung, 1971). Another type of indicator looks at the general (rather than the dyadic) dependence of a country on foreign capital: flows into and accumulation of exogenous capital within a given country in the form of either direct investment in the economy or loans extended to the state.

Rubinson (1977) analyzes the impact of export partner concentration, foreign investments, and public debt on government revenue per capita between 1955 and 1970 and finds the expected pattern: higher levels of dependence diminish the growth of the fiscal power of the state. Thomas and Meyer (1980) show that export partner concentration has negative effects on fiscal growth, especially among poorer countries. Studies using different research designs and controlling for several other variables, including economic dependence, have demonstrated a positive impact of fiscally powerful states on national economic development in the post-World War II era (Rubinson, 1977; Meyer et al., 1979; see also Chirot, 1977). Gobalet and Diamond (1979) show that the direct negative effects of foreign capital dependence on development are weaker in countries with stronger states than in countries with weaker ones. This result is also found when the relation between foreign "value" penetration and development is examined. Horowitz (1972) and Portes (1973) argue that the institutionalization of foreign values within a dependent country increases mass consumption and thereby attenuates endogenous capital formation. Delacroix (1977), using the number of imported foreign films as an indicator of foreign value penetration, finds the hypothesized direct negative effect on economic growth. Furthermore, the negative influence of foreign value consumption is weaker among countries with stronger state apparatuses. These studies suggest that foreign capital penetration, whether conceptualized and measured in "economic" or "cultural" terms, is most detrimental to national economic growth in countries with relatively weak fiscal state structures.

Another process of interest concerns the relationship between levels of economic and military dependencies and the extent to which military dependencies may weaken the extractive capacities of the state. The imperialist phases of worldwide capitalist development strongly suggest linkages between the penetration of foreign capital and the appearance of foreign forces. Although a wave of merchants and missionaries may follow the initial thrust of soldiers, as indeed was the case in the Spanish colonization of the New World and the Philippines during the Pax Americana, the volume of economic dependency would seem to have causal priority over the extensiveness of military dependency. That is, high levels of dependency on foreign capital may generate high levels of dependency on military aid to suppress antiforeign or anticapitalist movements. Using the dollar value of military aid (arms transfers) received by a nation as a percentage of its total military expenditures as an indicator of the level of military dependency, Lanfranchi (1979) finds a positive relationship between economic and military dependence.

Nativist resistance to foreign capital penetration, though seldom taking the form of revolutionary movements, will nevertheless be directed at the state in various reformist demands, calling for the expansion of state authority over the national economy. This process is often undermined either by the dominant coalition of foreign capitalist and local *compradores* (Horowitz and Trimberger, 1976) or by the lending policies of international agencies that favor private-sector development (Hayter, 1971). Therefore, in addition to its direct negative effect on state power and its indirect effect through the importation of consumption-oriented foreign values, economic dependency may weaken the state apparatus through increases in military dependency.

At this point, there seems to be good support for dependency arguments which recognize that the fiscal power of the state plays an important role in dependence and development. The struggle for national development requires freedom from the domination of foreign capital. Without overturning the world capitalist system, the strategic possibilities open to the less developed countries are limited (Wallerstein, 1974b). The Chinese experiment with autarky is an implausible model of development for most other countries, given the unique vastness of China's population and resource base (Krauss, 1979). In the post-World War II era the establishment of a relatively sound fiscal state serves as a buffer, mitigating the detrimental influence of dependence and stimulating national economic growth; but initial high levels of dependence decrease the likelihood of establishing a fiscally strong state organization.

Figure 7.1 suggests two major research issues that should be pursued. First, we should examine the influence of the degree of centrality in the world-economy, along with economic dependence, on the fiscal power of the state (and on economic development). This would differentiate between the effect of dyadic dependence relations and position in the larger system. Most research concerned with this issue controls for a country's economic development, but a more direct approach examines the consequences of cross-national variations in the percentage of world trade controlled by a country. Boli-Bennett (1980) uses this indicator of centrality in the world-economy and finds no significant relationship between it and the extractive power of the state in cross-sectional analyses taken every ten years from 1910 to 1970, as well as in analyses that pool all of the cross-sections. We propose a more dynamic longitudinal study over the same period.

Second, we need to examine more explicitly the thesis that strong states can offset the detrimental effects of dependency. Presumably, one mechanism through which this process takes place is via the reduction of the degree of dependency itself. It will be informative to study the effects of government revenue on different dependency measures over time, as well as on such intervening factors as endogenous capital accumulation. Such analyses will clarify whether the expansion of the public sector diminishes the dependence on foreign interests. Note that an implicit assumption is that the expansion of the extra-active powers of the state will lead to increased government spending on national development projects, not merely to the construction of modern palaces and secular cathedrals. This assumption may indeed be axiomatic in the contemporary world-system, but its lawlike appearance may be contingent on the character of the world-system instead of some inherently functional relationship between state revenue and national economic development.

THE DEPENDENCY MODEL: DIALECTICAL CONSIDERATIONS

We significantly alter the dynamics of Figure 7.1 by focusing on another dimension of state structure: the degree to which political authority is centralized. In *Lineages of the Absolutist State* (1974), Anderson makes clear that one should distinguish between the administrative power of the monarchies and the extent to which they successfully advanced absolutist claims. To illustrate, in the seventeenth and eighteenth centuries, the English monarchy had attained a level of administrative power comparable to that of the French monarchy, though royal absolutism was by far more institutionalized in France than in England. Or, to cite another historical example, the Hapsburg dynasty in Spain during the sixteenth century never attained the level of fiscal strength that would characterize later monarchies (only its vast overseas dominions prevented an earlier fiscal crisis), but its ideology of royal absolutism was never matched in England.

The distinction between the amount of power the state wields and the degree to which state powers (whatever their scope) are concentrated in some visible organ is strongly emphasized throughout the comparative institutional analyses undertaken by

Huntington (1968; Huntington and Moore, 1970). The distinction is also acknowledged in studies of state-formation processes in Latin America which recognize that a degree of political central-ism is often attained prior to the actual expansion of the extractive power of the state. For example, an extensive review of the litera-ture on state-building in Mexico (1917–1924) from a world-system perspective illustrates the process of centralizing what little political power is available to the national state (Tardanico, 1979). In work on the development of single-party states in the African continent, Wallerstein (1969) analyzes a similar process. Recent changes in the state structures of many Asian countries may be characterized as increases in the levels of political centralism. Although there are different ways of conceptualizing and measuring political centralism, in the world-system as presently constituted the development of a single-party regime is a good indicator.

Diverse attempts have been made to explain the rise of centralist regimes in different countries. The most common general explana-tory variables are (1) conditions of economic underdevelopment; (2) successful coalitions of specified interest groups; (3) patterns of cultural authoritarianism; and (4) various forms of political instability, including those based on ethnic fragmentation. While the earlier literature was critical of centralist regimes, more recent discussions suggest that "hard" states are more likely to undergo economic growth.

Recent quantitative research has shed some light on these is-sues, allowing us to make some tentative assertions concerning the antecedents and consequences of centralism. Figure 7.1 summa-rizes studies which focus on the extractive power of the state; Figure 7.2 adds to this an assessment of research on centralist regimes—usually one-party and/or military regimes. To parallel our earlier discussion, we first consider the effects of economic dependencies on centralist regimes. Various longitudinal analyses show that through the period 1950–1978 economic dependency increases the likelihood of centralist regimes (Thomas et al., 1979; Lanfranchi, 1979). The process seems to operate especially in

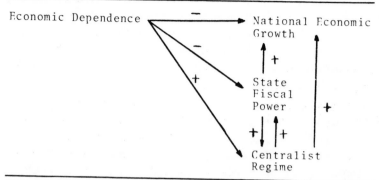

Figure 7.2: Dialectical Dependency Model of Statism

countries that gained independence after World War II. Also, these studies uniformly show that the less economically developed countries are more likely to give rise to centralizing regimes, but the dependency effects are obtained over and above the effect of "underdevelopment."[2]

Turning to the effects of centralizing regimes on national economic development, the pattern of results is strikingly similar to the evidence for the influence of fiscally powerful states on economic growth. In the post-World War II era, centralist regimes stimulate economic growth, and this positive impact is strongest in the poorer countries (Meyer et al., 1979; Delacroix and Ragin, 1978).

It is crucial to understand the relationship between centralization of authority and the fiscal power of the state. Recently, it has been shown that in countries gaining independence after World War II, strong fiscal states lead to a larger number of regime changes toward centralized authority (one-party or military regimes). Furthermore, there is indirect evidence that in poor, peripheral countries, centralization leads in turn to fiscally stronger states (Thomas and Meyer, 1980). For rich, noncommunist countries, unitarian systems which tend to be more centralized politically than federalist ones are more likely to expand the level of government revenue (Cameron, 1978).

Figure 7.2 transforms Figure 7.1 not merely by adding one further variable to consider but rather by altering the logic of dependency arguments from a simple Aristotelian one (with voluntaristic nuances) to a more complex dialectical one with no references to the intentions of foreign capitalists or their liaison elites, or the groups or classes that oppose them. The very processes of capitalist penetration that hinder economic development, in part by undermining the organizational capacities of the state, generate charismatic centralist movements that institutionally glorify the national milieu (nation-building under conditions of relatively weak state formation) and promote state development through mobilizing strategies. These mobilizational processes ultimately weaken the stranglehold of foreign capital. Another way of expressing the same idea is to note the contradictory requirements of capitalist penetration in the present world-system: On one hand, capitalist penetration undermines state organization insofar as capitalist penetration emphasizes private-sector instead of public-sector development. On the other hand, capitalist penetration and development within a larger hostile environment are facilitated by better-integrated and larger-scale organizations. The development of the ultimate authority of the nation-state facilitates this process by reducing within-nation variations in legal and business practices.

It should be emphasized that there is nothing intrinsic about centralized structures that should trigger greater development within countries with such structures. Some of the most successful developers in prior historical eras were countries (Great Britain and the United States) with relatively low levels of political centralism (Bendix, 1964). Likewise, the historical record is repleté with examples of highly dependent countries as well as countries that slipped from the core to the semiperiphery that did not develop politically centralized authority. The relationship between levels of economic dependency and centralist regimes must also be understood within the contextual properties of the world-system as presently constituted.

The findings summarized in Figure 7.2 suggest that a major research direction is to study the impact of centralist regimes on the degree of economic dependence. This parallels research on the effects of state fiscal power on dependence relations; taken together, these studies will increase our knowledge of whether expanded state power and/or centralism directly reduces the degree of economic dependence.

The proposed research should be undertaken keeping in mind that throughout the twentieth century the proportion of national societies under fiscally powerful states and/or centralized regimes has expanded worldwide (Boli-Bennett, 1980; Thomas et al., 1979). This upward secular trend tends to be ignored in many discussions of the association between state organization and internation dependency relations. Moreover, centralist regimes have undergone a qualitative change, from being passively authoritarian primarily concerned with preserving the status quo to being more oriented to mobilization and more actively pursuing development goals (Huntington and Moore, 1970).

A WORLD-SYSTEM MODEL OF STATISM

Within the dependency framework researchers do not clearly distinguish between the *degree* of national incorporation into the world-economy and the *form* of the national linkages to the world-economy. Most dependency studies deal with the latter issue, discussing the antecedents and consequences of specialized versus flexible economic roles within the world-system while ignoring cross-national variation in political-economic involvement in the world-system.

We contend that research must take into account the extent to which a country is incorporated within the world-system: the degree to which a society is dependent on the dynamics of the world political economy as a whole. This should not be conceptually equated with economic dependency ties, often discussed as dyadic relations; nor should measures of the level of national incorporation be lumped together with indicators of dependent forms of involvement in the larger political-economic environment. We contend that the national consequences of incorporation differ

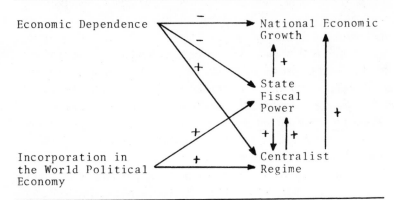

Figure 7.3: World-System Model of Statism

from the effects of inter-nation dependency processes, as shown in Figure 7.3.

The comparative literature suggests the following indicators of the level of national incorporation within the world political economy: (a) the volume of diplomatic exchanges, (b) the number of conjoint treaty memberships, (c) the extensiveness of memberships in international organizations, and (d) the degree of participation in world trade—the value of a country's total trade as a proportion of its gross national product.

There are several analyses of the relationship between trade involvement and state fiscal growth: The pattern of results consistently differs from the findings of conventional measures of economic dependency. Boli-Bennett (1980) shows a positive association between the national level of trade involvement and the fiscal power of the state for 1920, 1930, 1960, and 1970. (A positive but statistically insignificant relationship held in 1938.) Thus, after World War II, those nations that were most involved in world trade were most likely to have fiscally strong states, except during a period of world economic contraction. In a panel analysis covering 1960–1975, Cameron (1978) reports the same findings for a sample of industrialized noncommunist countries, observing that exposure to world trade is the strongest predictor of the expansion of state fiscal powers. Rubinson (1976) finds that trade participation usually has small positive effects on government revenue as compared to negative effects of the standard indicators of economic dependency.

Further exploration of these ideas would include analyses of incorporation not only on state fiscal power but also on centralization and economic development.[3] Total trade participation for poor or dependent countries is probably highly correlated with internation economic dependence: for these countries, trade constitutes dependent trade. Therefore, analyses of the effects of incorporation into the world-system should control for the level of internation economic dependence.

We doubt that the relationship between different forms and degrees of participation in the world political economy and the development of national state structures and economies is a historical constant. For example, the lack of a positive relationship between involvement in world trade and state fiscal power in 1938 (Boli-Bennett, 1980) suggests that such a relation holds only when the larger system is expanding. Comparative trade information and other relevant data are available for some countries from 1800 to 1975, making long-term historical analyses feasible (see Krasner, 1976; Banks, 1975). This would allow us to track changes in patterns of relationships against changes in historical context.

Further Structural Consequences

The findings we have reviewed support the interpretation that state power and authority are expanded in part due to the incorporation of the national society into a larger world political economy. Central to this development is the paradoxical relation between mobilizing people around collective purposes and conferring large degrees of autonomy and individuality on them. Any theory of statism must account for this dialectic between state mobilization and individualism. We discuss briefly some of its aspects by extending the model to include the effects of expanded states on egalitarianism and repression, as shown in Figure 7.4.

We discuss research findings on two aspects of egalitarianism: income equality and equality between the sexes. The proliferation

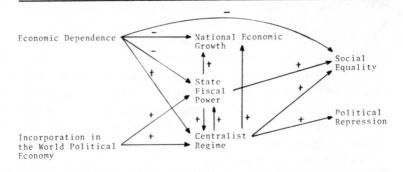

Figure 7.4: World-System Model of Statism: Consequences for Political
            Repression and Social Equality

of cross-national studies of income inequality is impressive. A voluminous literature on the status of women in society has developed; a few inquiries utilize the formally comparative research designs and statistical analyses that characterize much of the income inequality literature. A basic finding that runs throughout these studies is that dependence relations increase income inequality (Bornschier et al., 1978; Frank, 1972; Dos Santos, 1971) and inequality between the sexes (Boserup, 1970; Chinchilla, 1970).

While we know of no studies that examine the effect of centralism on income inequality, it appears that in the period following World War II strong fiscal states lower income inequality. Stack (1978), using a measure of government expenditures that is highly correlated with government revenue, shows the equalizing effect of "direct government involvement in the economy." This study includes communist countries, giving rise to some criticism of the comparability of his measure between communist and noncommunist countries, but this finding is consistent with a study of government revenue and income inequality for noncommunist nations (Rubinson, 1976). This is also consistent with what is known about the relationship between government fiscal power and income distribution in communist (Michal, 1973) and noncommunist countries (Wilensky, 1975).

Studies of sex inequality show that relative levels of female participation in mass or secondary schooling and in the paid labor force are increased by fiscally more powerful states (Stewart and Winter, 1977; Ramirez and Weiss, 1979) and by one-party regimes

(Ramirez and Weiss, 1979). These findings are interpreted as a process of political incorporation: Conditions of expanded state power and authority increase the likelihood of women being endowed with citizenship status within the national collective.

There is no intrinsic relation between state expansion and income and sex equality. Historically, state expansion has gone hand in hand with the emergence of individualism, and the state/individual dynamic has dominated Western life since the Middle Ages (Gierke, [1881] 1958). However, in the history of state formation in Western Europe, fiscally powerful and centralized bureaucracies were created primarily at the expense of the peasantry, which shouldered the burden of increased taxation. The eventual extension of citizenship rights to the lower classes was more than offset by the concomitant suspension of traditional prerogatives and privileges. Likewise, the early expansion of the state in Western Europe was not accompanied by the incorporation of women into the economy. The triumph of industrial capitalism is often associated with the establishment of the bourgeois state, and it is further argued that both of these historical forces led to the privitization of family life and the restriction of women to the domestic sphere (Zaretsky, 1976).

We emphasize, however, that while it is a mistake to argue ahistorically that state expansion and particular levels of realized equality go together, it is equally inaccurate to extrapolate earlier relationships to the mid-twentieth century. In our contemporary world the expansion of the state does not result in increased differentiation between "the public" and "the private." The national state/individual citizenship model is the institutionalized political mode of organization throughout the world-system. (Even in fundamentalist Islamic republics, such as Iran, the people are expected to vote, and adult males *and* females constitute "the people.") The expansion of the state helps integrate the public and private spheres via the expansion of citizenship rights and duties and the extension of citizenship status to greater numbers within the population.[4] Of course, not all forms of inequality are automatically defined as violations of citizenship rights (for example, many urban/rural inequalities of access to education and other social services are ignored even in the USSR and other Eastern European countries). But, increasingly, some forms of inequality are classified as social inequities, and national states are expected to eradicate or at least reduce the level of inequality.

We emphasize that this elaboration of the individual and the increase in egalitarianism takes place within a context of collective, national mobilization. Boli-Bennett (1979) has forcefully shown that the rights of individuals become increasingly defined as citizen rights derived from the state. As such, they can be suspended for the sake of the collective. Also, Hubretch (1978) has shown that countries with more centralized states more severely violate human rights. Bergesen (1977) finds that one-party states engage in greater levels of political witchhunting and are more likely to undertake these activites across the greatest number of institutional spheres. This holds true when controlling for the coercive power of the state. These studies suggest that in centralized states the collective purposes of the nation (modern absolutist claims) permeate all aspects of life.

We have argued that expanded state organization and claims arise in part as a function of the incorporation of a region into the world political economy. The expanded state, in turn, creates elaborated definitions of the individual and equality in the context of citizenship and mobilization, according to rules residing in the larger world political environment. Two interesting questions arise out of this interpretation: (1) Does incorporation to the world-system have direct effects on egalitarianism and repression independent of state structure and dyadic dependence relations? (2) Are structural consequences of expanded state power and enhanced centralism contingent on the form and degree of national incorporation in the world-system?

THE WORLD POLITICAL ECONOMY:
SOME PRELIMINARY CONSIDERATIONS

The world political economy is capitalist and statist. Throughout the world, capitalism is the dominant mode of production, and statism is the dominant mode of political organization. The global dimensions of these phenomena are historically unprecedented. There are some socialist movements, but no widespread socialist mode of production (Wallerstein, 1974a). There are some nation-building movements that are only loosely coupled with state organization, but even these invoke statist ideology, and those that do are much more likely to survive as legitimated political entities in the world system (Meyer, 1980). The world-system of state organizations cannot be reduced to the world capitalist economy (Skocpol, 1979; Modelski, 1978). These institutional structures are interrelated and mutually constrain one another. At the global level, capitalism may hinder the formation of a world state, while the international system of states stigmatizes colonialism and other capitalist links among territories that undermine the development of statist ideology.

Even as Western intellectuals bemoan the decline of confidence in the idea of progress among Western peoples (Nisbet, 1980), a theory of progress mandating state-managed economic and social development has become firmly rooted throughout the world.

The world political economy is the foundation of this theory of progress, with state capitalism as its underlying logic. Incorporation into the world political economy involves exposure not only to technical processes of rationalized exchange and production, but also to enormous pressures, external to national societies, to organize all areas of life within political categories: States and only states are ultimately responsible for economic and social development. This leads to the consolidation of national authority and social responsibility within the state. Therefore, incorporation into the world political economy increases not only the monetarization of exchange and the commodification of life, but also the politicization of an expanding sphere of relationships and activities: State expansion and monetarization are two dimensions of the same systemic process. The emerging world-system is therefore best conceptualized not as a reduced number of "capitalist *firms* producing commodities for the world market" (Chase-Dunn and Rubinson, 1979: 292, italics added), but rather as a reduced number

of more or less capitalist *states*. Indeed, these states produce commodities for the world market; but as a world-system these states
also create and maintain worldwide conventions that reflect and
extend the logic of state capitalism. National states are expected to
incorporate their people as individual citizens, to educate and mobilize their populations around economic and social development
goals, and to promote welfare and equality through public programs and the expansion of citizenship rights. These responsibili-
ties are rooted in often repressive state authority and power relative
to other internal organizations and in state sovereignty vis-à-vis
other states. Even controversial national states are expected to
participate, not withdraw from the world-system of national
states.[5]

Some scholars who note that involvement in the world market
positively affects the fiscal powers of the state contend that these
high levels of participation expand the internal level of occupational specialization, thereby generating new taxing opportunities
for the state (Delacroix and Ragin, 1980). When it is recognized
that incorporation into the world-system increases contact with not
only merchants and financiers, but also diplomats, bureaucrats,
and transnational civil servants, it becomes apparent that the
growth of the national state apparatus results not only from expanded internal taxation but also from increased external authori-
zation and legitimation.

We have sought to synthesize many research findings and to
indicate further lines of inquiry. Neither our arguments nor these
findings can be extrapolated in total to other historical periods (for
example, the positive impact of stronger and more centralized
states on economic development and social equality). The findings
we have cited in this paper should *not* be conceptualized as ahis-
torical functional interrelationships among state, economy, and
society. We must keep in mind the current world historical context,
for these findings reflect ongoing substantive processes linked to
long-run historical changes in the world political economy.

In coming to grips with the evolutionary development of the
system as a whole, it is crucial to understand that the dynamic of

increased state power and centralization is not a simple diffusion process from core to periphery: Note that neither the free enterprise ideologies nor the relatively decentralized state structures of the last two hegemonic powers (Great Britain and the United States) have diffused throughout the world. Furthermore, this increase is not a result of each country independently adapting to a capitalist market environment. Just as capitalist organization and technology develops in country after country due to the impact of world capitalism, world statism dictates statist organization and ideology across the diversity of human societies. Incorporation into the world political economy, even to some degree as an economically dependent country, expands the legitimacy of the state to mobilize society in line with worldwide conventions regarding progress and development. Ours is a world-system of state capitalism; understanding its dynamics requires understanding a world political economy that underlies a theory of progress mandating state-managed development.

NOTES

1. For an interesting exegesis on the writings of Marx on the state, see Tarschys (1972).

2. Since many of these one-party regimes espouse socialist and nationalist ideologies and policies, it is awkward to interpret the effect of dependency as the mechanical imposition of a centralist puppet by some dominant foreign power. Moreover, although economic dependency generates military dependency, high levels of military dependencies do not increase the likelihood of the formation of centralist regimes (Lanfranchi, 1979). This observation further weakens the case for interpreting the rise of centralist regimes as primarily the intended product of external coercion.

3. In some analyses, world trade involvement is unrelated to economic development (Delacroix and Ragin, 1980), while other analyses show positive effects (Snyder and Kick, 1979).

4. This line of reasoning is more fully developed in Chapters 5 and 14 in Meyer and Hannan (1979).

5. Some of these ideas are further developed in Meyer (1980).

REFERENCES

AMIN, S. (1974) Accumulation on a World Scale. New York: Monthly Review Press.

ANDERSON, P. (1974) Lineages of the Absolutist State. New York: Schocken.

BANKS, A. S. [ed.] (1976) Political Handbook of the World. New York: McGraw-Hill.

BENDIX, R. (1964) Nation-Building and Citizenship. Garden City, New York: Doubleday.

BERGESEN, A. (1977) "Political witch hunts: the sacred and the subversive in cross-national perspective." American Sociological Review 42: 220–233.

BLOCK, F. (1977) "The ruling class does not rule: notes on the Marxist theory of the state." Socialist Revolution 7 (May–June): 6–28.

BOLI-BENNETT, J. (1979) "Human rights or state expansion? Cross-national definitions of constitutional rights, 1870–1970," in J. Scarritt and V. Nanda (eds.). Boulder, CO: Westview Press.

––––––– (1980) "Global integration and the universal increase of state dominance. 1910–1970," in A. Bergesen (ed.) Studies of the Modern World-System. New York: Academic Press.

BONILLA, F. and R. GIRLING [eds.] (1973) Structures of Dependency in Latin America. Stanford, CA: Institute for Political Studies.

BORNSCHIER, V., C. CHASE-DUNN, and R. RUBINSON (1978) "Cross-national evidence of the effects of foreign investment and aid on economic growth and inequality: a survey of findings and reanalysis." American Journal of Sociology 84: 651–683.

BOSERUP, E. (1970) Woman's Role in Economic Development. New York: St. Martin's Press.

CAMERON, D. (1978) "The expansion of the public economy: a comparative analysis." American Political Science Review 72: 1243–1261.

CHASE-DUNN, C. (1975) "The effects of international economic dependence on development and inequality." American Sociological Review 40: 720–738.

––––––– and R. RUBINSON (1979) "Cycles, trends, and new departures in world-system development," pp. 276–296 in J. Meyer and M.

Hannan (eds.) National Development and the World System: Educational, Economic, and Political Change: 1950–1970. Chicago: University of Chicago Press.

CHINCHILLA, N. (1970) "Industrialization, monopoly capitalism, and women's work in Guatamala." Signs 3: 38–56.

CHIROT, D. (1977) Social Change in the Twentieth Century. New York: Harcourt Brace Jovanovich.

DELACROIX, J. (1977) "The export of raw materials and economic growth: a cross-national study. American Sociological Review 42: 795–808.

———— and C. RAGIN (1978) "Modernizing institutions, mobilization, and third world development: a cross-national study." American Journal of Sociology 84: 123–149.

———— (1980) "Structural blockage: a cross-national study of economic dependency, state efficiency, and underdevelopment." Sociology Department, Indiana University. (unpublished)

DOGGAN, M. [ed.] (1975) The Mandarins of Western Europe: The Political Role of Top Civil Servants. New York: Halsted Press.

DOS SANTOS, T. (1971) "The structure of dependence," pp. 225–236 in K. Fann and D. Hodges (eds.) Readings in U.S. Imperialism. Boston: Porter Sargent.

FRANK, A. (1972) "The development of underdevelopment," pp. 3–17 in J. Cockcroft, A. Frank, and D. Johnson (eds.) Dependence and Underdevelopment. Garden City, New York: Doubleday.

GALTUNG, J. (1971) "A structural theory of imperialism." Journal of Peace Research 8: 81–117.

GIERKE, O. (1958 [1881]) Political Theories of the Middle Age. Boston: Beacon Press.

GOBALET, J. and L. DIAMOND (1979) "Effects of investment dependence on economic growth: the role of internal structural characteristics and periods in the world economy." International Studies Quarterly 23 (September): 412–444.

GOLD, D., A. CLARENCE, Y. LEE, and E. WRIGHT (1975) "Recent developments in Marxist theories of the capitalist state." Monthly Review 27 (November): 36–51.

HAYTER, T. (1971) Aid as Imperialism. Baltimore: Penguin.

HOROWITZ, I. L. (1972) Three Worlds of Development. New York: Oxford University Press.

_____ and E. K. TRIMBERGER (1976) "State power and military nationalism in Latin America." Comparative Politics 8: 223–244.

HUBRECHT, W. (1978) "Political repression and the monolithic state." Master's thesis, Department of Sociology, San Francisco State University. (unpublished)

HUNTINGTON, S. (1968) Political Order in Changing Societies. New Haven, CT: Yale University Press.

_____ and C. MOORE [eds.] (1970) Authoritarian Politics and Modern Societies. New York: Basic Books.

KRASNER, S. (1976) "State power and the structure of international trade." World Politics 28: 317–347.

KRAUSS, R. (1979) "Withdrawing from the world-system: self-reliance and class structure in China," in W. Goldfrank (ed.) The World System of Capitalism: Past and Present. Vol. 2, Political Economy of the World-System Annuals. Beverly Hills, CA: Sage.

LANE, D. (1976) The End of Inequality? Stratification Under State Socialism. Manolia, MA: Peter Smith.

LANFRANCHI, C. (1979) "Centralist regimes: a cross-national study of the capitalist world." Master's thesis, Department of Sociology, San Francisco State University. (unpublished)

LIPSET, S.M. (1960) Political Man: The Social Bases of Politics. Garden City, New York: Anchor.

MAZURI, A. (1976) A World Federation of Cultures: An African Perspective. New York: Free Press.

MEYER, J. (1980) "The world polity and the authority of the nation state," in A. J. Bergesen (ed.) Sociological Studies of the Modern World-System. New York: Academic Press.

_____ and M. HANNAN (1979) National Development and the World System: Educational, Economic, and Political Change, 1950–1970. Chicago: University of Chicago Press.

_____ R. RUBINSON, and G. THOMAS (1979) "National economic development, 1950–70: social and political factors," pp. 85–116 in J. Meyer and M. Hannan (eds.) National Development and the World System: Educational, Economic, and Political Change, 1950–1970. Chicago: University of Chicago Press.

MICHAL, J. (1973) "Income distribution of earnings and household incomes in small socialist nations." Review of Income and Wealth 19: 407–428.

MODELSKI, G. (1978) "The long cycle of global politics and the nation-state." Comparative Studies in Society and History 20: 214–235.

MOORE, B. (1966) Social Origins of Dictatorship and Democracy: Lord and Peasant in the Making of the Modern World. Boston: Beacon Press.

NISBET, R. (1980) History of the Idea of Progress. New York: Basic Books.

PORTES, A. (1973) "Modernity and development: a critique." Studies in Comparative International Development 8: 247–279.

RAMIREZ, F. and J. WEISS (1979) "The political incorporation of women," pp. 238–249 in J. Meyer and M. Hannan (eds.) National Development and the World System: Educational, Economic, and Political Change, 1950–1970. Chicago: University of Chicago Press.

RUBINSON, R. (1976) "The world-economy and the distribution of income within states: a cross-national study." American Sociological Review 41: 638–659.

——— (1977) "Development, government revenue, and economic growth, 1955–70." Studies in Comparative International Development 12: 3–28.

SCHUMPETER, J. (1954) "The crisis of the tax state," pp. 5–38 in A. Peacock et al. (eds.) International Economic Papers: Translations Prepared for the International Economic Association, Vol. 4. New York: Macmillan.

SKOCPOL, T. (1979) States and Social Revolutions. Cambridge: Cambridge University Press.

SNYDER, D. and E. KICK (1979) "Structural position in the world system and economic growth, 1955–1970: a multiple-network analysis of transnational interactions." American Journal of Sociology 84: 1096–1126.

STACK, S. (1978) "The effect of direct government involvement in the economy on the degree of income inequality: A cross-national study." American Sociological Review 43: 880–888.

STEWART, A. and D. WINTER (1977) "The nature and causes of female suppression." Signs 2: 531–553.

TARDANICO, R. (1979) "Revolutionary nationalism and state-building in Mexico, 1917–1924." Presented at the Annual Meetings of the American Sociological Association, Boston.

TARSCHYS, D. (1972) Beyond the State. Stockholm: Laromedelsforlaget.

THOMAS, G. and J. MEYER (1980) "Regime changes and state power in an intensifying world state system," in A. Bergesen (ed.) Sociological Studies of the Modern World-System. New York: Academic Press.

THOMAS, G., F. RAMIREZ, J. MEYER, and J. GOBALET (1979) "Maintaining national boundaries in the world system: the rise of centralist regimes," pp. 187–206 in J. Meyer and M. Hannan (eds.) National Development and the World System: Educational, Economic, and Political Change, 1950–1970. Chicago: University of Chicago Press.

TILLY, C. [ed.] (1975) The Formation of National States in Western Europe. Princeton: Princeton University Press.

WALLERSTEIN, I. (1969) Africa: The Politics of Independence. New York: Random House.

———— (1974a) The Modern World-System. New York: Academic Press.

———— (1974b) "Dependence in an interdependent world: the limited possibilities of transformation within the capitalist economy." African Studies Review 17: 1–26.

WILENSKY, H. (1975) The Welfare State and Equality. Berkeley: University of California Press.

ZARETSKY, E. (1976) Capitalism, the Family and Personal Life. New York: Harper & Row.

PART 4

CYCLES AND TRENDS OF
WORLD-SYSTEM DEVELOPMENT

Chapter 8

INTERMEDIATE CLASSES
IN A BIPOLARIZING STRUCTURE

Dale L. Johnson
Livingston College, Rutgers University

Perhaps the most debated thesis of the Marxist theory of social classes is that, under capitalism, the main historical process—the basic factor determining a wide range of social phenomena—is the polarization of classes. Development of the capitalist mode of production involves, at one pole, the concentration and centralization of property and control, wealth and power, in the hands of a reduced class of capitalists; at the other pole, development propels an ever-greater proportion of the population into the proletarian condition. Artisans, peasants and farmers, small businessmen, national minorities, and—lately—women and other unpaid producers of use values are dispossessed of alternative means of living and are irresistibly drawn into the orbit of capital—reduced to dependence on wages, relegated to the social position of producer of value appropriated by capital. As historical development proceeds within nations and internationally, all social relations prevailing in world society are increasingly defined by the basic social relation: that between capital and labor, bosses and workers, exploiters and exploited, oppressors and oppressed.

Much of the intellectual work of sociology over the last century, and especially since Max Weber, has been produced in an explicit or implicit attempt to refute this thesis. At the same time, contemporary Marxists have been concerned to amplify and in many respects to modify the thesis of class polarization—or, at least, to try to account for the social existence of intermediate classes which in the history of Marxist thought have been relegated to incidental formations.

The generalization I want to try to develop is that *capitalist development, through its distinct stages and phases, has been and remains characterized by a multi-class complex of class relations in a bipolarizing structure.*

A few brief illustrations of the thesis follow. In the transition to capitalism in seventeenth- and eighteenth-century Europe the bourgeoisie/proletarian relation had not yet become the central axis of class relations and socio-economic development. These relations were still engulfed within, yet increasingly penetrating, those of the feudal order of lords, peasants, and guild artisans. The bourgeoisie remained burghers, primarily a mercantile formation; the landed gentry only gradually, with the lure of commercial gain, underwent embourgeoisment; the working class was mainly a youthful and feminine appendage of the peasantry and artisan groupings—peasant families and guildsmen were forced to send their women and children into the new factories as their traditional way of life was being destroyed by the commercial and incipient developments of the era. Yet, an imperative of capitalist accumulation, spearheaded by mercantile interests and facilitated by absolutist states, was restructuring *all* class relations. The central antagonism was not yet bourgeoisie and proletariat, but a *systemic one* of a decaying feudalism and an emerging international capitalism, crystallized in the merchant-aristocracy and colonial relations of the transitional stage of capitalist development. The structure of the *totality* of multiclass relations was eroding precapitalist relations and moving toward the salience of bipolar relations.

Yet, during the nineteenth-century stage of competitive capitalism, an ample intermediate class, a petty bourgeoisie (independent
farmers, skilled craftsmen, and professional practitioners), was
formed as a result of the economic dynamic of the era and as a
refuge for ex-peasants and former artisans facing proletarianization. The forces of twentieth-century monopoly capitalism—the
concentration and centralization of capital and the forceful corporate absorption of wage labor, the polarization of industrial capital
and industrial labor—utterly destroyed this petty bourgeoisie. And
the same unraveling of forces formed a new intermediate class, the
salaried middle class. Indeed, the middle class of the twentieth
century is mainly an *expression* of the class polarization process.
The middle class of the emerging epoch, though, unlike the bourgeoisie and working class and like the old petty bourgeoisie, is a
transitory formation. The internal structure and character of the
bourgeoisie change, and the fractionalization and composition of
the working-class change with successive stages and phases of
development. But as long as there is capitalism, there will be a
bourgeoisie and a working class. The intermediate classes, on the
other hand, do not simply change in structure; they are always in a
process of fundamental transformation, of eclipse and eventual
disappearance, or of becoming qualitatively new formations. In
the case of the salaried middle class of the twentieth century, this is
so because the various fractions (such as technical personnel, administrative agents, and service professionals) that make it up at
any one historical point reflect specific *forms* that the polarizing
class relations of capitalist development take on in specific historical circumstances. This is why there is so much conceptual confu-
sion about what to label the class: "new middle class" (Carchedi,
1978), "new petty bourgeoisie" (Poulantzas, 1975), "new class"
(Bruce-Briggs, 1979), "new working class" (Mallet, 1963, 1975),
"professional-managerial class" (Ehrenreich and Ehrenreich in
Walker, 1979), *"capas medias"* or *"couches intermédiates"*
(various Latin American and French authors), or simply "strata"
occupying "contradictory locations" (Wright, 1978). Different
analysts have mistaken specific forms of these relations in particu-

lar conjunctures for more generalized class phenomena. For example, the "new working class" concept that today is given little credence seemed to make sense in the French situation of 1968 (the total revolt of youthful aspirants to the middle class and millions of salaried employees); the "post industrial society" thesis (Bell, 1973) seemed somewhat plausible in the American celebration of the 1950s and the economic expansion of the 1960s; while theories of the "professional-managerial class" and "new class" reflect opposite political responses to the social structural *appearances* of the United States in 1970s.

CAPITAL ACCUMULATION
AS CLASS FORMATION

All classical and contemporary variants within a historical materialist framework, in which world-systems theory can be located as one perspective, depart from an understanding of history as moving through distinct stages of development, including stages of underdevelopment and dependent development in peripheral formations. These are stages propelled by the accumulation process and impelled by class struggle. To understand bipolarization and the place of intermediate classes within this historical process, it is necessary to view the accumulation of capital as a good deal more than the movement of productive forces within national economies or on a world scale. Capital accumulation is not simply investment in production; it is a historical process of changing class relations, of the formation and dissolution of classes. As such, the accumulation process underlies the forms of class struggle in different stages and phases of development. For example, in the contemporary interlocked phases of development of monopoly capitalism of the core and dependent development on the periphery, the primary relation is between corporate/finance capital of the core and the working class on a world scale, a relation mediated by a complex of intermediate formations, also on a world scale. The intermediate classes include the middle classes whose members man the administrative and technical apparatuses of modern empire within the core and the local, dependent bourgeoisies and salaried middle classes of the periphery.

I will briefly touch on capital accumulation as a process of changing class relations.

The opening of new historical avenues of accumulation had a profound effect on the social structure, the social conditions of the population, and the social struggles accompanying capitalist development—all of which involved augmenting the space accorded new social elements in a growing, complex social division of labor. In a recently completed book, *Social Class and Social Development* (forthcoming a), I examine the principal sources of accumulation and their impact upon the formation of the salaried middle classes in the course of the development of the monopoly stage of the core and the stage of dependent development in parts of the periphery.

I emphasize that, while there are different sources of accumulation, it should always be kept in mind that in the final analysis all rest upon the basis of changing social relations. For example, in the United States after 1870, an era of vast accumulation through railroad extension and new technologies, an increasing proportion of the population became initiated into the wage labor to capital social relation. This permitted the appropriation of surplus previously produced outside the sphere of capital. In the twentieth century, accumulation proceeded more and more on the basis of the transformation of the population into a dependent mass of wage workers who remain, on one hand, in the employment of capital and, on the other hand, consumers of marketed commodities. Most production became commodified in the age of what Harry Braverman (1974) termed "universal markets." As the twentieth century progressed, the average family became more dependent on commodified relations and less dependent on communal exchanges of use values. Middle-class professionals penetrated the life cycle of the average American from the slap of the doctor's hand at birth to the grooming of the mortician's hand at death.

The middle class was formed in the context of the increased salience of the capital-to-labor relation. The productivity of the mass of workers, employed in new areas of production, was constantly augmented by the activities of proliferating groups of scientists, engineers, and organizational experts; workers were subjected to routinized, dequalified work, and the skills they were stripped of were transferred to the new experts; control of the extended and complicated labor process required layer upon layer of supervisors; and the reproduction of the growing wage labor force was technically managed by an expanding number of professionals.

The massive incorporation of persons into the wage labor to capital relation depended upon new areas of large-scale investment. In the twentieth century, the automobile, electronics, cheap energy, and computers revolutionized the world of work and with it the contours of social structure and forms of social relations. Employees who swelled the ranks of new occupations came to form a class set squarely between the polarizing relations of increasingly concentrated and centralized capital and the growing mass of proletarianized workers.

The internalization of North American capital as a principal source of accumulation also carried with it a change in the social structure at home. The establishment of the United States in the post-World War II period as the technological and administrative center of transnational capital and "free world" empire caused considerable expansion of the middle class, strengthening of corporate capital, and a change in the composition of the American working class. To a certain degree, the American middle class (like the English merchants of the eighteenth century and the English industrial bourgeoisie of the nineteenth century) has been fed by "the spoils of imperialism."

Finally, the development of the positive state is also intimately involved in the process of accumulation and class formation. The closure of opportunities for livelihood outside the sphere of waged labor, the misery among the masses of urbanized, dependent workers, the increased level and complexity of social struggle, and the periodic crises accompanying capitalist development caused the state to greatly enlarge its scope of activity. The extension and proliferation of state agencies to confront crises and facilitate accumulation, to manage repression on domestic and foreign fronts, to assume overall responsibility for reproduction of the social order, and to provide for social needs that could not otherwise be met in the new social conditions of industrialism and urbanism—all swelled the ranks of the middle class. The middle class came to inhabit all the interstices of the "warfare-welfare state."

Historically, each of these developments—the incorporation of most of the population into the wage labor to capital social relation, the great technological and organizational innovations, the internationalization of capital, and the growth and proliferation of functions of the state—has had the effect of forming a labor force of professional, administrative, scientific, and technical employees that increased at a much faster rate than other sectors of the labor force, especially from the end of World War II to 1970. In the United States this consolidated a middle class that by 1970 included 17 million employees, or one-fifth of the labor force. However, the future of this class may not be as bright as its history was favored. Elsewhere (forthcoming-a: chap. II), I argue that most of the historical avenues of accumulation that once swelled the American middle class have nearly reached the limits of their expansion, greatly affecting its class situation.

BIPOLARIZATION AS A HISTORICISM
AND PROBLEMS OF SPECIFICITY

In attempting to come to grips with the fluid character of intermediate classes and the great variety of actual national class formations, a historicist perspective that does not deny historical specificity is necessary. The study of intermediate classes requires a historical understanding of a wide range of specific forms of multiclass relations in the context of the fundamental historical process of bipolarization. Recent Marxist theories of social class are not adequate to the task. Primarily analytic or functionalist conceptualizations of class, such as that of Poulantzas (1975),

Wright (1978), Carchedi (1978), and the Ehrenreichs (in Walker, 1979), not only shift attention away from questions of historical formation and a relational conception of class, but also are seldom posed in a manner facilitating analysis of the social-political role of the social forces that emerge from the middle class in different times and places. For these reasons, a greater respect than is generally prevalent today for historicist Marxism is required.

Marxist historicism has at least three virtues. It views classes as a relational process of acting subjects, it conceptualizes dialectical movement in terms of a historical totality, and it poses history as class struggle. Unfortunately, these virtues are not easy to disassociate from their roots in a neo-Kantian and Hegelian philosophical rather than materialist idea of history.

A historical and dialectical sociology has as an end the study of classes as historical actors. In this broad sense the historicism of Lukacs, Korsch, Gramsci, and others is sound. It is quite misleading, though, to conceive, as was Lukacs' tendency, of a social class with an "ascribed consciousness"—as a monolithically constituted, acting subject with an assigned historical mission. Gramsci comes closer to a view of classes as composed of subjects who live out the relations of social class—relations of exploitation, of social inequality, of power and struggle—on a day-to-day basis. Classes as collectivities of people formed in and acting out social relations are also identifiable historical entities that engage in collective actions, but only under the most unusual circumstances are classes clearly defined groups with specific programs that are well organized to engage in purposive actions. We can infer from the historicists that classes become historical antagonists because they are composed of acting subjects. Working within an abstraction of the historical totality, in which most historicist thinking is located, it is difficult to move to a more concrete level on which individual subjects come together to form clusters of collectivities occupying similar relational positions in the system of exploitation and domination. These relations, because they are conflictive, bring similarly situated people together in opposition to their adversaries. This opposition, in dialectical interrelation with the movement of productive forces in the accumulation process, constantly reshapes classes and gives form to class relations.

Historicist Marxism's main concern has been with classes as historical actors, but the bipolar concept of class in Lukacs in particular must be modified to be able to locate the place of different concretely located nonbourgeois and nonproletarian classes in the relations of the two principal classes.

The traditional Marxist focus upon a bipolar class structure, most clearly stated within the historicist tradition but reaffirmed in recent analytic approaches to class determination (such as Poulantzas, Carchedi, and Wright), is a necessary starting point in historical analysis; but it is not a conception that by itself enables an understanding of the complexities of the movement of social history in its variations in different national contexts.

A political sociology of intermediate classes should proceed from the basis of dialectical movement originating at different levels: at the level of capital accumulation and the movement of productive forces, which forms classes and broadly structures class relations; at the level of basic structural antagonism of the historical totality, the inherent opposition of polarizing classes that is expressed in diverse forms, including the formation of intermediate classes, and with varying intensities; and at the level of opposition of historically shaped and conjuncturally active social forces—among which prominently figure forces that are neither bourgeoisie nor working class. The opposition of temporal forces, formed in the process of accumulation, always takes place within the basic structural antagonism and within specific conjunctures. The different formations that emerge from within the middle classes in Europe, in North and South America, and in other parts of the world are among the crucial social forces of the contemporary era: They have to be considered in their specific manifestation, but always within the broader context of a bipolarizing structure of world capitalist development.

I will conclude with a few notes on intermediate classes in societies immersed in relations of dependency. (See also Johnson,

forthcoming-b, for an analysis of class formation under conditions
of dependency.)

INTERMEDIATE CLASSES
ON THE PERIPHERY

Both the global historicist perspective stated above and the specificity of temporal social forces are particularly important in the
study of social structures formed under conditions of dependency.
While broadly structured under the impulse of the internationalization of monopoly capital, these social structures nevertheless differ radically from region to region and nation to nation. On one
hand, the explosion of worldwide activity by transnational corporations sets the stage for an accelerated pace of bipolarization as
an international process that is less nationally specific and uneven
than in previous stages of development. On the other hand, the
relation of concentrated transnational capital and an international-
ized working class is mediated by a variety of new class formations
and national institutional arrangements.

In general, it is clear that the middle formations of the colonial,
postcolonial, and contemporary peripheral, dependent societies
have been among the principal social forces internationally. The
circumstances of their historical ascendance and their places in
local and international class relations are quite distinct from the
middle classes of the advanced capitalist countries.

The legacy of colonial rule resulted in the overall effects of (1)
blocking industrial development and the formation of a modern
bourgeoisie, while it (2) strengthened precapitalist modes of production, landowning oligarchies, and agrocommercial or purely
merchant bourgeoisies and (3) nurtured new middle groups that
first administered colonial relations, then agitated for independence and finally wrested control of postcolonial states that over-
see dependent capitalist development.

In some postcolonial countries, because of weak formation of
local bourgeoisies—which themselves can be seen as dependent,

intermediate classes—and the limited formation of national working classes, the roles of middle classes are central ones (extreme
examples are Bangladesh and perhaps Afghanistan). In cases such
as the Southern Cone of South America, where the local bourgeoisies are stronger and closely associated with transnational capital
and the military acts as the political directorate of this alliance of
capitals, the middle classes, while amply formed and extremely
important in the prior stage of national development (1930s to
1950s), today have a less salient (though still significant) role.

Today, in most of Asia, the Middle East, the Caribbean, and all
of Latin America, there are two distinct and sizable "middle"
classes: the petty bourgeoisie (classically understood) and the salaried sectors of administrative, technical, and professional employees. Dependent capitalist development in the Third World has not
annihilated the petty bourgeoisie, as in Europe and North
America, especially in Asia and Africa, though it has been in rapid
eclipse where (as in the Southern Cone of South America and
Mexico) dependent development has proceeded furthest. Artisan
producers have been all but wiped out by modern industry wher-
ever industrial developments, through import substitution industrialization or large-scale investments by transnational corporation, have taken root; but the commercial and service sectors of
dependent countries are by and large organized through small-
scale entrepreneurship. The same pattern of development has
formed the basis for rapid expansion of a salaried "new" middle
class. Large-scale transnational corporate investments and industrialization sponsored by state and local capital have created a
considerable demand for skilled technical and educated administrative labor. The interventionist character and rapid expansion of
the scale of state activity has substantially augmented the new
middle class. In fact, the development of the state in colonial and
postcolonial Asia, under the conditioning situation of new relations of international dependence, is coterminous with the formation of a middle class. Yet, this class, whether in Asia or Latin
America, often resembles a petty bourgeoisie (or, with increased
statist development, an incipient bourgeoisie) in that persons

within it do not live by salary alone but by their wits in multiple activities, including small-scale entrepreneurship which salaried, bureaucratic posts give them access to (including graft).

The arguments stated here on the historical formation of intermediate classes in the process of capitalist development in the core and the brief notes on peripheral formations indicate that the idea of a multiclass complex of class relations in a bipolarizing structure is a necessary foundation for understanding the historical development of the modern world-system.

REFERENCES

BELL, D. (1973) The Coming of Postindustrial Society. New York: Basic Books.

BRAVERMAN, H. (1974) Labor and Monopoly Capital. The Degradation of Work in Twentieth Century America. New York: Monthly Review Press.

BRUCE-BRIGGS, B. (1979) The New Class: New Brunswick, NJ: Transaction.

CARCHEDI, G. (1978) On the Economic Identification of the New Middle Class. London: Routledge & Kegan Paul.

JOHNSON, D. L. (forthcoming-a) Social Class and Social Development: Comparative Studies of Class Relations and Intermediate Classes.

———— (forthcoming-b) "Economism and determinism in dependence theory." Latin American Perspectives VII.

MALLET, S. (1963) La Nouvelle Classe Ouvriere. Paris.

———— (1975) Essays on the New Working Class (D. Howard and D. Savage, eds.). Telos Press (St. Louis, Mo: Washington University).

POULANTZAS, N. (1975) Classes in Contemporary Capitalism. London: New Left Books.

WALKER, P. [ed.] (1979) Between Labor and Capital. Boston: South End Press.

WRIGHT, E. O. (1978) Class, Crisis and the State. London: New Left Books.

Chapter 9

LONG ECONOMIC CYCLES
AND THE SIZE OF
INDUSTRIAL ENTERPRISE

Albert Bergesen
University of Arizona

*Downturns are always a moment of increased concentra-
tion of capital. This is done at the level of the firm.*
—Immanuel Wallerstein

The capitalist world-economy grows and expands in fits and
starts, in what are variously termed "long waves" or "long cycles."
In previous research I have identified two long waves associated
with an expansion of formal colonial rule, rising tariffs, and a
multicentric-unstable core (Bergesen, 1980; Bergesen and
Schoenberg, 1980). In this paper I want to discuss another set of
cycles: the expansion/merger cycle.

AUTHOR'S NOTE: I would like to thank Arthur L. Stinchcombe, John W.
Meyer, Walter L. Goldfrank, Chris Chase-Dunn, and Michael Hout for helpful
comments on an earlier draft of this paper.

The expansion/merger cycle involves different ways in which the capitalist enterprise has grown since the inception of industrial capitalism at the end of the eighteenth century. One way is for the firm to expand its volume of business and basic organizational structure. The other way growth occurs is for a number of firms to merge into a larger unit of production. These two procedures alternate with the expansion and contraction of the world-economy. During periods of economic expansion, the firm grows by *expanding* its organizational framework and volume of business. During periods of economic contraction or stagnation, growth comes through *merging* of a number of firms, the well-known idea that downturns bring a consolidation and centralization of capital. This is a cyclical process because in empirical fact these two methods of growth alternate and because the expansion phase plants the seeds for the following contraction, which in turn removes the blockage that allows the process of expansion to continue. It is very possible that these sorts of cycles began prior to the emergence of industrial capitalism at the end of the eighteenth century. For instance, there have been discussions of the consolidations that occurred during the famed "crisis of the 17th century" (Frank, 1978; Wallerstein, 1980b). It has also been suggested that the long waves of economic expansion and contraction that occurred under the feudal mode of production are linked to the very inception of the modern world-system in the sixteenth century (Wallerstein, 1980a). In this paper, though, I will be dealing only with transformations of the industrial enterprise that emerged at the end of the eighteenth century.

CYCLES OF ECONOMIC EXPANSION
AND CONTRACTION

The capitalist enterprise seems to grow and expand until it reaches some natural limit where its very growth and activity become dysfunctional for the overall process of accumulation, like the overproduction and competition at the end of the nineteenth century and the world slump which began in 1974–1975. At that point world economic expansion turns to stagnation, or contraction, and this crisis helps unblock the stalled accumulation process by eliminating many of the competitive firms through mergers, which in turn creates capitalist enterprises that are larger but fewer in number. This in turn provides the institutional arrangements, the organizational forms, for a renewed wave of capital accumulation and another boom or upswing in the world-economy.

The association of mergers and economic downturns was recently discussed by David Gordon (1980), who argued that there are specific institutional arrangements associated with the accumulation process—what he called the "social structure of accumulation." When this breaks down, a new structure must appear before accumulation can continue. The capitalist world-economy, with its long waves of expansion and stagnation, has passed through a number of these social structures of accumulation, which in succession constitutes a series of "stages of capitalist accumulation." The history of long waves in the world-economy is in some sense the history of successive stages of capitalist accumulation.

Following Marx, Gordon also noted that crises and downturns, while representing stagnation in the accumulation processes, can have positive effects in that they remove some of the problems which might have generated the crisis in the first place. In this regard he comments how the downturn at the end of the nineteenth century was accompanied by mergers which reduced competition and helped put the accumulation process back on its feet.

Robert Heilbroner, following from Gordon's discussion, goes on to argue that one of the tendencies of repeated crises was

to bring into being an economy of giant enterprises. Each crisis encouraged the formation of large enterprises because smaller and weaker firms were the typical victims of economic hesitations and downturns, while stronger and larger firms survived to buy up and integrate the assets of their competitors [1978: 73].

In this way crises act to remove the blocks to the accumulation process, and allow it to move forward again.

> The business cycle, in other words, is not just a wavelike movement of production, but a movement of the whole socio-economic order through history; and the measure of the cycle therefore requires that we pay heed not alone to its quantitative effects on production or prices or employment, but also to its qualitative impact on the organization of the society itself [1978: 72–73].

With downturn fostering consolidation, upturns seem to involve overall expansion of the firm in response to favorable market conditions and growing demand. Downturn/consolidation, upturn/expansion: This appears to be the general way the capitalist enterprise grows. We can divide the history of industrial capitalism into four general periods which correspond to ups and downs in the world-economy and to changes in the business enterprise.

1790–1873, Economic Upturn, and Expanding Individual Enterprises

This first period is the classic age of competitive capitalism, when the single firm, individually owned or in small partnerships, dominated production. There were few monopolies. During some of this period growth was quicker (the 1790–1815 and 1848–1873 booms) and some periods were slower (1816–1847). The world-economy was expanding, and so was the individual firm.

This period also correlates with other cycles (Bergesen and Schoenberg, 1980). The first wave of colonialism was collapsing with the loss of the British colonies in 1776 and the collapse of the Spanish and Portuguese-American empires in the early nineteenth century. Mercantile regulations of core-periphery trade gave way to free trade in the 1820s, and after 1815 peace broke out among the great powers under British hegemony.

This period of expansion appears to have planted the seeds of overproduction and excessive competition which came to fruition during the Great Depression of 1873–1896, which inaugurated a period of general downturn and stagnation in the world economy and a fundamental change in the shape of the capitalist enterprise.

1874–1945, Economic Downturn, and Merged Enterprises: Large Corporations and Monopoly Capitalism

By the end of the nineteenth century, all of the cycles I have mentioned were moving in the opposite direction. Colonialism was now increasing—"the Rush for Africa"—free trade was giving way to rising tariffs and neomercantile policies; British hegemony was declining in the face of German and American industrial growth; and tensions were rising among the great powers that would eventually result in the "Second Thirty Years War" of 1914–1945. There was also a general downturn in the world-economy, which began with the 1874–1896 depression and, except for the short upturn from the end of the 1890s through 1914, continued through the 1920s and 1930s.

With the economic crisis at the end of the nineteenth century firms failed, and the appearance of an unprecedented wave of mergers brought about the modern industrial corporation. In the United States the merger process began in the 1880s in the refining and distilling industries (Standard Oil) and then spread to manufacturing industries and, by the 1920s, to large retailing outfits. By the 1920s the organizational format of the modern corporation was by and large set (Chandler, 1978). With the emergence of giant corporate firms a new era of monopoly capitalism appeared, reflecting the demise of the excessive competition of the first era and the tremendous size of the newly consolidated enterprise.

1945–1973, Economic Upturn, and
Expanding Enterprise: The Era of
the Multinational Corporation

Again the shift. Colonialism retreated, high tariffs gave way to free trade (GATT), American hegemony brought peace among the core powers, and the capitalist enterprise was once again expanding its size and scope. The organizational innovation of the last downturn was now growing: the corporation was becoming the multinational corporation. This time growth was through expansion of the corporate format, rather than organizational restructuring through consolidation and merger. There were mergers during this period and a dramatic wave of mergers termed "conglomerates" during the 1960s. But the conglomerate represented more of a financial takeover of firms in different industries than the concentration of productive power within one industry that was accomplished by the plant closings and internal reorganization involved in the initial wave of mergers at the turn of the century. With conglomerates much of the internal functioning of individual firms was left intact.

1974–, Economic Downturn, and Mergers:
The State Enterprise

The great 1945–1973 boom was similar to the earlier mid-nineteenth-century period of expansion in that it also planted the seeds for later contraction and stagnation. Rapid growth in plant and production in the industrialized world resulted in problems of overproduction and excessive competition by the early 1970s. Beginning in 1974–1975, the world-economy entered another slump and the beginning of another period of economic contraction and stagnation. The analysis of this world downturn is trickier than the past one, as the benefit of hindsight is not available. We are just entering this period, and as such we hope to identify the correct trends. But we may not, and this caution should be remembered in the following discussion of possible organizational outcomes resulting from this downturn. Just what should we expect? First, there should be another wave of mergers and consolidation of capital as individual firms go under and others combine to attain a strong position in the world market.

Signs of this can be seen in the auto industry, which was one of the hardest hit by problems of overproduction and excessive competition. As late as 1972 foreign producers held only 14.5 percent of the American auto market, a figure which jumped to 28.5 percent by early 1980, with Japanese imports alone accounting for a larger share of the American market than either Ford or Chrysler (Newsweek, April 28, 1980). With world competition heightening in the 1980s auto experts predict that as many as 15 of the present 30 companies operating in the nonsocialist world-economy will fail. Smaller firms will be able to survive by serving only marginal or protected markets, or by merging with a larger firm, as the recent dealings between the faltering AMC and Renault may suggest. Some experts predict that the only sure survivors of the present downturn and market wars of the 1980s will be GM, Ford, VW, and Japan Inc. (Newsweek, April 28, 1980), while others broaden the list to include Peugot-Citroen, Fiat, and Renault (Moberg, 1980).

The auto industry also suggests another possibility—the merger of state and firm—as seen in the takeover or nationalization of faltering multinational firms. The Chrysler "bail-out" in which federal guarantees for loans to keep Chrysler from bankruptcy suggests that firms increasingly will go to the state for aid, and that the appearance of state firms or state enterprises may provide the structural readjustment that will eliminate the present blockage to world accumulation and usher in a new era of expansion and upswing in the world-economy. As the merged individual enterprises led to corporations, so will the merger of multinational corporation and state lead to an era of state enterprises. Now, the active participation of the state in the world-economy is not new, as Wallerstein and others would rightly argue. Further, much of the nationalization of the European economies occurred during the 1930s and 1940s, and the American state has also been deeply involved in managing the national economy. Still, the point here is not so much that this is the first role of the state in the world-economy, but a particular response to the crisis of the last quarter of the twentieth century. Also, the presence of a new wave of nationalizations in European industry during the 1970s suggests that the present downturn is again spurring consolidation and centralization (Walters and Monsen, 1979). The present attitude of the American state toward managing the economy also seems different from its earlier role, which centered more on monetary and fiscal policy and propping up demand through its role as consumer and contractor. The issues of the 1980s seem more questions of the actual planning of production, of turning the United States into a gigantic conglomerate, with the success of "Japan, Inc." clearly being the model. For example, a former secretary of transportation in the Carter administration, commenting on how to "modernize the auto industry" and make it competitive worldwide, spoke of a

> new era of cooperation between government and industry in which goals were jointly established, and Detroit—by tax incentives and direct grants, if necessary—was assured the wherewithal to meet them [Adams and Bracy, 1980: 15].

This kind of talk is what is generally found in discussions of the "reindustrialization" of the American economy, which usually refers to some sort of tripartite "social compact" among business, labor, and government in which collective decisions can be made on how to develop more competitive "sunrise" industries and how to phase out older, less competitive "sunset" industries—in effect, a national planning of production to be competitive on the world market.

What the present world downturn will generate, it seems, is a world-economy dominated by state enterprises and a state/firm fusion that will be the structural equivalent of the consolidated corporation that emerged a century ago. This new organizational innovation will eliminate the present blockage to the accumulation process, facilitating an upturn in the world-economy probably sometime during the early twenty-first century.

The irony here is that the nationalization of production, while creating the possibility of "socialism" within states, is the very organizational response necessary to facilitate the survival of capitalism on a world scale. Socialism at home will ensure the survival of capitalism on a world scale.

FUTURE EXPANSION
MERGER CYCLES

If there is an upswing in the twenty-first century, enterprises should once again expand in their new, reorganized format. The dominant enterprise will now be the state/firm fusion, although there will still be everything from individual enterprises to corporations to multinational corporations to merged multinational corporations. But the state/firm will dominate world production and usher in a new era of world capitalism. Now, if the process continues, we would expect another contraction, with failures, consolidations, and mergers. Since the state is now one with the firm, the question is raised as to whether this will also involve political consolidation along with the previous economic consolidation. While there is no way of knowing these things, certainly this is one mechanism for political consolidation that will move the world-system toward having a single world state.

Finally, I suppose, there is the question of whether this process of expansion and merger will go on forever. Certainly, those who favor regular periodicity in their cycles, like the 40–60 year Kondratieff, see a world continuing with its ups and downs. The cycles of colonialism, tariff/free trade, hegemony/multicentricity, and war/peace I have identified (Bergesen and Schoenberg, 1980), though, do not have a regular periodicity. Their frequency is increasing, which suggests that at some point the cyclical process will be so short as to be negligible. Since the expansion/merger cycles correspond to the other cycles, there may also be a point at which the expansion and consolidation dynamic ends or turns into something else. There is simply no way of knowing. What we do know is that there are a lot of movements in the world-system which exhibit the same general periodicity. What remains to be uncovered is the deep logic which governs these movements.

REFERENCES

ADAMS, B. and T. BRACY (1980) "Moving the U.S." Arizona Daily Star (April 16): Section A, p. 15.
BERGESEN, A. (1980) "Cycles of formal colonial rule," pp. 119–126 in T. K. Hopkins and I. Wallerstein, (eds.) Processes of the World-System. Beverly Hills, CA: Sage.
———— and R. SCHOENBERG (1980) "Long waves of colonial expansion and contraction, 1415–1969," pp. 231–277 in A. Bergesen (ed.) Studies of the Modern World-System. New York: Academic Press.
CHANDLER, A. D. (1978) "The United States: evolution of enterprise," pp. 70–133 in P. Mathias and M. M. Postan (eds.) The Cambridge Economic History of Europe. Volume 7. Cambridge, MA: Cambridge University Press.
FRANK, A. G. (1978) World Accumulation, 1492–1789. New York: Monthly Review Press.
GORDON, D. (1980) "Stages of accumulation and long economic cycles," pp. 9–45 in T. K. Hopkins and I. Wallerstein (eds.) Processes of the World-System. Beverly Hills, CA: Sage.
HEILBRONER, R. L. (1978) Beyond Boom and Crash. New York: W. W. Norton.
MOBERG, D. (1980) "The car crash." In These Times (May 28–June 3): 7–10.
WALLERSTEIN, I. (1980a) "The future of the world-economy," pp. 167–180 in T. K. Hopkins and I. Wallerstein (eds.) Processes of the World-System. Beverly Hills, CA: Sage.

———— (1980b) The Modern World-System II. New York: Academic Press.

WALTERS, K. O. and R. J. MONSEN (1979) "State-owned business abroad: new competitive treat." Harvard Business Review (March/April): 160–170.

PART 5

THEORETICAL ISSUES

Chapter 10

PRODUCTION AND REPRODUCTION OF EVERYDAY LIFE

Roberta M. Spalter-Roth
Eileen Zeitz
American University

This paper has four starting points: (1) Marx's definition of material life, as presented in *The German Ideology:*

> But life involves before everything else eating and drinking, a habitation, clothing and many other things. The first historical act is thus the production of the means to satisfy these needs, the production of material life itself. . . . Men, who daily remake their own life, begin to make other men, to propagate their kind: the relations between man and woman, parents and children, the family [Tucker, 1972: 120];

(2) a growing conviction that a feminist theoretical perspective has much to gain from the use of world-system theories of uneven

development to understand everyday issues such as housework; (3) the recognition that, at present, no synthesis of world-system and feminist theory has been achieved; and (4) an interest generated by a New York *Times* story about a Japanese Women's Christian Temperance Union protest against a major Japanese tourist industry commodity—male sex vacations in the Philippines. This article is discussed later in the paper when prostitution as commodity circulation is analyzed. The issue is addressed from the perspective of whether it fulfills a material need and analyzed in terms of "who benefits" and "at whose expense" in the context of patriarchy and capital.

Starting from these points, the aim of this paper is (1) to critique recent work that attempts to integrate women's work into a world-system model; (2) to develop a theoretical framework that integrates women's work and special oppression into a world-system model by both laying out the questions that need to be addressed by the theory and pointing out the elements the theory should include; (3) to apply the theoretical framework to the case of Japanese sex vacations, and (4), having done so, to point out the methodological difficulties entailed in using this theory.

CRITIQUE OF THE LITERATURE

Much of the work of the world is for the reproduction of people rather than commodities. Most of this reproductive work is the task of women. World-system/dependency theory lacks the richness required to address the daily production and reproduction of social life insofar as it is concerned almost exclusively with class relations or relations among nations. World capitalist system theory defines the relations between people in the production of commodities as a worldwide class system, but ignores those dimensions of life other than the structure of capitalist commodity production (Jalee, 1968; Anderson, 1974). Dependency theory emphasizes the creation of sectoral backwardness in so-called "underdeveloped countries" and the constraints placed on Third World development by the economic hegemony of industrialized nations through the control of technology and markets (Elliott, 1977). Currently, dependency theory is the subject of elaborate debate. However, without entering this arena, it is still possible to observe that these two theoretical models concentrate on the structure of capitalist production and the relations between nations and/or social classes. An examination of the literature leads to the conclusion that much of world-system/dependency theory not only abstracts from the whole of social life, but frequently treats the processes of production and accumulation as sex-neutral.

Recent work by Marxist-feminist scholars in the area of dependency theory demonstrates that women's work within the household is necessary as an adaptive, low-cost production center which feeds, clothes, shelters, and maintains its members despite the vicissitudes of the market economy (Elliott, 1977). Others have shown that the incursions of monopoly capital undermine the household mode of production (Kandiyote, 1977; Jelin, 1977). In order to survive, women must perform the same reproductive labor in the informal sector as paid domestics, prostitutes, and vendors in their work as wives and daughters in the household (Arizpe, 1977).

The work of these scholars is important in that it moves beyond the sex-neutrality of male authors; however, the analyses retain weaknesses. First, the majority of these analysts perceive the survival activities of women as being functional only for capital. Women's activities in their own households maintain the reserve labor armies capital throws off (Dalla Costa and James, 1972; Wallerstein et al., 1979). In the informal sector their activities benefit a local elite (Chinchilla, 1977). However, these analyses fail to examine the ongoing, interacting class and sex struggles that do not necessarily work in the interests of capital. Moreover, these analysts do not move socialist feminist theory forward. Thus, when sex relations are analyzed at all, they are explained either in terms of "the needs of capital" or in terms of "culture" or the "survival of traditions."

In a fall 1977 article, "Mobilizing Women: Revolution in the Revolution," Norma Stoltz Chinchilla argues that it is necessary to elaborate an overall theory, strategy, and tactic linking women to the class struggle in order "to mobilize the full potential of women's militance." Although critical of "economist" Marxists for denying the necessity for women to struggle on behalf of their own liberation, she states that the conditions for women's liberation can be created only in the process of fighting for socialism. Having put this constraint on her analysis, Chinchilla proceeds to follow the narrow economist model, contrasting the economic exploitation of capitalism with ideologies that defend capitalism such as male supremacy. Thus, patriarchy is seen as an ideology that defends capitalism. Therefore, patriarchy has no material base in itself, nor does it have a structural integrity of its own. It is, in Chinchilla's analysis, functional merely for capitalism.

Because Chinchilla sees patriarchy (male supremacy, as she calls it) as reinforcing capitalism through ideology, she can come up with no theoretical argument for women's liberation—only a tactical one. She argues that if Marxist movements fail to organize women around "family issues" such as food and day care, it becomes easy for the rightwing bourgeoisie to manipulate women's concerns (as they did in Chile). Hence, Chinchilla sees a need for women's movements, but this praxis comes out of no feminist or socialist feminist theory. In the type of analysis she presents, the structures that surround women for most of their lives are analyzed only as "pre-capitalist remnants." Activities such as bride pricing, child marriage, exclusion of widows, and prostitution are seen as traditional customs rather than economic or social relations. If explanations such as custom or tradition are unacceptable to dependency theorists in explaining sectoral underdevelopment, why should such explanations be acceptable in explaining women's work? A feminist world-system theory will explain how men and women, as well as commodities and classes, are produced and ask who benefits. This requires more than simply tacking on cultural survival and/or male supremacist ideology.

TOWARD A THEORETICAL INTEGRATION

To develop this theory, the following questions must be addressed: (a) In both class and sex relations, how are men and women differentially reproduced? Within the context of interaction among the world capitalist system; a worldwide sex-gender system; specific nation-states; local tribes and communities; and household economies, how does this differential reproduction occur? (b) Within these interacting systems, how are the necessary goods and services (food, clothing, shelter, sex, and children) produced, extracted, distributed, and consumed by class and sex members? (c) Who benefits from the existence and maintenance of this differential reproduction? Thus, interest is focused on the following theoretical elements: circulation and distribution, as well as production; interaction among social forms; sex as well as class; and surplus extraction. These questions are derived from socialist feminist theory, generally based on Engel's premise that there is a mode of reproduction of people in addition to a mode of production of necessities of daily life. Socialist-feminist theorists such as Eisenstein, Hartmann, Rubin, and Bridenthal see these modes (reproduction of people versus commodities) in dialectical relationship; the mode of reproduction of people is not simply a reflection of commodity production, but a separate element. Several socialist feminist theorists have attempted to identify the structures and/or relations of production that reproduce people as well as commodities. Our own attempts to identify these structures/relations is a synthesis of the work of Mitchell (1971), Rubin (1975), and Edholm, Harris, and Young (1978). These structures/relations are listed below.

(a) Production. This structure/relation includes the conventional examination of commodity production. However, the questions have been expanded by asking: How are the basic necessities of daily life—primarily food, clothing and shelter—produced? In addition, the transformation of commodities back into use values

is addressed by asking questions concerning cooking of food, servicing of people, and maintenance of commodities.[1]

(b) Reproduction of the species by class and sex. The authors we have cited identify two aspects of this category: (1) the reproduction of labor power, which is usually analyzed in social class terms, and (2) the reproduction of gender, which is seen as social rather than biological. According to Edhom et al.,

> the reproduction of the labour force is itself an underdeveloped concept. Firstly, it has to be distinguished from human or biological reproduction, and then within the concept we must distinguish two further meanings: on the one hand, maintenance of the labour force in the here and now, on the other allocation of agents to positions within the labour process over time [1978: 106].

It is obvious that reproduction by class and sex includes far more than reproduction of the labor force, particularly if one is discussing everyday life. For example, out of the vast human plasticity, how are people, through social relationships, reproduced by gender? This is the second aspect of reproduction of the species by class and sex; what Rubin (1975) has called the sex gender system.

(c) Sexuality. How are sexual objects produced, distributed, and consumed? We are separating sex from reproduction for two reasons: (1) to avoid viewing sex as inextricably linked to biological reproduction and (2) because traditionally this has been the most taboo dimension of women's lives (Mitchell, 1971). We realize that this definition is limited to the examination of sex as a commodity. However, this seems reasonable in light of the fact that women are perceived everywhere as sexual property. Moreover, this property is treated as a commodity for use and exchange. This is illustrated later by the example of Japanese sex vacations.

Within any specific social formation, each of these structures may be shaped by a world market, a domestic economy, the state or patriarchy, private and/or collective activity, or some combination of these. How and why this occurs are questions for analysis. The labeling of specific historical formations as patriarchy, capitalism, or socialism as existing in reality should not be accepted until the work of uncovering these structures and relations is more developed. Before labeling we suggest examining and categorizing the specific structures of production, reproduction of labor power, gender and sexuality within formations on the basis of their mode of appropriation, or extraction of surplus.

Why define social formations by their mode of appropriation? First, this approach will answer a fundamental Marxist question: How is surplus extracted from the prime producer? Second, to answer what Frank (1975) states is a fundamental question and a key to analyzing development and underdevelopment: What is done with the surplus? Further, the analysis of surplus has been a fundamental concern of socialist feminists. This concern is reflected in the debate over whether productive housework labor creates a surplus value for capitalism. Major participants in this debate (Dalla Costa and James, 1972; Gardiner, 1976; Hartmann, 1979) agree that capital at least benefits from the surplus labor involved in housework. The issue of whether men, as a group, benefit remains a point of contention. We agree with Hartmann's argument that both patriarchy and capital benefit from housework. The many more extra hours spent by women than men in working for their households shows that surplus labor is produced by women (usually wives) and appropriated by men (husbands and sons). In Hartmann's terms, this surplus is appropriated by men, who use women to provide them with many personal and sexual services, to bear and rear their children, and to relieve them of many unpleasant tasks both within and beyond households. In short, the mode of appropriation being described in patriarchy, one of the three modes we discuss. Patriarchy can be individual— benefiting individual male household heads—or collective—

benefiting men as a social group through the differential reproduction of gender. The existence as well as the description of patriarchy should be historically analyzed.

The second mode of appropriation, capitalism, is broadly defined as a system of private property ownership and control of persons and things through wage labor and commodity production. Under the capitalist mode of production, class is analyzed in terms of expropriation of surplus value through wage labor and commodity production. Surplus value has a restricted meaning: In Mandel's words, "surplus value is nothing but the difference between the value created by the worker and the cost of maintaining him" (1970: 88). This restricted definition is used when asking: Does capital benefit? Within the capitalist beneficiaries there are, of course, class fragments. There are national elite or *compradore* surplus extractors, as well as international or multinational surplus extractors. For the present, analysis of class fragments or types of capital is limited to national or international dimensions.

The third mode, socialism, is broadly defined as a system of centralized state planning with collective ownership and control of production and distribution of commodities. Whether international socialism can be defined as a system of extraction is clearly debatable. However, to the extent that socialist countries define themselves and act in the world marketplace as blocs, it is argued that this division is appropriate.

State apparatuses are not presently integrated into this analysis in a satisfactory way. Currently, the position is taken that, under capitalist modes of production, the state is more than "the executive committee of the ruling class"; it often acts as a quasi-independent entity mediating class and sex struggle. Under socialist modes of production it is harder to make an analytical separation between the state and the mode of production. Hence, the state is treated as a separate entity, with the recognition that, in the case of socialism, this may remain an empty cell.

The primary socialist-feminist questions are thus: Within each of the specific structures, does one of these systems of extraction benefit at the expense of the others, or are coalitions formed such that two or more may benefit? There are a number of possible answers to the question "who benefits" from the division of labor, mode of cooperation, and distribution with each structure. The possibilities are outlined schematically in Table 10.1. All of the

TABLE 10.1

| | | Capitalism | | Socialism | | | Patriarchy | |
		Nat'l	Intnat'l	Nat'l	Intnat'l	State	Indiv.	Collect.
Benefits	all	+	+	+	+	+	+	+
Benefits	NC	+	−	−	−	−	−	−
Benefits	IC	−	+	−	−	−	−	−
Benefits	NS	−	−	+	−	−	−	−
Benefits	IS	−	−	−	+	−	−	−
Benefits	ST	−	−	−	−	+	−	−
Benefits	IP	−	−	−	−	−	+	−
Benefits	CP	−	−	−	−	−	−	+
Benefits	N & IC	+	+	−	−	−	−	−
Benefits	NC & NS	+	−	+	−	−	−	−
Benefits	NC & IS	+	−	−	+	−	−	−
Benefits	NC & ST	+	−	−	−	+	−	−
Benefits	NC & IP	+	−	−	−	−	+	−
Benefits	NC & CP	+	−	−	−	−	−	+
Benefits	IC & ST	−	+	−	−	+	−	−
Benefits	IC & IP	−	+	−	−	−	+	−
Benefits	IC & CP	−	+	−	−	−	−	+
Benefits	NS & IS	−	−	+	+	−	−	−
Benefits	NS & ST	−	−	+	−	+	−	−
Benefits	NS & IP	−	−	+	−	−	+	−
Benefits	NS & CP	−	−	+	−	−	−	+
Benefits	IS & ST	−	−	−	+	+	−	−
Benefits	IS & IP	−	−	−	+	−	+	−
Benefits	IS & CP	−	−	−	+	−	−	+
Benefits	ST & IP	−	−	−	−	+	+	−
Benefits	ST & CP	−	−	−	−	+	−	+
Benefits	IP & CP	−	−	−	−	−	+	+
Benefits	all but CP	+	+	+	+	+	+	−
Benefits	all but IP	+	+	+	+	+	−	+
Benefits	all but ST	+	+	+	+	−	+	+
Benefits	all but NS	+	+	−	+	+	+	+
Benefits	all but IS	+	+	+	−	+	+	+
Benefits	all but IC	+	−	+	+	+	+	+
Benefits	all but NC	−	+	+	+	+	+	+

NC = national capitalism; IC = international capitalism; NS = national socialism; IS = international socialism; ST = State; IP = individual patriarchy; CP = collective partriarchy systems in question dominate women. However, questions arise concerning: (a) When are the systems in accord? (b) When are they in conflict? (c) What circumstances create conflict? (d) When conflict arises, how is compromise achieved? (e) If compromise is not achieved, who wins? (f) Do women ever win? These questions will be analyzed within the structures of production, reproduction of the species by class and sex, and sexuality.

AN APPLICATION

The analysis of sexuality has been historically peripheral to both Marxist theory and practice. Marxist-Leninists have been vitriolic in their criticism of socialist feminists who have analyzed or organized prostitutes. Remember Lenin's scolding of Clara Zetkin:

> I understand that in Hamburg a gifted Communist woman is bringing out a newspaper for prostitutes, and is trying to organize them for a revolutionary struggle. . . . They are the unfortunate double victims of bourgeois society. . . . [T]o understand this is one thing—how shall I put it—to organize the prostitute as a special revolutionary guild contingent and publish a trade paper for them. Are there really no industrial working women left in Germany who need organizing, who need a newspaper, who should be enlisted in your struggle? This is a morbid deviation [Weinbaum, 1978: 57].

We wish to class ourselves with the morbid deviationists. Of course, in *The Family, Private Property and the State,* Engels saw the relationship between two conditions of women: (1) as private property of their husbands, or (2) submitting to sexual relations for wages.

Prostitution defined as an exchange relation raises theoretical as well as methodological problems. Is sex a material need for men? Is sexual power a commodity for extraction? How do you describe the surplus in terms of socially necessary labor time? And, clearly, unlike bauxite, there is nothing approximating accurate data on the exchange, extraction, and circulation of this commodity.

Nonetheless, case studies exist that allow examination of what is produced, who produces it, the relations of production, and who benefits. While it is methodologically incorrect to simply isolate prostitution from the whole context of productive/reproductive relations, failure to complete a historical analysis can also be criticized. However, it is felt that the present research can be extremely fruitful in spite of these limitations.

Shortly after hearing about the New York *Times* article on sex vacations, the investigators discovered an article by Lin Neumann in *The Southeast Asia Chronical,* "Hospitality Girls in the Philippines." In the Philippines, according to Neumann (1978):

- prostitution has always flourished in places where there is a heavy concentration of foreigners;

- tourism, a major governmental development priority, had grown to the fourth-largest source of foreign exchange by the late 1970s;

- as the closest rich, core country, Japan provides much of the new tourist business (about one-third of all visitors are Japanese; 85 percent of whom are men);

- prostitution has been banned in Japan since 1958, and easy acccess to women has long been offered as an inducement for core men to visit the poorer peripheral countries of Asia;

- with such a market, both foreign and local tour operators have been quick to organize both the women and the visiting men via package tours;

- sources in business report that men on tour pay an average of $60 per night for a woman. Of this, the woman gets about $5; the balance goes to clubowners, hotels, tour operators, local guides, and Japanese guides;

- government built, multinationally leased hotels also benefit through additional fees charged when men bring prostitutes to their rooms;

- police and government officials are paid about $1.50 per night out of the prostitutes' take for protection;

- most prostitutes are women coming to Manila in flight from rural poverty. Usually they are women who "have been wronged" and cannot marry because of loss of virginity. Many send wages back for use by their families (including sending brothers through school); and,

- while a number of philanthropic institutions such as the Catholic church try to rehabilitate these women, the ostracism they face in nearly all sectors of society is a major obstacle to their rehabilitation. Another obstacle is that prostitution pays better wages than clerical or sales work for women in Manila. And, as long as male tourism is encouraged, there will be a demand for prostitutes.

Neumann sees these women as "bearing the double burden" for accumulation of foreign capital. Indeed! Clearly, what is described is not simply a buyer/seller relation. Rather, different segments of the bourgeoise and petty bourgeoisie, both Japanese and Filipino, are selling the sexual power of the prostitute to the buyer, benefiting from her labor. Men both distribute and consume this commodity. Most, although not all, of these men are members of the bourgeoisie.

This particular example requires analysis of an additional set of relations, those of kin. These relations have been identified by Batya Weinbaum, who, in *The Curious Courtship of Socialism and Feminism,* develops a methodology for comparing fathers, wives, brothers, and daughters as social groups with both contradictory and binding relations as they face production and reproduction over time (1978: 149ff). Using these kin categories, we can reexamine our example as follows: Japanese men (usually temporarily unattached from their families) buy the sexual power of Filipino sisters and daughters. In doing so, they do not share a portion of the wages they have received (or surplus they have extracted) with their wives and children for their reproduction (or the reproduction of the labor force or the reserve labor army). However, the wages not given to the Japanese families are sent home by the prostitutes and used for the differential reproduction of their own Filipino families by gender (and age). This is a circuit of patriarchy! Looking at both sets of relations (capital and patriarchy), who benefits, and how?

- International (or multinational) capital benefits (for example, hotel corporations).
- National or local bourgeoisies and petty bourgeoisies benefit, such as tour operators, guides, and clubowners.
- The state (state capitalism) benefits in its effort to collect foreign dollars via increasing tourism. There are direct pay-offs to police and state officials. And the state (in its role of public patriarch) maintains control over sexuality, its economic function, and public order.
- Collective patriarchy benefits from their collective daughter or sister prostitute. As kin members, they may receive a portion of her wages. And women's sexuality is owned and/or controlled by men who will marry only virgins but are quite willing to use prostitutes.
- Individual patriarchs (fathers and brothers) may benefit a bit from their sister/daughter's earnings, but they always risk discovering that their daughter/sister, or even wife, is a prostitute. Women are sometimes killed after such a discovery.

Asking "who benefits" provides a tool for bringing class and sex struggle into the model. It enables analysis of conflicts and collusions between and within these ideal types. Moreover, examining who benefits in each of these structures avoids conflating mode of production of commodities with mode of production of people.

METHOD

An analysis has been initiated using prostitution. However, it should be noted that the data required for analysis of sex as a commodity are not readily available. The only systematic comparable data that exist on a worldwide basis describe the exchange of commodities that produce a surplus for capital. Other types of data are either unavailable or presented in sex-neutral form. Data concerning world literacy rates, date of first marriage; labor force statistics for certain countries; and differential salary rates for certain countries can be obtained. In addition, world trade statistics are available by country, although frequently they do not include the Eastern European countries. There are, of course, volumes of ethnographic studies available, but while these are not without interest, their focus tends to be local or comparative: either among tribes, between urban and rural areas, or between two or more countries. These data sometimes offer information concerning bride prices, dowries, female infanticide, or disenfranchisement of women, but little material has been found concerning prostitution and/or what is termed "white slavery." As a result, it has been difficult to work out an appropriate method for this investigation.

CONCLUSION

By concentrating on how people are differentially fed, clothed, and provided with sex, we have developed a framework that allows for the following:

(1) inclusion of women's nonmarket and informal sector work in production and reproduction;
(2) inclusion of the whole of social life (that is, eating, drinking, sexing, childrearing), rather than narrowly defined production activities;
(3) avoidance of treating the benefits of production and reproduction as sex-neutral;
(4) uncovering of additional linkages within and between structures and men and women's work on a worldwide basis; and

(5) explaining important contradictions between women's production and reproduction activities.

As we have indicated, systematic data are not available. However, we believe that there are other data sources that can be drawn upon and pieced together, and we will be continuing this work in the future.

NOTE

1. This comes closest to Edholm, Harris, and Young's category of social reproduction (1978).

REFERENCES

ANDERSON, C.H. (1974) The Political Economy of Social Class. Englewood Cliffs, NJ: Prentice-Hall.

ARIZPE, L. (1977) "Women in the informal labor sector: the case of Mexico City," in the Wellesley Editorial Committee (eds.) Women and National Development: The Complexities of Change. Chicago: University of Chicago Press.

BRIDENTHAL, R., E. ROSS, and R. RAPP (1979) "Examining family history." Feminist Studies 5 (Spring).

CHINCHILLA, N.S. (1977a) "Mobilizing women: revolution in the revolution." Latin American Perspectives IV (Fall).

——— (1977b) "Industrialization, monopoly capitalism and women's work in Guatemala," in the Wellesley Editorial Committee (eds.) Women and National Development: The Complexities of Change. Chicago: University of Chicago Press.

DALLA COSTA, M. and S. JAMES (1972) The Power of Women and the Subversion of the Community. Bristol, England: Falling Wall Press.

EDHOLM, F., O. HARRIS, and K. YOUNG (1978) "Conceptualizing women." Critique of Anthropology 3: 101–130.

EISENSTEIN, Z. [ed.] (1979) Capitalist Patriarchy and the Case for Socialist Feminism. New York: Monthly Review Press.

ELLIOTT, C. M. (1977) "Theories of development: an assessment," in the Wellesley Editorial Committee (eds.) Women and National Development: The Complexities of Change. Chicago: University of Chicago Press.

ENGELS, F. (1972) The Family, Private Property and the State. New York: International Publishers.

FIRESTONE, S. (1971) Dialectic of Sex. New York: Bantam Books.

FRANK, A. G. (1975) On Capitalist Underdevelopment. London: Oxford University Press.

GARDINER, J. (1976) "Political economy of domestic labor in capitalist society," in D. L. Barker and S. Allen (eds.) Dependence and Exploitation in Work and Marriage. London: Longman.

HARTMANN, H. (1979) "The family as the locus of gender, class and political struggle: the example of housework." Unpublished manuscript, October.

JALEE, P. (1968) The Pillage of the Third World. New York: Monthly Review Press.

JELIN, E. (1977) "Migration and labor force participation of Latin American women: the domestic servants in the cities," in the Wellesley Editorial Committee (eds.) Women and National Development: The Complexities of Change. Chicago: University of Chicago Press.

JOHNSON, D. L. (1972) "Dependence and the international system," in J. D. Cockcroft, A. G. Frank, and D. L. Johnson (eds.) Dependence and Underdevelopment. New York: Anchor Books, 1972.

KANDIYOTE, D. (1977) "Sex roles and social change: a comparative appraisal of Turkey's women," in the Wellesley Editorial Committee (eds.) Women and National Development: The Complexities of Change. Chicago: University of Chicago Press.

MANDEL, E. (1970) Marxist Economic Theory, Vol. 1. New York: Monthly Review Press.

MITCHELL, J. (1971) Women's Estate. New York: Pantheon Books.

NEUMANN, L. (1978) "Hospitality girls in the Philippines." Pacific Research 9 (July–October): 5–6.

RUBIN, G. (1975) "The traffic in women: notes on the 'political economy' of sex," in R.R. Reiter (ed.) Toward an Anthropology of Women. New York: Monthly Review Press.

TUCKER, R.C. [ed.] (1972) The Marx-Engels Reader. New York: W.W. Norton.

WALLERSTEIN, I., W.G. MARTIN, and T. DICKINSON (1979) "Household structures and production processes: theoretical concerns, plus data from Southern Africa and nineteenth-century United States." New York: Fernand Braudel Center for the Study of Economics, Historical Systems and Civilization.

WEINBAUM, B. (1978) The Curious Courtship of Women's Liberation and Socialism. Boston: South End Press.

Chapter 11

DEPENDENCY,
NATIONAL ECONOMY,
AND INEQUALITY

Sally K. Ward
University of New Hampshire

INTRODUCTION

As a relative neophyte to the world-system perspective, I raise questions here which lie on the periphery of the issues and concerns addressed in several other papers in this volume. The prime question I raise is: "What can community and urban sociologists learn by examining the body of work that falls under the world-system label?" In brief, recent work in comparative stratification has relied on the world-system assumption that nations do not represent separate systems of economic production, "but rather, that all countries are part of a single system of production which

AUTHOR'S NOTE: I thank the participants in the Fourth Annual Conference on the Political Economy of the World-System for their comments on a version of this paper.

contains multiple political units within it" (Rubinson, 1976: 639; see also Wallerstein, 1974). This assumption bears marked similarity to assumptions of community research, representing a variety of theoretical perspectives. This research has long recognized the limitations of treating communities as units independent of the larger society. At both this and the comparative levels of analysis, it has been argued that *interdependence* is an important concept that must be included in models developed to explain internal characteristics of the unit under study, such as degrees of income inequality. The purpose of this paper is to discuss explicitly the convergence of theoretical insights from the two bodies of research, particularly regarding the question of the relationship between interdependence and income inequality, and to present a preliminary empirical test, for a sample of U.S. communities, of hypotheses derived directly from comparative work. Areas of divergence between the two bodies of work will be discussed in light of the empirical results presented. I will organize my task by discussing, first, the work in community sociology that could benefit from an examination of world-system theory; second, two major areas where world-system theory can make a contribution to community-level work; third, a first-step empirical assessment of the contributions; and, finally, the limitations of drawing an analogy between world-system and community sociology work.

INTERDEPENDENCE AMONG COMMUNITIES

The concepts of interdependence, dominance, and dependency have been cited in the literature on communities within one nation-state, most commonly U.S. communities. A variety of theoretical perspectives relies on these concepts, yet the links between the perspectives are frequently left undeveloped. Specifically, human ecology and "nonecological" community studies are two fields that address a similar range of conceptual issues.

The concept of dominance is used extensively in the field of human ecology. It has been used, however, in two quite different ways: First, there is the use of dominance to analyze power distributions *within* communities (for example, Hawley, 1963). This usage, while most relevant for discussions of community power, is not directly germane to the primary issues raised here. The second use of the concept of dominance by ecologists is that which is useful for an analysis of relationships *among* communities; this second use of the concept is of concern here. This branch of work is primarily addressed to the interdependence among communities that has evolved with increasing urbanization and metropolitanization of society. Dominance has been used to describe one dimension of this interdependence. Bogue's work on classifying communities as dominants, subdominants, influents, and subinfluents (1949) and the discussion by Duncan et al. (1960) of a system of cities are illustrative.

Building on the work of Gras (1922) and McKenzie (1929), Bogue (1949) attempts to refine the general theory of urban dominance, which

> assumes there is a system of interdependency among cities, and that there are considerable differences between the activities of individual cities. It maintains that the organizing agent, and one of the forces making for intercity differentiation, is the metropolis [p. 528].

To this end, he classifies cities along a scale of dominance consisting of four locations or points: dominants, subdominants, influents, and subinfluents. Movement "down" this scale is characterized by two types of change in dominance: "(1) decreasing range or area of dominance, and (2) decreasing number of functions over which dominance is exercised" (p. 536). A dominant community or metropolis controls many functions over a broad area, while communities lower on the dominance scale perform limited functions vis-à-vis other communities and exert influence over a more limited area. In general, Bogue's work is restricted to what is labeled here the *dominance dimension* in its explanation of the interdependence among communities—interdependence can be explored by analyzing the relative presence or absence of dominance.

The work of Duncan et al. (1960) is in the same tradition as that of Bogue. The frame of reference adopted in this work "assumes that what cities are like depends at least in part on what cities do (their functions), and that the functions of cities are in some measure a reflection of intercommunity relationships" (p. 46). Their approach concentrates on interdependence as reflected in a "system of cities" and in the "nesting" of dominance relations; their classification of large metropolitan areas into categories based on metropolitan functions and regional relationships (p. 271) illustrates the same concern with the dominance dimension of intercommunity relationships that is evident in the work of Bogue.

While ecologists were developing and refining their study of intercommunity relations, community sociologists were traveling parallel paths but using different labels. Specifically, Warren's (1963) work on the concept of vertical ties or the vertical pattern of a local community directly addresses the issue of a community's interdependence with the larger society. The local community's vertical pattern is defined as "the structural and functional relation of its various social units and subsystems to extracommunity systems" (Warren, 1963: 161–162). This can be compared to a community's horizontal pattern, which is defined as "the structural and functional relation of its various social units and subsystems to each other" (p. 162). There is a very clear parallel here to the human ecology concern with community interdependence, although citations from one approach to the other are not common.

Turk's (1970) work falls in the same camp as the Warren contribution, but, again, a different label is applied. Turk discusses the role of extralocal integration in affecting the level of interorganizational activity within a local community. The degree of extralocal integration is defined as "the number of organizational linkages with the broader society" and is operationalized by the number of national headquarters of voluntary associations (p. 4).

One of the major differences between the ecological and community sociology perspectives is that the latter work includes explicit reference to phenomena such as absentee-ownership of manufacturing plants as an aspect of the vertical system of a local community. Absentee-ownership can be classified with what is labeled here the *external control dimension* of a community's interdependence with other communities or the larger society. Ecologists have largely ignored this dimension of interdependence, insofar as ecological work can be read as implying that the absence of dominance as a characteristic of a community's place in the system of cities is equivalent to the presence of external control; that is, if a community's level of dominance is low, its level of external control is high.

THEORETICAL CONVERGENCE

The major argument I would like to make at this juncture is that the discussions of interdependence in world-system work and community sociology are markedly similar and that hypotheses and findings from the former may be equally appropriate for the latter. The explicit link between the two literatures is clear— ecological and nonecological community research has questioned the utility of treating communities as units independent of the larger society; world-system work has begun to question the utility of treating nations as units independent of the larger world-economy. At both levels, it has been argued that interdependence is an important concept that must be included in models attempting to explain internal characteristics of the unit under study.

If the link is valid, there are at least two productive contributions the world-economy perspective can make to work on communities within a national economy. The first contribution is insight regarding the dimensions of linkage in the world-economy.

Although at least two dimensions of the relationship between local communities and the national society have been analyzed in community-level work (referred to above as the dominance and external control dimensions), the two are rarely brought together. There are some notable exceptions, as in the work of Lincoln (1976), but the tendency is for the exploration of one dimension only in specific studies of communities. World-system work provides insight regarding the multidimensional nature of the phenomenon of linkage or control and, more importantly, insight regarding the processes of such control. For example, Rubinson's (1976) exploration of the proposition that a nation's position in the world-economy will have a direct bearing on the extent of income inequality within its borders includes reference to several mechanisms of dominance and control in the world-economic system. As Rubinson points out, the three specific mechanisms of control he analyzes—state strength, economic penetration, and dependence on external markets—"are not necessarily highly correlated, and states may rank differently on all three" (Rubinson, 1976: 643). The intercorrelations among his measures of dominance (or control) are consistent with the assumption that states may rank differently on different dimensions of the control process. There are 15 correlations among the six indicators of control, and the range of the absolute value of these is .041 to .652. The weakest correlations among the 15 possibilities suggest that dominance or control is a multidimensional phenomenon; if all measures were tapping the same dimension, the correlations would be consistently substantial in absolute value. In short, the concept of control in the world-economic system is a multidimensional one, and dependence (or, more precisely, *in*dependence) is one of several possible dimensions of such control.

Lauder (1979) makes similar reference to the multidimensional character of dominance and control in his work on structural inequality. He distinguishes between a state's position in the world-economic system and economic dependency by arguing that "economic dependence is different from position in the world-economic system in that it is analytically possible for a state to be located in the core and be economically dependent upon a country within the periphery" (Lauder, 1979: 5).

Finally, elsewhere in this volume, Ramirez and Thomas argue that dependence is a multidimensional phenomenon. These three works are representative of the world-system perspectives on the processes of linkage or control in the world-economy, and this literature may provide important clarification regarding the operation of these processes at the community level. That the processes may be similar across the two levels of analysis has not gone entirely unnoted in the community literature. Lincoln (1977: 43–44), for example, explicitly refers to the world-economy perspective in his discussion of community structure and dominance:

> As the metropolis controls the functioning of its satellites, so does the industrial nation control the economies of the underdeveloped countries of the world. The organizational mechanisms are largely the same at both levels of analysis. In the urban system, national corporations make investments of capital, equipment, and expertise in small, undeveloped communities creating a pattern of local dependence for wages, employment, and status on large absentee-owned plants. In the international system, similar corporations based in industrial countries make investments in productive facilities in developing countries, creating a pattern of dependence and fostering a narrow economic specialization.

Clearly, the link between the two levels of analysis makes sense on a theoretical level. The question remains as to whether or in what ways the theoretical similarities will be supported by empirical evidence.

A second major area of contribution of world-system literature to community studies is the former's suggestion in comparative stratification work that position in the world-economic system is related to the internal income distribution of a nation (see, for example, Rubinson, 1976; Chase-Dunn, 1975; Bornschier and Ballmer-Cao, 1979; Bornschier et al., 1978). This suggests that, if the theoretical processes of control are similar at the two levels under discussion here, a community's income distribution may be affected by the community's role in the national division of labor. As far as I can determine, quantitative studies of the extent of income inequality in U.S. communities have largely ignored this possible relationship (see Foley, 1977; Reich, 1971). One exception is the important work of Summers and Clemente (1976), in which the effects of the development of a major corporate plant in rural Illinois on the income distribution in the area are examined. Their findings are roughly parallel to the finding in comparative stratification work of a positive effect of dependency on income inequality.

Returning to the discussion of the dimensions of community interdependence, there are two such dimensions: dominance and external control. A dominant community is one in which various control functions of the national society are located. An externally controlled community, on the other hand, is one which is dependent on the larger society for viability. Following the logic of the world-economic system perspective, two hypotheses are plausible:

(1) the greater the dominance of a community in the national system, the lower the extent of income inequality; and
(2) the greater the degree to which a community is externally controlled, the greater the income inequality within the community.

If the theoretical insights from the world-system approach are appropriate for this level of analysis, we might expect empirical confirmation of these hypotheses. I turn now to a preliminary test of the hypotheses for a sample of U.S. communities.

ANALYSES

The test of these hypotheses requires the operationalization of three concepts for the sample of U.S. communities I am working with.[1] *Dominance* is measured by an index based on four components: number of home offices of manufacturing corporations, number of voluntary association headquarters, banking activity, and number of colleges and universities.[2] *External control* is the level of absentee-ownership of manufacturing plants in the community in 1966, defined as the proportion of manufacturing employees in plants owned by the largest 500 industrials with home offices outside the community.[3] Finally, *income inequality* is measured by the Gini index of income concentration, calculated on the basis of 1970 census data.[4] A fourth variable plays a role in the analyses to follow: the ratio of employment in manufacturing industries to employment in other industries in the city. This measure is included for several compelling reasons. First, human ecologists have argued that the extent of manufacturing is an indicator of a city's relation to the national division of labor (Duncan et al., 1960; Lincoln, 1976). Second, relying again on world-system work, it has been suggested (Rubinson, 1976) that one of the important characteristics of *core* states is the presence of a large, strong manufacturing class, as opposed to the small, weak manufacturing class characteristic of states in the periphery. If the concept of core state finds a parallel in community work, it is plausible to conceive of the strength of the manufacturing class as relevant to the dominance issue. Finally, on an intuitive basis, it is likely that the size of the manufacturing class will be related to the strength of labor unions, which will be related, in turn, to the extent of income inequality. If labor unions are strong, the effect of external control on income inequality may be quite different from that suggested by world-system theory.

The test of the hypotheses is relatively straightforward; this is not intended as a complete test of a well-developed causal model. Obviously, a full model of the determinants of income inequality in U.S. communities would include a range of additional predictive factors, including other economic characteristics, demographic factors such as growth rate, and some indicator of the racial composition of the community. However, since my purpose is to explore the utility of predictions derived from the world-

TABLE 11.1   Means, Standard Deviations, and Zero-Order Correlations
               for Core Characteristics and Income Inequality (N = 193)

	Gini Index	External Control	Dominance Index	Manufacturing
Gini Index	1.000			
External Control	.159	1.000		
Dominance Index	.357	−.093	1.000	
Manufacturing	−.347	−.127	−.112	1.000
Mean	.3459	.5025	880.42	44.60
Standard Deviation	.0398	.3736	332.20	18.57

system perspective rather than to make a definitive statement
about the causes of income inequality, the statistical tests are ap-
propriately limited.

The zero-order correlations presented in Table 11.1 provide
insight regarding the processes of linkage and control in the system
of cities. Interpreting external control, dominance, and manufacturing as indicators of linkage and control, it is clear that the
processes represented are diverse; the correlations are quite weak,
and the cities included here rank differently on different dimensions, much as states rank differently on the several dimensions of
control in Rubinson's (1976) work. Furthermore, there is ambi-
guity here regarding the interpretation of the role of manufacturing
employment. If both the dominance index and manufacturing are
indicators of core status, they should be positively correlated; yet
their correlation is not only weak but negative. Thus, the argument
based on world-system theory that core states will have a large,
strong manufacturing class may not be appropriate for this level of
analysis.

The effects of each measure of linkage and control on income
inequality are assessed in Table 11.2, which presents the results of
the regression of income inequality on these measures. Even
though the model being tested is not meant to be a comprehensive
model of the determinants of income inequality, it does a respect-
able job by explaining almost 25 percent of the variance in the
dependent variable. The effect of external control is as predicted;

TABLE 11.2   Results of the Regression of Income Inequality
on Core Characteristics (N = 193)

Variable	Regression Coefficient (standard error)	Beta
External Control	.0163 (.0068)	.153
Dominance Index	.00004 (.00001)	.339
Manufacturing	−.00062 (.00014)	−.289
Adjusted R^2 = .234		

the regression coefficient is significant and positive, yet it is not particularly strong (Beta = .153). The effect for manufacturing is also in the predicted direction; whether manufacturing is interpreted as a measure of core status or as an indicator of the strength and effectiveness of labor unions, the expectation is for a negative effect on income inequality. The effect that emerges from this analysis is negative, significant, and moderately strong (Beta = −.289). The strongest explanatory variable, however, is the dominance index, and here the effect is the opposite of that predicted by world-system theory.

These results represent only the additive effects of the three independent variables in income inequality. However, if the argument that relations between a place (community or nation) and the larger system (nation or world-system) are multidimensional is accurate, an examination of additive effects is necessary but not sufficient for understanding the complexities of the system. In short, if dominance and external control are separable dimensions, it is reasonable to expect that the effect of each will be strongest when the other is "absent" or takes on a low value. In statistical terms, there may be an interactive effect of the two dimensions on inequality. The measures I am using are clearly not tapping the same dimension of a community's position in the larger national society, as indicated by the low correlations between the

TABLE 11.3 Interaction Effects: Correlations Between Income Inequality and Core Characteristics, by Various Sample Subsets

	RELATIONSHIP			
	Gini Index and External Control		Gini Index and Dominance Index	
Manufacturing	Dominance Index		External Control	
	High	Low	Low	High
Low	.094	.310	.407	.396
	(n=53)	(n=45)	(n=43)	(n=55)
High	−.153	−.063	.319	.401
	(n=40)	(n=55)	(n=51)	(n=44)

three measures (see Table 11.1). To explore the possible role of interactions, several relevant correlation coefficients were recomputed for subsets of the larger sample. The results are presented in Table 11.3.

The table presents the zero-order correlations between either the dominance index or external control and the Gini index of income inequality for eight subsets of the larger sample. To produce the subsets, each of the measures is divided at its median into a high and low class. The results are interesting in their variation across the sample subsets. The relationship between income inequality and external control is strongest in those cities where both dominance and manufacturing take on low values ($r = .310$). In contrast, the relationship is negative where both dominance and manufacturing are high ($r = −.153$). Where there is a mix of core and periphery characteristics, the effect of external control is quite weak (.094 and −.063).

The variations for the relationship between the dominance index and income inequality are not as large or as consistent as those for external control. The most important variation in the second half of Table 11.3 is the relatively low correlation where external control is low and manufacturing is high ($r = .319$). Again, manufacturing and the dominance index do not behave in similar ways; the dominance index has its *weakest* effect when manufacturing is *high* and when, as predicted, external control is low. But here, as in Table 11.2, the most important aspect of the dominance index findings, whether in terms of additive or interactive relationships, is the positive effect on income inequality, in contrast to the negative effect predicted on the basis of world-system theory.

In summary, these preliminary findings suggest that the world-system perspective is relevant for the analysis of inequality within communities. The direct relevance, however, is restricted to the role of external control, as measured by absentee-ownership, and to the role of the size of the manufacturing class.

AREAS OF THEORETICAL DIVERGENCE

It appears that predictions from the world-economy perspective "work" for a community-level analysis, but only up to a point. The unexpected positive effect of the dominance index on economic inequality is not consistent with the theoretical processes which have been supported in comparative stratification work. If the findings presented here had been consistent, I might have been in a position to argue that there is, in fact, no unique "urban" theory, insofar as processes at the international and national levels are simply replicated at the city or (urban) community level (see Clark, 1978). However, the findings are not entirely consistent, and the processes operating at the community or city level appear to be different in important ways. There is a body of work, however, relatively new and still developing that is similar to the world-system perspective in its emphasis on the role of the operation of the modern capitalist system; this work, represented by Harvey (1973), Castells (1976), Gordon (1978), and Hill (1976), provides an explanatory framework for the effect of dominance on economic inequality. It also points to those areas where the analogy between nations within a world-economic system and cities within a national-economic system breaks down.

To recapitulate the findings presented above, dominant cities (core or center cities in alternative terminology) are characterized by high levels of income inequality when dominance is conceived in terms of the presence of various control functions. The benefits of housing control functions for the society do not flow consistently to the urban resident population. A major difference between treating nations as the unit of analysis and treating cities within one nation as the unit of analysis is that the political border limiting a city is considerably more permeable in terms of the residential location of both workers and elites. Conventional analyses of U.S. urban development emphasize the costs, in terms of fiscal problems and decay, of the exodus of central-city residents to the suburbs, especially the white middle class. This accounts for the relative concentration of poverty in central cities in the United States. However, this approach does not fully explain the relative concentration of income inequality in large central cities. Approaches which emphasize the "uneven" development of the urban system do a better job at analyzing class-based inequality.

At least until the early 1970s, the period roughly corresponding to the measurement of dominance presented here, the large central cities, my dominant cities,[5] had retained "the major directional and organizational activities and several major cultural and symbolic institutions" of the society (Castells, 1976: 8) and of the world-system. These same cities have lost manufacturing and retail sales jobs, along with a sizable portion of their resident middle class, in the process of suburbanization. However, they have also retained an elite class which has chosen not to move. Their behavior relative to the middle class has been examined by Harvey (1973: 173):

> The rich possess the political and economic power to resist encroachment, while the socioeconomic group immediately below them is unlikely to be as unacceptable in its behavior as is the poorest group. The richest of all will probably not move unless they prefer to.

The presence of an urban elite class, presumably representing the leaders of the control functions tapped by the dominance index, in conjunction with a large urban lower class that is not able to find employment in the administrative offices found in dominant cities (that is, the urban/surburban "mismatch" of jobs and workers), are sufficient to account for the relationship between dominance and income inequality.

SUMMARY AND CONCLUSION

In summary, there is uneven development in the capitalist world-economy both *among* nation-states and *within* nation-states—a "nesting" of unevenness. Within a core state such as the United States, there is a degree of unevenness which parallels that among states in the world-system. The extent of inequality within a core state such as the United States is, of course, less than the extent of inequality between nation-states in the world-system. But the variations in equality can be specified in terms that have been developed for studying the latter. The role of the dynamic operation of the capitalist system seems clear. Empirical work on communities needs to recognize and incorporate this in the future.

There are three specific suggestions for future research along these lines, in addition to the general suggestion that world-system theory is relevant for community-level work. First, the concept of dominance or control needs to be more clearly specified if we are to rely on world-system theory. In the United States, the size of the manufacturing class may not be a valid indicator of dominance or core status as it is in comparative, cross-national work. Unless we are willing to argue that the concept of dominance, as well as the concept of linkage with the larger system, is multidimensional, then it will be necessary to respecify the role of manufacturing vis-à-vis administrative and control functions tapped by the dominance index used here.

Second, the question of the appropriate unit of analysis for work within one nation-state is relevant for future work. The analyses here have relied on politically defined municipalities as the unit of analysis. Yet, it might be argued that a more accurate unit is the

Standard Metropolitan Statistical Area (SMSA), which ignores political boundaries in favor of a more complete economic unit. Arguments for both sides of the issue are compelling, and its resolution may require empirical tests which are beyond the scope of this paper.

The third and final suggestion is that there is a second avenue for integrating world-system and community-level work. The avenue chosen here is to look at the appropriateness of world-system theory, as applied to an analysis of varying degrees of income inequality among states, to the analysis of income inequality among communities. The alternative avenue is to include reference to a *community's* place in the world-system in models of inequality and in models addressed to other aspects of a community's quality of life. Gary, Indiana, for example, is affected by its place in the national economy; the national economy is affected by the position of the United States in the world-economic system; by extension, Gary is also affected by dynamics occurring in the larger system. Some means of including those dynamics in the development of community-level models is a fruitful avenue for future work.

NOTES

1. The sample consists of 200 cities in the United States with populations 50,000 or greater in 1960. The six largest communities (New York, Chicago, Los Angeles, Philadelphia, Detroit, and Houston) have been excluded, since they represent extremes on several key variables.

2. The index was formed by averaging the standard scores of the four components. The dates for which the data were collected and the sources are: home offices, 1970 (Moody's Investors Service, 1970); voluntary association headquarters, 1970 (Gale Research Co., 1970); colleges and universities, 1968 (American Council on Education, 1968); and banking activity, 1964 (U.S. Bureau of the Census, 1972).

3. The data were recorded from *Fortune Magazine* sources (1966) and are restricted to absentee-ownership in the manufacturing sector.

4. The source for the index is U.S. Bureau of the Census (1970). See Allison (1978) and Schwartz and Winship (1980) for discussions of measures of income inequality.

5. The correlation between the dominance index and city size is very high, as might be expected.

REFERENCES

ALLISON, P. (1978) "Measures of inequality." American Sociological Review 43, 6: 865–879.

American Council on Education (1968) American Universities and Colleges, 10th Edition (O. Singletary, ed.). Washington, DC: American Council on Education.

BOGUE, D. (1949) The Structure of the Metropolitan Community. Ann Arbor: Horace H. Rackham School of Graduate Studies, University of Michigan.

BORNSCHIER, V. and T. BALLMER-CAO (1979) "Income inequality: a cross-national study of the relationships between MNC-penetration, dimensions of the power structure and income distribution." American Sociological Review 44, 3: 487–506.

BORNSCHIER, V., C. CHASE-DUNN, and R. RUBINSON (1978) "Cross-national evidence of the effects of foreign investment and aid on economic growth and inequality: a survey of findings and a reanalysis." American Journal of Sociology 84, 3: 651–683.

CASTELLS, M. (1976) "The wild city." Kapitalistate 4/5 (Summer): 2–30.

CHASE-DUNN, C. (1975) "The effects of international economic dependence on development and inequality: a cross-national study." American Sociological Review 40, 6: 720–738.

CLARK, T. (1978) "There is no urban theory." Comparative Urban Research 6, 2/3: 9.

DUNCAN, O. D. et al. (1960) Metropolis and Region. Baltimore: Johns Hopkins University Press.

FOLEY, J. (1977) "Trends, determinants and policy implications of income inequality in U.S. counties." Sociology and Social Research 61, 4: 441–461.

Fortune Magazine (1966) Plant and Product Directory. New York: Fortune.

Gale Research Company (1970) Encyclopedia of Associations, 6th Edition. Detroit: Gale Research Company.

GORDON, D. (1978) "Capitalist development and the history of American cities," pp. 25–63 in W. Tabb and L. Sawers (eds.) Marxism and the Metropolis. New York: Oxford University Press.

GRAS, N. S. B. (1922) An Introduction to Economic History. New York: Harper & Row.

HARVEY, D. (1973) Social Justice and the City. Baltimore: Johns Hopkins University Press.

HAWLEY, A. (1963) "Community power and urban renewal success." American Journal of Sociology 68: 422–431.

HILL, R. (1976) "Fiscal crisis and political struggle in the decaying central city." Kapitalistate 4/5 (Summer): 31–49.

LAUDER, S. (1979) "Structural inequality: a synthesis of research and theory." Presented at the Annual Meeting of the American Sociological Association.

LINCOLN, J. (1976) "Power mobilization in the urban community: reconsidering the ecological approach." American Sociological Review 41 (February): 1–15.

——— (1977) "Organizational dominance and community structure," pp. 19–50 in R. Liebert and A. Imershein (eds.) Power, Paradigms and Community Research. Beverly Hills, CA: Sage.

McKENZIE, R. (1929) The Metropolitan Community. New York: McGraw-Hill.

Moody's Investors Service (1970) Moody's Industrial Manual. New York: Moody's Investors Service.

REICH, M. (1971) "The economics of racism," pp. 107–113 in D. Gordon (ed.) Problems in Political Economy. Lexington, MA: D.C. Heath.

RUBINSON, R. (1976) "The world economy and the distribution of income within states: a cross-national study." American Sociological Review 41, 4: 638–659.

SCHWARTZ, J. and C. WINSHIP (1980) "The welfare approach to measuring inequality," pp. 1–36 in K. Schuessler (ed.) Sociological Methodology, 1980. San Francisco: Jossey-Bass.

SUMMERS, G. and F. CLEMENTE (1976) "Industrial development, income distribution, and public policy." Rural sociology 41, 2: 248–268.

TURK, H. (1970) "Interorganizational networks in urban society: initial perspective and comparative research." American Sociological Review 35 (February): 1–19.

U.S. Bureau of the Census (1970) Census of Population, General Social and Economic Characteristics. Washington, DC: Government Printing Office.

———— (1972) County and City Data Book, 1972. Washington, DC: Government Printing Office.

WALLERSTEIN, I. (1974) The Modern World-System: Capitalist Agriculture and the Origins of the European World-Economy in the Sixteenth Century. New York: Academic Press.

WARREN, R. (1963) The Community in America. Chicago: Rand McNally.

PART 6

DYNAMICS OF
DEVELOPMENT OF THE WORLD-ECONOMY

Chapter 12

STRUCTURAL
TRANSFORMATIONS OF
THE WORLD-ECONOMY

Terence K. Hopkins
Immanuel Wallerstein

State University of New York,
Binghamton

PREFACE

We start from some assumptions all of us presumably share: A set of interrelated processes effect the capitalist development of the modern world-system. These processes work through a massive, world-scale complex of relational networks or social structures, which the processes produced, continually reproduce, and also continually modify. Together this ensemble of generative processes and channeling structures form a coherent, historical, social system—the capitalist world-economy. As a historical social system, this world-economy is time-specified in two constitutive ways: it is temporally bounded, having beginnings, middles, and end points that can in principle be located on conventional time scales; and it is temporally patterned, having distinctive periodicities and durations.[1]

Of immediate concern are the periodicities given by the long waves in the overall rate of growth of the historical system as a whole. These Kondratieff cycles trace and reflect constitutive phasings of the capitalist development of the modern world-system. Both changes in the scope and depth of the system's relations of production (its social structure) and changes in the scale and composition of the forces of production (its historical role) are similarly patterned. Two to three decades of overall relative social stability and declining growth in production and productive capacity precede two to three decades of relatively rapid change in the social structure of production/accumulation and of relatively rapid growth in production and productive capacity. The period of expansion is then followed by another of stagnation, which in turn is followed by another expansion, and so on.

The general reason advanced for these patterned phases of capitalist development premises a recurrent opposition between two sets of the system's processes: those expanding the forces of production, notably the accumulation processes, and those reproducing the existing constellation of relations of production, among which figure prominently processes of the organization of force, stratification/legitimation, and institutionalization. In the expansion phase or A-phase of a cycle, the broadening and deepening of the social structure of the world-economy provide, in the imagery most of us work with, ample social space for the expansion of productive forces. But in time that expansion fills up that social space, as it were, while the effectiveness of the stabilizing processes (abetted by the growing stagnation they help produce) precludes alternative relational structures. This is a cycle's stagnation phase or B-phase. If capitalist development continues to expand the world's productive forces, it does so, in this formulation, only because the existing constellation of relational networks, through which accumulation processes operate, are periodically broadened, deepened, and reconstituted.[2]

The structural feature often singled out for attention here, in explanations of stagnation and of recovery from it, is the world-scale distribution of income or purchasing power, especially the distribution among states and, within states, among households. For this determines the world-scale structure of effective demand, especially for wage goods. Income distribution is determined (and continually reproduced) by processes of the world-economy's social structure (notably armed struggles between states and class struggles within them). It thus becomes increasingly stabilized in the course of a cycle over the A-phase, just as the forces of production and world-output as a whole are being rapidly expanded. It is this growing contradiction that leads into the B-phase. Recovery takes place in this view, then—that is, a new A-phase of expanding accumulation begins, insofar as the restructuring of the constellation of relational networks entails a significant redistribution of world-income or purchasing power among states and among households, and through this a renewed effective demand.

Of concern to us here are structural transformations of this sort—that is, cyclically specified transformations of the world-economy's social structures of production/accumulation (and the income distributions specific to them). What follows, however, as was indicated above, is not a coherent theoretical sketch but only a set of notes on topics germane to the subject, structural transformations of the world-economy.

ON CAPITALIST DEVELOPMENT

A distinction is often drawn between two directions of structural transformation, the broadening of the capitalist world-economy and its deepening, to use the well-known pair of terms. One refers to the historical expansion of its geographical space, by the successive elimination via incorporation of areas external to it. The capitalist world-economy thus broadens geographically, from the limited arena in which its axial division of labor took shape during the sixteenth century (an arena thereby formed into a locus of a world-economy), to its present occupancy of the whole of the globe (and, indeed, even beyond, if the minuscule footholds on outer space provided by orbiting satellites may be counted). The other refers to the historical extension of its social space (to use that metaphor) via the successive elimination, or the fundamental reconstitution, of social relations external to it. The world-economy thus deepens socially, from the highly circumscribed and subordinate place its organizing processes occupied initially, in the geographical area where they operated, to their present place of dominance and reach throughout the length and breadth of contemporary human affairs.

These are distinguishable directions of the changes periodically transforming the world-economy's social structure. But they are hardly separate domains of inquiry—the one forming the domain of capitalist development, the other the domain of something fundamentally different (for example, a sort of ongoing original accumulation)—which some would make them out to be. For the processes responsible for the transformations are intimately related in theory and interwoven in history, and their continual joint result has been both an increasingly uneven and an increasingly combined development of the world's productive forces, to use a second well-known pair of terms.

Increasingly uneven development, to pursue this pair for a moment, translates into a growing difference in productive capacity, a polarization between the two kinds of production zones which the world-economy's axial division of labor forms, its core, and its periphery. (There is as well an increasingly *different* development of the two zones, which is discussed briefly below.) And increasingly combined development translates into a growing integration between them. This latter is a bit more complex. At one level it entails the products of each zone increasingly becoming capital goods for the production processes of the other, or wage goods (or luxuries) for the households of the other (or, we might add, means of governance, such as guns or paper clips, for ruling or rebelling groups of the other). At another level, distinguishable from and less visible than such material flows, is a growing centralization of capital. This is effected through several kinds of structural change, but a significant one is a growth in the scale and in the array of organizations that directly and indirectly administer the circulation of their capital as it goes through its circuits of successive forms and expands. Collectively (whether competitively or collusively) they effectively shape the structuring and operation of the processes of accumulation on a world-scale, to a large extent by altering the conditions of existence of other kinds of units of the world-economy (states, households, petty producers, and so forth). But most importantly, they do so by decisively influencing where, geographically, productive capacity is expanded (that is, where expanded reproduction takes place materially and means of production, as capital, thereby accumulate), where it is only reproduced (maintained but not expanded), and where it is run down and abandoned as capitalized means of production.

A quite common (if also usually tacit) misconstruction of the concept "capitalist development" should be noted here (one almost all of us commit at one time or another). This error occurs when the capitalist development of the modern world-system is tacitly equated with, and so confined to, the capitalist development of the world's forces of production. It thus eliminates from immediate view—if not always from theory altogether—the structured constellations of relational networks (the relations of production writ large) through which the abstractly organizing capital/labor relation is materially and heterogeneously formed and re-formed and the processes of accumulation thereby made, in effect, operative. Capitalist development can then be construed as a scalar quantity and rendered monotonically, as more-ness or less-ness, in particular as more-ness or less-ness or economic development or, even, progress. Globally, capitalist development is understood to have taken place (or to be taking place) largely in advanced countries (what we call the core) and to have taken place very little, if at all, in other areas (what we call the periphery), which is why the core is "developed" and the periphery "backward," or undeveloped, or even underdeveloped, in comparison with the core.

As we said above, in the perspective from which and on which we work, what capitalist development develops is the capitalist world-economy as a whole. This has entailed, integrally, the development of the world's forces of production, including the world-scale socialization of production (or labor) which that development implies. But it has also entailed much else. And it is the "much else" that theoretically explains and historically provides for not only the development of productive forces on a world-scale (accumulation of capital) but even more for the unevenness of the development—from which the overall or worldwide extent of such development has to be abstracted to be constructed as a quantity.

ON PERIPHERIES

The unevenness with which productive forces are developed on a world-scale, then, *is* the pattern which the accumulation processes—forming, working through, reproducing, and altering the axial division of labor—necessarily give their development (necessarily, in virtue of the theory of capitalist development). If this claim is construed as a premise, and so as a procedural directive, at the next level down in the theoretical movement from abstract to concrete (that is, in the movement from historically unspecified theoretical categories to theoretically specified historical interpretations), we must imagine the capitalist development of the world-economy as working in opposite and complementary ways, to develop cores-in-relation-to-peripheries and peripheries-in-relation-to-cores.

The historical patterns descriptive of core formation are relatively well known. They are variously depicted in every textbook on European or U.S. economic history and are the subject of that body of European theoretical writings formed by the label "Classical Sociology" (which serves simultaneously to draw readers to them and to distance readers from them). The historical patterns descriptive of periphery formation are, again, relatively unknown. They are depicted largely from the perspectives and in the languages of (conceptually, but also literally) the core areas; and they have not been—save for a few works whose titles can be quickly rattled off—the subject of a collection (let alone a body) of theoretical writings. Accordingly, we are all commonly drawn into detailing what the capitalist development of peripheries-in-relation-to-cores is *not* (which undoubtedly helps explain the tendency for many of us to commit the error observed above).

There are, nevertheless, at least four well-known features of periphery formation, which, as we collectively move to subvert and replace the scholarly paradigms and practices responsible for the unevenness of our substantive knowledge and the imbalanced form of our theoretical knowledge, it would seem well to keep prominently in view.

(1) There is the way areas and peoples structurally external to the capitalist world-economy are brought within it, to form its broadening, with their production processes thereby becoming increasingly integrated with others of the axial division of labor and their governing processes thereby increasingly integrated with others of the interstate system. This changed condition for an area and its peoples, from being outside to being within and of the world-economy, we construe as a one-time result for the area of a complex set of processes and circumstances, which are recurrent for the historical system as a whole but specific for the instance. These we briefly discuss below under the heading "incorporation."

(2) There is the construction of an area's labor processes into specific production chains feeding toward an output of a few kinds of products, each of which is produced within a definite, world-structured division of labor as a capital good for core-area production processes or a wage good for core-area labor forces (households). Such specialization in production, of goods consumed (in

one way or the other) elsewhere, is commonly rendered as the commodities which the area specializes in producing for sale on the world-market. (This rendering, we might note, is not objectionable if understood metaphorically but if taken literally entails both reification—areas as such do not produce—and an often erroneous presumption—intrafirm or interstate relations, for example, rather than specifically market relations, may well integrate the peripheral-area and core-area production/consumption processes in question).

(3) There is the transformation of workers (the population) into labor-in-relation-to-capital—whether directly (as fieldhands in relation to planters) or indirectly (as small producers in relation to merchant/transporters in relation to bulk processors—and, in particular, into low-wage labor-in-relation-to-capital). If one could do the accounts, the cost to capital for labor (whether as wage payments or their computed equivalents, whether paid in money, in kind, or in usufruct) would amount to little more than is needed, in actual or imputed expenses at conventional levels of living, to maintain the workday energy levels of individual workers while functioning as labor. It would not specifically amount to enough to cover, in actual or imputed expenses, what it takes to maintain and reproduce the household communities which supply the workers as labor and thus in effect subsidize capital to that extent. In accounting terms, the necessary labor time, in this form of the capital-labor relation, is that much less than it would be, and so surplus labor time that much more, were the households fully proletarianized and the costs of generationally reproducing the labor force therefore borne within the capital-labor relation.

(4) There is the reproduction of capital in its simpler versions, insofar as it is reproduced at all. That is, there is the textbook version of simple reproduction (stocks replenished, equipment maintained or replaced) with no changes in scale, technical division of labor, or technical (organic) composition of capital; and there is simply expanded reproduction, whether as a scalar expansion of existing units of production or as a numerical expansion of similarly scaled units, but with little or no change in the technical

division of labor or, specifically, in the technical composition of capital. Production procedures thus are, or become in time, customary; the tasks of workers as labor are or become habitual; labor intensities remain by definition at or about the same levels for long periods; and technical improvements in tools or organization are, also by definition, few and far between and have few or no structural ramifications when they do occur.

Three observations may be briefly made about these. First, as sketched here, these features are conditions or developmental tendencies, not processes—a point which needs to be made because words ending in -*tion* in English are ambiguous on this score, the suffix indifferently denoting both a condition or state of affairs and an action or process.

Second, the conditions are, first and foremost, features of peripheries-in-relation-to-cores, and only on that fundamental relational ground are they secondarily or derivatively features of peripheral areas in comparison with or in contrast to features of core areas. With respect to the latter three—a high degree of product specialization, relatively "unlimited supplies" of low-wage labor, and customary production procedures (which thus become, competitively speaking, increasingly backward)—these conditions are positive, continual results of the accumulation process as it operates on the world-scale it has created, and in particular as it works through and reproduces while doing so the world-economy's axial division of labor. Such conditions are thus in no sense "distortions" of capitalist development, as some would have them be—a description having meaning only in what we earlier mentioned is a serious misconstruction of the concept of capitalist development—but conditions integral to the concept.

Third, for that reason extensive changes in these conditions in a particular area signal not merely that area's economic growth or development. More importantly, they signal (a) its zonal relocation, to use that figure of speech, from the system's periphery to its thereby enlarging semi-periphery; and so (b) the ongoing occurrence of a sea change in the social structuring of the world-economy's production/accumulation processes—that is, a complex structural transformation of the system as a whole, of which the changes in question are but one part and the area in question but one locus (see Fröbel et al., 1977).

ON INCORPORATION

The Axial Division of Labor

The capitalist world-economy's broadening has occurred through the geographical expansion of both its axial division of labor and its interstate system, from the limited arena ("world") which they formed when first developed during the sixteenth century to their present reach across the globe. This broadening took the form of the successive elimination of areas external to the system through their successive incorporation into it. And this elimination of its external arena took place not piecemeal and continuously so much as in large chunks, as it were, and in several recurrent waves (see Bergeson and Schoenberg, 1980).

These waves of the system's zonal expansion in part entailed and in part prefigured (at least until the completion of the territorial constitution of the modern world-system in this century) successive, cyclical structural transformations. And each of these transformations, beginning during a period of increasing stagnation, provided a substantively extended and relationally reorganized structuring of the world-economy—a wider and redesigned field for the processes of capitalist development to continue to expand, to interrelate, and to concentrate the world's forces of production on a global scale.

Regarding any particular place in the world-economy's external arena, expansion into it constitutes incorporation into the system, as a definite, relationally named and located, geopolitically bounded area and jurisdiction within the modern-world system.

As the complex process through which the world-economy expands territorially, then, incorporation operates, for each area it forms, once and for all, over a delimited period, and in historically specific form. Everywhere the process is theoretically the same and everywhere, historically distinctive.[3]

Generally, the transition for an area from being external to the world-economy to incorporation in it seems to have taken some 50–75 years. It is a period constituting a definite break in the area's history, a period of extensive, basic structural change, most apparent in two of its interwoven fundamental relational networks: that comprising and shaped by its processes of production and that comprising and shaped by its processes of governance or rule. We shall discuss each briefly.

With respect to the restructuring of production processes, the changes here form the beginnings of the construction of the area's labor processes into sequenced production operations resulting in the regular flow of products from the area to other (principally core) areas of the axial division of labor. Sometimes this meant the introduction of production processes totally new to the area (plantation sugar production into the Caribbean); sometimes the grafting of partially new production processes (cotton production in Uganda); sometimes, at first, mainly the redirection of flows of products already regularly produced (wheat production in the Ottoman Empire). But everywhere this reconstitution of the production processes in a once external area into part processes of the capitalist world-economy entailed (1) the transforming of workers into labor-in-relation-to-capital, whether in relation directly or in one or another mediated form; (2) the forceful conversion of workers into labor in this sense, and so an increasing and increasingly extensive coercion of labor; and (3) a more or less rapid, more or less extensive decline in the material well-being of the population in the area from what it had been.

The second of these claims, regarding labor-coercion, we treated as an organizing hypothesis in an about-to-be completed exploratory or pilot study done at the Fernand Braudel Center.[4] In particular, we focused on the ways in which the complex process of incorporation worked in three different periods of the world-system's development in forming three of its areas—1650–1690, the Caribbean; 1750–1815, the Ottoman State (formerly the Ottoman Empire, later Turkey); 1870–1920, southern Africa. It would take us too far afield even to outline here the premises and procedures of the pilot inquiry as a whole, since this kind of research entails departing from methodological canons in several ways and each such departure needs its own justification. It is a propos, however, to report briefly this: We treated degree of labor coercion, *inter alia,* as an observably varying condition, one whose changes at least were ordinally measurable (more-ness or less-ness). We devised a classificatory schema for changes in work relations designed to show whether, in each of five respects, there was more or less labor coercion when any two of the historical kinds of work relations encountered within each of the situations studied were compared. We found the schema to be adequate for the numerous descriptive reports we examined on each time-place and to provide a reasonably simple order of the principal kinds of work relations within each, in terms of the degree or extent of labor coercion characteristic of each kind when compared to the others. We found that, virtually without exception, the historically specific changes in work relations recorded for each time-place indicated changes in direction of the sort stated in the general claim (toward kinds characterized by more labor coercion).

These preliminary results are, of course, encouraging. Nevertheless, it is important to point out that they are preliminary: In particular, while we feel fairly confident that labor coercion did indeed increase markedly in each area during the respective times in question, we could not even try (within the confines of the exploratory study) to propose, then to formulate, and then to examine alternative reasons (that is, reasons alternative to the expansion of the world-economy) for this being so; nor could we reach the point of trying to rule out such reasons. The results are thus encouraging but, by design, provisional at best.

The Interstate System

A second domain of change during incorporation is that of the network(s) of governance or rule in the area in question. In this respect incorporation entails the expansion of the world-economy's interstate system. But before proceeding, there is a certain terminological point to be made.

It is very common to refer to politically centralized areas of the world-economy's external arena as "states" (the Chinese state in the seventeenth century, the Zulu state in the nineteenth). This practice, we think, is a mistake because it is confusing. At the very least, it obscures (if not eliminating entirely) a point of basic theoretical importance: "The state system of modern Europe" is fundamentally different from and is to be distinguished "from the political life of all previous and [all] non-European civilizations of the world" (to use Walter Dorn's [1963] version of the point). Stateness, to put the point differently, is not a generic category of political life (whose varied forms are to be traced within and across civilizations), but a historically specific category, one distinctive to the relationally formed jurisdictions (the sovereignties and partial sovereignties) of the initially European-centered interstate system. It is a category conceptually given by, because factually imposed by, the developmental processes of the capitalist world-economy. (The Ottoman Empire, by virtue of internal and external agencies acting in relation to one another, was turned into the Ottoman state, which, in turn, by virtue of a similar network of interrelated acting agencies, was turned into the state of Turkey. What is true of the constituted empires of the external arena is *a fortiori* true of the states (Argentina) and regions (the Caribbean) formed into units through the workings of the expansion/incorporation process.)

But the point under discussion is terminological only to begin with. For the stateness of an area/population, in relation to other constituted jurisdictions of the world-economy, is nominally given by its diplomatic (interstate system) classification, which results from and changes by virtue of very real alignments of forces (the imperial-national opposition being a principal one but hardly the sole one). The claim holds, too, for the boundary relations at once separating and integrating nominally sovereign jurisdictions in relation to one another: Their directional openness and closure, in many different respects, reflect very real alignments of forces, and more or less changing ones at that. Interstate relations and the interstate system overall, then, in part express and in part circumscribe or structure the world-scale accumulation/production processes. In short, the relational networks forming the interstate system are integral to, not outside of, the networks constitutive of the social economy defining the scope and reach of the modern world-system.

Even more fundamentally, can one imagine production/accumulation processes operating as a totality except in and through relational networks defined, guaranteed, and informed by state-centered processes? Are such abstruse categories as money, private property, and contract to be given abstracted definitions independent of the real relations giving them material substance in world-economy and, as well, a certain kind of abstractness today in the realm of concepts? The duality of state and economy (market) reflects a nineteenth-century historical interlude, a brief condition in a small part of the world which was generalized into a principal ground of liberal social thought. It has no place as a basic theoretical duality in political economy.(To say this, however, is not to deny a central place in theoretical work to explanations of the rise and demise of the historical condition of duality.)

Insofar as external areas are incorporated, then—and in the singular development of the modern world-system all have been—the transition period framing incorporation encloses definite directions of change in a once external area's arrangements and processes of rule or governance. Briefly, more or less rationalized and centralized structures of domination (in Weber's sense) are developed, or constructed from scratch, that minimally have these three features: Each center claims and/or is more or less widely accorded jurisdictional responsibility within the interstate system for a defined geopolitical area and the population(s) within it; each is or becomes strong enough in relation to local (internal) forces to assure flows of goods, people, and value in money from across the borders of its geopolitical jurisdiction and so into other similarly bordered areas (mainly core); and each is or becomes weak enough in relation to other jurisdictions (mainly core) to be incapable of blocking such flows, should those in strategic posts in the apparatus under construction be or come to be disposed to do so.

The study mentioned above—on the incorporation and formation of the Caribbean, the Ottoman Empire/state, and southern Africa as world-system areas—also traced structural changes in their governing arrangements, with an attempt to determine whether and to what extent the formulation just advanced was tenable, at least in these instances. As parts of the external arena, the three were obviously descriptively different. The Ottoman Empire by definition encompassed a geopolitically circumscribed, relatively centralized area. The Caribbean was the opposite; it was not a predefined region but consisted of a large number of island territories, as well as some mainland reaches, none of which was integrally related to any other or centralized. Southern Africa was somewhere in between. It, too, was not a predefined area, but substantial portions of it were marked off by several centralizing administrative operations, albeit within large stretches characterized by what some anthropologists call "acephalous" political systems.

To put our tentative findings in a sentence or two, the information we have collected and assembled on each time-place establishes, first, that in each a transformation of rule took place; second, that it resulted in the formation of state-like relational structures and processes which were of the sort and had the effects sketched theoretically in our general construction of the process of incorporation; and, third, beyond that, that the transformations took highly distinctive forms in each instance, the state-forming sequences, events, and conditions which occurred in each amounting to historically original versions of the incorporation process at the level of the (expansion of) the interstate system. The last is hardly surprising, perhaps, but worth mentioning owing to the persisting belief in the paradigmatic virtue of rigorously comparative inquiries despite mounting evidence of their inappropriateness in the empirical study of the capitalist world-economy, save for their occasional usefulness in summarizing results already obtained or for preliminarily "scouting the terrain" in advance of conducting focused inquiries.

We should, though, add one point about procedure. It was, of course, necessary to pay careful attention to the various meanings which strength-of-state may have and so to the numerous ways in which this relational property of putative centers may vary (within ranges, sometimes independently of one another) and be observed in these ways to vary over time (here, not over places). Without going into details, we found it indispensable, not only to distinguish strength in the interstate system (vis-à-vis other world-system centers) from strength internally, as it were (vis-à-vis regions or regional centers in the area), but also to distinguish within these broad relational settings strength/weakness with respect to what. Here we worked pragmatically with several concerns and organized our information in terms of relational strength/weakness of centers over time (now versus then) with respect to relative control over means of force, means of legislation and adjudication, means of jurisdiction (boundaries), means of production (notably land), means of circulation (notably currency, also prices), means of distribution (taxation, other structured appropriational opportunities).

Again, the exploratory nature of this research provided us with enough room to establish, with some degree of confidence in light of information considered as evidence on the matter, that transformations of rule took place in each area during the times in question along the lines sketched. But its limited scope precluded our formulating, let alone ruling out, reasons for these changes alternative to those we worked with in designing and conducting this trio of studies on expansion/incorporation.

Finally, we consider the structural transformation of each area's processes of production and rule, through which its incorporation into and definition within the world-economy was effected: (1) equally a structural transformation *of* the world-economy (a locus of its expansion); (2) a site or part of an at-that-time wider set of cyclical transformations of the world-system's social structuring of accumulation/production; and (3) a consequence of the world-system's stagnation-expansion periodicities and, as such, to have occurred when it did (although not where it did, which is another question). That complex claim, obviously, has to remain no more than a disciplined speculation or orienting thesis. For nothing in the design or conduct of the exploratory research allows us even indirect or casual checks on its plausibility. That plausibility, however, is specifically what we are planning to examine directly in a larger, follow-up study now being designed.

ON STRATIFICATION

The exploratory study we have mentioned concerns the structuring and results of core-periphery relations over three centuries, as well as their periodic transformation in part through the expansion/incorporation process. In the course of this work, and in other studies we are doing together or singly, we find ourselves frequently making use of arguments and constructs that are not as prominent in the array of theoretical ideas we say we work with as they turn out to be in the narrative/explanatory sketches we construct and employ. In effect, in any particular inquiry, we find ourselves moving out theoretically, along the ligaments of the world-economy as presently conceived, and at a point invoking a complex process that proves to be more central, in the narrative account of the structural change under examination, than it had been in the preliminary abstract sketch of the processes we initially drew up to guide the inquiry.

It accordingly seems desirable to begin paying more explicit attention to some of the processes we regularly invoke in analysis but have yet to bring into systematic relation, at the appropriate abstract level of discourse, to such central general processes in our work as accumulation, division of labor, and state formation. And so we conclude this presentation with some observations about one such complex process: stratification/legitimation. There are others we would like to bring up, such as household formation and the world revolutionary movement, but there is not enough space to do so. We add only that we have nothing particularly novel to say about this familiar subject, stratification/legitimation, except perhaps that which comes from locating it as a theoretical focus in world-economy studies and construing it as a process of the modern world-system.

Stratification, we are taught by modern sociological writings, comprises the processes of consciousness that establish, reproduce, and alter the relative standing, in terms of deeply held sentiments of worth, of socially defined groups and categories in relation to one another.

These processes, seen from a world-historical perspective, are invariably localized, and their respective settings—usually, if tacitly, core-zone nation-states—are treated as totally unconnected. It is as if in this regard each setting were an enclosure infinitely extended in its own time. And the writings, as is their wont, do not address the substantive establishment, reproduction, or alteration of the groups and categories whose relational worth it is the province of the localized stratifying processes to provide. Modern sociology deals with given contexts of interaction, not with how they came to be given. Neither do the writings even raise questions about the construction and continuing modification of the working social dictionaries, which provide the groups and categories in direct or mediated relations with one another with their relational definitions of each other. It is as if the material constitution of groups and categories, their social definition, and their hierarchical evaluation were each entirely separate, mutually irrelevant sets of processes.

That is quite a complex presumption. In effect, to form the subject matter of stratification as construed by modern sociology, one has to fasten onto localized versions of a world-system process as separable occasions of its operation and then tacitly eliminate from consideration (1) the locale's setting within the modern world-system (even as the West), although one of that system's general processes in specified form provides the subject matter; (2) the processes of consciousness, world-scale and in localized forms, which shape and carry the nomenclature and criteria people construct and use to distinguish among the material groups and categories structuring their social world, although the defined forms of these are what localized stratifying processes (also processes of consciousness) supposedly provide with commonly received evaluations and ranks; and (3) the actual relational networks which are in part stabilized, in part changed, by the workings of localized stratifying processes, although it is through the networks, in any case, that the processes invariably operate. A theory of stratification, built on whatever remains after eliminating all that, is indeed an "analytic" theory, with a vengeance.

It is small wonder that, on the ground remaining, the process of stratification in the abstract is likened to a continual measuring and apportioning operation. It is imagined that:

(1) There is an array of values widely shared among the people of the local setting and deeply internalized in each.
(2) This array is fashioned by some unspecified process into something like a footrule or yardstick whose increments represent degrees of social worthiness (degrees of realizing the common values).
(3) In this form, as a yardstick of worthiness, the array of common values is used by people to gauge the relative worth of each group and category they distinguish and define.
(4) The evaluative judgments so reached, about the various groups and categories, are similarly reached by everyone and by and large shared and reinforced in the course of everyday activities.
(5) The standing of a group or category, within the array of evaluative judgments, attaches by some unspecified process to the understood social definition of the group or category in question.

(6) There results a widely believed and therefore stable ordering of the groups and categories, according to their respective, commonly agreed upon, relative social worth.

(7) This ordering by some unspecified process actively guides the processes recurrently affecting the actual distribution, among the people in the setting, of material and immaterial well-being.

(8) Hence it is that the well thought-of are well-off and the poorly thought-of, poorly off (making quite spurious any suggestion that the abstract association of attributes is because the poorly off come to be poorly thought-of and the well-off, well thought-of); and that those in high esteem are powerful and those in low esteem, powerless (making quite spurious, etc.).

(9) The continuing, socially visible correspondence between the ideal and the real distributions affirms the ideal as ideal, the real as justified, and the reigning common values as the ultimately right ones of a just social order.

What is perhaps most remarkable about this version of the mechanism of stratification is not that it was formulated—social theory is full of supercilious ideas—nor that it has survived—social research as currently carried out is a far poorer form of scientific editing than experimental research and leaves much to be desired in its blue-pencilling activities, its canons of procedure often blocking consideration of plausible ideas, and its actual procedures often giving the stamp of approval to implausible ideas (such as the present one). It is not even that this mechanism became the centerpiece of modern sociological theoretical work—that figures, to use that dismissive expression. What is most remarkable is that, despite its manifest absurdity in the circumstances, it remains ensconced there, like a child-emperor in a barricaded temple, occasionally under attack from the house nobles (conflict theorists) but far removed from the border skirmishes with the barbarians (materialists) and so, throughout all, unscathed on the surface and unchallenged in its centrality.

We cannot seriously entertain, then, the possibility of using modern sociological constructions of stratification in our work, except perhaps in bits and pieces, here and there. Yet, we agree with Talcott Parsons that stratification is indeed an absolutely fundamental aspect of any social system and that as both condition and process it is in large measure what one means by a social system. Moreover, as one of us put it a few years back, we can "only speak of social change in social systems" (Wallerstein, 1974: 7), so that the mutual relevance of stratification and social change has been from the start, as it were, a presumed principle. The central point of course remains, however, that "the only [total] social system [is] the world-system" (1974: 7). And from this point of departure we are left with the notion of a singularly developing, in time globally extensive, complex of stratifying processes, whose changing form and reach are as integral to the broadening and deepening of the capitalist world-economy as the related changes in the axial division of labor and the interstate system. And so we are left to do two things, if not from scratch, surely from a novel angle of vision: first, track the fundamental processes of stratification, those constitutive of the modern world-system, as they have evolved and operated historically, in and across the localized settings of the capitalist world-economy; and, second, ground anew the theory of stratification, here the theory of the historically singular complex of processes forming an elemental component of the capitalist development of the modern world-system, and in this way put the division and integration of solidarities on a world scale on a par theoretically with the division and integration of production processes and the division and integration of domains of rule.

Were this direction of inquiry to be accepted, one could thereupon suggest moving to the study of the sequenced versions of the ideas promoted by factual ruling groups to legitimate their rule, their modes of taxation or tribute collection, their forms of labor coercion, and so on, and then, in approved contrapuntal style, to the sequenced versions of the ideas formed in opposition to these. Winthrop Jordan, for example, did something like this in his book *White Over Black*. We think, however, that this would be the wrong way to go about so basic a business. Such an approach to the task(s) would have to presuppose, *inter alia,* a mechanism not unlike that used in modern sociology, and it would thus have to presuppose what in our judgment is precisely in need of detailed depiction and reflective conceptualization. There is a place for anthropomorphic analogies in studying social processes and social change, but we are well beyond that place in the study of stratification. It is not general inquiries into the hegemonic ideas of the modern world-system that seem needed, then, or into the non-Western and/or popular ideas appearing in opposition to them and treated as just that. Conventional undergraduate courses in Western Civilization, after all, do all this and not that badly, given the framework. What seems wanted, rather, are focused studies on the emergence, reproduction, and change of hegemonic ideas and of the opposing ideas defining them, in particular periods of change in the modern world-system and in particular locales, all without presuming the framework of "Western Civ."

In tracking the broadening and deepening of the capitalist world-economy—and in particular in tracking the structural transformations which mark its singular history as increasingly the modern world's centrally organizing social system—we need to monitor in the course of our studies the workings of its stratifying processes in particular locales over particular periods. This means at the least addressing such evidently derived concerns as these, to list but four:

—the establishment of customary wage levels in locales and the subsequent changes that occur in them (and, more generally, in what is customarily regarded, by whom, as adequate returns to or for labor, or even in what is customarily regarded, by whom, as adequate conditions and levels of living);

—changes in the scope, depth, contents, and so forth of legitimations justifying the use of force and other practices in the ever-present struggles, manifest or latent, between ruling and ruled classes or strata in locales;[5]

—the extension and contraction of individual and collective rights and freedoms (in the Western sense), particularly those regarding property in produced means of production and produced means of subsistence, appropriation and alienability of land, freedom/unfreedom of labor and of associations of workers, inviolability of contract, eminent domain, freedom/unfreedom of capital and of associations of capitalists; and, to leave the matter at this for now,

—the recurrent contradictions in locales, especially national formations, between status-consciousness and class-consciousness (to use the formulation of Lukacs).

But this sort of derived, and in that sense subordinate, place of stratifying processes only opens up their larger place in world-system studies. Equally accessible to us from this perspective—and in the light of our present knowledge probably of more importance—are such concerns as these, again to list a few:

—the changing terms and structure of the world-economy's nomenclature (its system of relational names for peoples and places), over the course of its development as a singular historical social system, in tandem with the material reconstitution, creation, and elimination both of the peoples forming its populations and of the places forming its areas;

—the persistence in some settings of patriarchy (including its formed inversions and oppositions), its reconstitution or very introduction in others, as a defining and justifying structure of sentiments throughout an otherwise notably heterogeneous ensemble of relational networks and social conditions;

—the broadening and deepening of some linguistic communities, the narrowing and shallowing (and elimination) of others, and the reproduction, expansion, and contraction of multilingual zones and populations;

—the historical parallelism between the declining salience of the strata-divisions formative of national communities in core areas and the establishment or reconstitution and growing salience of such divisions in the populations of newly incorporated or continually peripheralized areas;

—but, perhaps most centrally, because equally extensive as ground
and consequence of the world-economy's stratifying processes, the
pervasiveness throughout its reaches of Fanon's Manichean world,
the centrality of the anchoring distinction of white versus nonwhite
(the very residual nature of the latter term reflecting, as it were, a
residualizing tendency or even process at work), and their corol-
lary, the domains of consciousness informing, emergent through,
and being recovered by the ongoing world-revolutionary movement.

There is one last matter to mention here, in concluding this
section and drawing this paper to a close. To repeat a general point,
there has been an overall secular growth in the dependence of
sovereignties on one another through the interstate system and in
the dependence of production processes on one another through
the axial division of labor. Analogously, there has been, for each
of the two great revolutionary movements of the modern world-
system, a sort of secular growth within each in the dependence on
one another of the successively joined, long-term struggles constituting each movement. Just as in the first world-scale revolutionary movement—the bourgeois—the successive struggles in locales became ideologically and structurally interdependent over
time, thereby generalizing as they did so an increasingly specified
and increasingly integrated world-scale complex of stratifying
processes, so too in the second world-scale revolutionary
movement—the socialist—the successive struggles in locales constitutive of the movement are becoming more and more ideologically and structurally interdependent over time.

Of course, the parallel is limited. The socialist revolutionary
movement takes shape in a world already made global by capitalist
development and so against an already world-scale bourgeois
movement. And for us at the present time, the world-scale stratifying processes that are being generalized, specified, and integrated
by the socialist revolutionary movement appear at once deeply
inconsistent internally and shrouded in the mists of presently
imagined possible future histories. Still, just as the bourgeois

world-revolution, by taking form in successive struggles in various locales, cumulatively evolved, in step-function fashion, the historically original ideas that came to inform its distinctive stratifying processes, and thus to define in consciousness its principal contradictions, so too, we may conjecture, something along the same lines is going on today.

In effect, we need to work with a weak version of an as-then-so-now procedural premise. This means conceiving of the socialist world-revolution of our time as, first, a historically singular world-scale movement; second, as being given increasing shape and substance through the cumulative succession of the loci of its constitutive struggle and the real relations among them; and third, as evolving through its stratifying processes the complex of historically original ideas that a long time hence will be seen as among the major differences distinguishing the capitalist era from the socialist era (if they will even be called that then). These stratifying processes, it should be understood, are presumed to be at work on a variety of levels—personality formation, household formation, labor-process formation, state formation, world-movement formation, and so forth.

True, on epistemological grounds alone our capacity even to begin to form concepts of the sort needed, in order to distinguish in the domain of consciousness what is progressive from what is not (to leave it at that for now), is seriously in doubt. Perforce, we are of our times, so is our consciousness, and so is all our work. Yet, we have no real choice in the matter, for two reasons. One is the situation we are in in relation to our subject matter. Magubane's observation is precisely to the point. It is about the study of southern Africa but holds much more generally:

> Revolutionary situations move by means of polarization, deepening the conflict, expanding its scope. Participants and observers, makers and victims cannot escape either the movement or the polarization. Disinterested analysis and commentary become thereby epistemologically excluded. Disinterested knowledge of

. . . revolutionary struggle is no more possible now than disinter-
ested knowledge of the religious wars of sixteenth-century Europe
was possible to contemporaries. There are no bystanders, no side-
lines, no refuges now. In particular, there is no press box from
which to describe the play on the field, and no spectators to whom
to describe the play. All are combatants, on one side or the other
[1977: 164–165].

The other reason is more narrowly methodological in nature.
Our analyses of contemporary events and trends, of the present as
history, logically entail in their concepts and arguments constructs
of coming states of affairs. These may be, as they are in much
current writing, liberal and Marxist alike, tacit projections of more
of the same, the implicitly projected conditions being capable of
differing from present conditions only quantitatively or propor-
tionately at best and specifically not qualitatively or structurally at
all. As students of long-term, large-scale social change, we presumably would rather read the present as a history admitting of
alternative futures and so construe the present as a historical transition or, specifically here, a period of structural transformation of
the modern world-system. In that case we have no choice but to try
to discern the shapes of these realistic historical alternatives alongside and before us and to form our concepts for grasping and
gauging the present in their light.
    The study of the stratifying processes of the world-scale so-
cialist revolutionary movement, and in particular the developments in the domain of consciousness they occasion and reflect,
thus has for us a double character of deep importance. It is, on one
hand, extremely difficult and demanding, with even its epistemological ground in need of rigorous formulation. We find the line of
inquiry being pursued by Abdel-Malek and associates under the
title of the Civilizational Project, profoundly instructive in this
regard.[6] It is on the other hand indispensable, as it turns out, to the
very formulation and elaboration of the theoretical ideas we work
with in analyzing the present and so the past—ideas which, to

compound the difficulties, are themselves part of the developments in the domain of consciousness we would study.

NOTES

1. On the cyclical patterning both of accumulation on a world-scale and, more generally, of the structural transformations marking the capitalist development of the modern world-system, see Hopkins and Wallerstein (1977; 1980, Part I), and Bergesen and Schoenberg (1980). For further readings, see Barr (1979).

2. This broadened understanding of the scope of the "theory of capitalist development" has the additional virtue of obviating some of the debate over endogenous versus exogenous processes—particularly if one makes explicit the general methodological principle that capitalists regularly "capitalized" historically on developments and situations they had no historical hand in creating. They regularly made endogenous processes that began exogenously, at least throughout much of the earlier decades of capitalist development of the modern world-system, and in this way continually enlarged the "theoretical system" of that development.

3. Compare this view to that of Popper (1957). We flag this point to call attention to its being, more generally, fundamental to the method of world-system or world-historical studies. As such, it obviously cannot be elaborated here; but there is speace and need to observe this: Only by relaxing the elemental tension in scientific inquiry, between theory and history, can one create the epistemological space needed to draw the distinction central to late nineteenth-century European thought, that between nomothetic and ideographic studies. That distinction in turn provides the indispensable methodological ground for the current dichotomy, as prevalent as it is false, between scientific and historical method or between scientific and historical interpretative or explanatory accounts. Once all that is (erroneously) granted, it becomes possible to claim, as Popper did, that any integration in practice of what everyone understands is philosophically separate in thought inevitably confounds two realms of discourse and so commits a grave error, the one to which Popper gave the name "historicism."

4. The research group conducting the study includes, besides our-
:elves, Robert Bach, Kenneth Barr, Eric M. Berg, Hale Decdeli, Juan
Giusti, Resat Kasaba, William G. Martin, Peter D. Phillips, and Robert
Russell.

5. The usual way of putting this topic is seriously one-sided and
inappropriately functionalist for studies of social change. To ask about
the legitimacy of a particular structure of domination is (1) tacitly to
approach the matter from the side of those in power in the structure; (2) to
inquire into a merely formal condition of an existing arrangement; and (3)
to take that arrangement, that structure of domination, as itself a pu-
tatively enduring "given" for the purpose of the inquiry without taking
into account the historically alternative arrangements which the structure's very existence presupposes, let alone those which the struggles
defining the structure's field and mode of operation prefigure.

6. There are by now a number of essays. See, for one, Abdel-Malek
(1979). Less far along in a comparable line of work, but no less instructive, are the writings of Robinson (1980).

REFERENCES

ABDEL-MALEK, A. (1979) "Historical surplus-value." Review III, 1
    (Summer): 35–43.
BARR, K. (1979) "Long waves: a selective, annotated bibliography."
    Review II, 4 (Spring): 675–718.
BERGESEN, A. and R. SCHOENBERG (1980) "Long waves of colo-
    nial expansion and contraction," pp. 231–277 in A. Bergesen (ed.)
    Studies of the Modern World-System. New York: Academic Press.
DORN, W. (1963) Competition for Empire, 1740–1763. New York:
    Harper & Row.
FRÖBEL, F., J. HEINRICHS, and O. KREYE (1977) "The tendency
    towards a new international division of labor." Review I, 1 (Summer):
    73–88.
HOPKINS, T. K. and I. WALLERSTEIN (1977) "Patterns of develop-
    ment of the modern world-system." Review I, 2 (Fall): 111–145.
———— [eds.] (1980) Processes of the Modern World-System, Vol. 3.
    Beverly Hills, CA: Sage.

JORDAN, W. (1977) White Over Black: American Attitudes Toward the Negro. New York: W. W. Norton.

MAGUBANE, B. (1977) "The poverty of liberal analysis: a polemic on Southern Africa." Review I, 2 (Fall): 164–165.

POPPER, K. (1957) The Poverty of Historicism. London: Routledge & Kegan Paul.

Review (1979) Special Issue on Cycles and Trends. Vol. II, 4 (Spring).

ROBINSON, C. (1980) "Notes toward a 'native' theory of history." Review IV, 1 (Summer): 45–78.

WALLERSTEIN, I. (1974) The Modern World-System I: Capitalist Agriculture and the Origins of the European World-Economy in the Sixteenth Century. New York: Academic Press.

NOTES ON THE CONTRIBUTORS

NESAR AHMAD teaches sociology at Bridgewater State College, Massachusetts. He was formerly Director of the Third World Studies program at Goddard College. He is presently completing his Ph.D. in sociology at the State University of New York, Binghamton.

ALBERT BERGESEN received his Ph.D. from Stanford University and is now Associate Professor of Sociology at the University of Arizona. He is currently working on the analyses of stages and cycles in the world-economy. He recently edited *Studies of the Modern World-System*.

WALTER GOLDFRANK is Associate Professor of Sociology at the University of California, Santa Cruz. He has been Director of the Interdisciplinary Graduate Program in Sociology and Chair of the Department of Sociology. He has published extensively on the Mexican Revolution and on fascism. He edited *The World-System of Capitalism: Past and Present, Volume 2* in the *Political Economy of the World-System Annuals*.

TERENCE K. HOPKINS is Professor of Sociology and Director of Graduate Studies in Sociology at the State University of New York, Binghamton. He is also Associate Director of the Fernand Braudel Center. He has written widely on the development of the world-system and is presently working on issues of concept formation and method for the study of the world-economy.

DALE L. JOHNSON is Chairperson of the Sociology Department, Livingston College, Rutgers University, and of the political sociology and development area specialization of the Graduate Department of Sociology. He has published three books on Latin America and various articles in the fields of political sociology and development. His contribution to this volume is drawn from his forthcoming book, *Social Development: Comparative Studies of Class Relations and Intermediate Classes*.

JAMES E. LUNDAY is completing his doctoral training in the Department of Social Relations, Johns Hopkins University. His interests are in the processes of state formation in the world-economy. He has written on development in Brazil and the United States.

KOSTIS PAPADANTONAKIS teaches economics at Essex Community College, Baltimore, Maryland. He has recently completed his Ph.D. thesis at Cornell University, "Greece: The Structure of Dependence," which he is planning to expand into a book. He has written numerous essays in American, Canadian, and Greek publications concerning the situation during and after the military dictatorship in Greece.

FRANCISCO O. RAMIREZ is Associate Professor of Sociology at San Francisco State University. He has done extensive cross-national research on the development of education and the development of the interstate system. He is also working on comparative analyses of the social status of women, writing a monograph on the political incorporation of women and editing a work on the status of women in education and occupational roles.

RICHARD RUBINSON is Associate Professor of Social Relations, Johns Hopkins University. He has worked extensively on cross-national studies of the relationships among dependency, inequality, and national development. He is presently researching processes of political transformation in the nineteenth century and is involved in a historical study of political change in the United States.

ROBERTA M. SPALTER-ROTH is writing her doctoral dissertation in the Department of Sociology, American University. The work is tentatively titled, "Dirt, Gentrification, Unmade Beds, Rent Control and Violence: Elements of a Feminist Dialectic of Shelter."

RICHARD TARDANICO is Assistant Professor of Sociology at Tulane University. He is currently studying state formation in revolutionary Mexico (1917–1940) as part of a larger project on the movement of countries from the periphery to the semi-periphery in Latin America. A previous analysis of the Mexican Revolution appeared in *Politics and Society*. He is now completing a book on Mexican state formation and the world-economy with Walter Goldfrank.

GEORGE M. THOMAS is a post doctoral fellow in the Sociology Department, Stanford University. His primary interest is in the interplay between long-term sociocultural change and religious and political movements. He is currently writing a monograph on nation-building and evangelical revivalism in the nineteenth-century United States.

MICHEL-ROLPH TROUILLOT is completing his doctoral training in the Department of Anthropology at Johns Hopkins University. A native of Haiti, he is interested in Afro-American history and culture. He is the author of *Ti Dife Boule*, a study of the beginnings of the Haitian Revolution, written in Haitian Creole.

IMMANUEL WALLERSTEIN is Distinguished Professor of Sociology and Director of the Fernand Braudel Center at the State University of New York, Binghamton. He is the author of *The Modern World-System: Capitalist Agriculture and the Origins of the European World-Economy in the Sixteen Century,* and *The Modern World-System II: Mercantilism and the Consolidation of the European World-Economy, 1600–1750*.

SALLY K. WARD is presently Assistant Professor in the Department of Sociology and Anthropology at the University of New Hampshire. She has done extensive research on the determinants of community structures and community power. She is currently studying patterns of industrial ownership in communities in the United States.

EILEEN ZEITZ is Project Director of the Sex and Violence Project at the Department of Sociology, American University. Her past work has been primarily in housing; she is the author of *Private Urban Renewal,* a study of gentrification in Washington, D.C.